Understanding Media Users

Understanding Media Users

From Theory to Practice

Tony Wilson

A John Wiley & Sons, Ltd., Publication

This edition first published 2009
© 2009 by Tony Wilson

Blackwell Publishing was acquired by John Wiley & Sons in February 2007. Blackwell's publishing program has been merged with Wiley's global Scientific, Technical, and Medical business to form Wiley-Blackwell.

Registered Office
John Wiley & Sons Ltd, The Atrium, Southern Gate, Chichester, West Sussex, PO19 8SQ, United Kingdom

Editorial Offices
350 Main Street, Malden, MA 02148-5020, USA
9600 Garsington Road, Oxford, OX4 2DQ, UK
The Atrium, Southern Gate, Chichester, West Sussex, PO19 8SQ, UK

For details of our global editorial offices, for customer services, and for information about how to apply for permission to reuse the copyright material in this book please see our website at www.wiley.com/wiley-blackwell.

The right of Tony Wilson to be identified as the author of this work has been asserted in accordance with the Copyright, Designs and Patents Act 1988.

Wiley also publishes its books in a variety of electronic formats. Some content that appears in print may not be available in electronic books.

Designations used by companies to distinguish their products are often claimed as trademarks. All brand names and product names used in this book are trade names, service marks, trademarks or registered trademarks of their respective owners. The publisher is not associated with any product or vendor mentioned in this book. This publication is designed to provide accurate and authoritative information in regard to the subject matter covered. It is sold on the understanding that the publisher is not engaged in rendering professional services. If professional advice or other expert assistance is required, the services of a competent professional should be sought.

Library of Congress Cataloging-in-Publication Data

Wilson, Tony, 1947–
Understanding media users : from theory to practice / Tony Wilson.
    p.   cm.
Includes bibliographical references and index.
ISBN 978-1-4051-5566-3 (hbk. : alk. paper) – ISBN 978-1-4051-5567-0 (pbk. : alk. paper)
1. Mass media–Audiences. I. Title.
P96.A83W55 2009
302.23–dc22
                                                    2008005945
A catalogue record for this book is available from the British Library.

Set in 10.5/13pt Minion by SPi Publisher Services, Pondicherry, India
Printed and bound in Singapore by Utopia Press Pte Ltd

001   2009

Contents

Acknowledgments

I acknowledge with thanks the several hundred students (particularly those from Southeast Asia) in my taught MA Media and International Communication classes at Monash University, Melbourne and Macquarie University, Sydney. Without these Australian sojourners the courses would not have been offered and my wages would not have been paid. Their papers and presentations convinced me that phenomenology and its practice could be established in audience analysis. Jayne Fargnoli at Blackwell further focused these thoughts in writing and I convey my appreciation for her energetic and supportive involvement in this project.

I also thank the Australia-Malaysia Institute for providing me with a research fellowship to which University Malaysia Sarawak (Faculty of Economics and Business) responded with the generous offer of accommodation both domestic and scholarly. If there are chapters here with value, much of their content was written peacefully adjacent to the campus mosque accompanied by its early morning call to prayer – *numen tremendum et fascinans*. I also wish to acknowledge the Titi turn in my theory of media use, the insights accruing from my Chinese researcher's invitation to interview in that west Malaysian town located amidst beautiful mountains and music.

My thanks to those who texted me while I wrote: they know who they are. I am grateful to the Chinese, Indian, and Malay scholars who joined me in research: they are mentioned by name in the pages of this volume. My mother passed away as *Understanding Media Users* came into being: I dedicate this book to her always-focused memory.

Research exemplars in chapters 6 and 9 draw selectively on empirical material published earlier in *New Media and Society* and *Tourist Studies*.

Introduction

Informed by my nomadic higher education research and teaching experience in Asia, Australia, and the UK, *Understanding Media Users* offers readers a philosophically rooted guide to audience studies which have emerged over the last quarter of a century. In chapter 1 I discuss European (Structuralist) and US (Effects) audience theory and dismiss both as irredeemably determinist. We respond to screens not as passive objects pushed around by greater forces but as active subjects critical and creative in our comprehension of screen content (see Wilson, 2004).

Media users are no "homogenized," "indistinguishable" mass (Zhong and Wang, 2006: 26). Researching "ordinary people's interpretative activities" (Livingstone, 2004: 75) we need to hear their particular justification for interpreting film or cellphone narratives in the way they do. Understanding screen content is a rational *process* which takes time. What are the psychological and social conditions enabling our success? Investigating media use must be "process-oriented rather than result-oriented, interpretive rather than explanatory" (Ang, 1990: 240). Our search is for the underlying universal structure of responses to cinema, soap opera, cyberspace, and cellphone (a *phenomenology* of perception), not for media stimuli causing passive reactions (*positivism*).

From chapter 2 we seek a route through what has become known (somewhat diffusively) as "active audience" theory. The phrase "active audience" has become part of the "shared knowledge" (Roscoe et al., 1995: 88) of media studies. I relate UK work examining screen responses as the viewer's final judgment on a text to wider European reader reception theory which considers the process of arriving at that judgment. Oddly, British communication studies has been less "sensitive" to the enriching "difference of European ideas" (Nightingale, 1996: 108) than the US school of consumer studies whose contribution I discuss in detail (chapters 7 and 8).

In writing these chapters my goal has been in presenting audience studies to emerge with a clearly focused claim deriving from media theory after structuralism, an account informed by the latter's philosophical rival, phenomenology. Seeing is *immediately* interpretative of its subject on screen. Looking initiates our *always* culturally located perception of pages, people, or programs *as* Asian or Caucasian, comprehensible content or enigmatic event, contestable or consensus gaining…. Sadly, there are no cross-culturally given uninterpreted "raw" data.

Nonetheless, there is a universal process of "reading the screen" at the heart of audience response everywhere. For media literacy is *ludic* – a term which here denotes the customary practice of viewing, not the counter-factual engagement with programs "as raw material with which to fantasize" (Liebes and Katz, 1993: x). As competent audiences, we are both "consumers of the spectacle" and "players in the game" (Ross and Nightingale, 2003: 147) of *Big Brother*.

The model of media use we shall be pursuing asserts it to be a continually future-oriented goal-focused play-like activity. In "everyday meaning-formation" (Hermes and Dahlgren, 2006: 259) we *project* and position content in television programs and web pages. Chapter 6 shows the theory's application to understanding cellphone use. Following a discussion of branding and consumer research guided by phenomenology, my final chapter draws on the model to offer an empirically responsive close analysis of audiences as consumer-citizens reading (creatively, critically) content on television and tourist websites.[1] Almost two decades ago researchers argued that the challenging task lying before them was to "open up the black box hiding the specific social-psychological processes behind and below the general process of reception" (Jensen and Rosengren, 1990: 232). Those processes are studied cross-culturally below.

Making Sense of/in Media Use:
Beyond Accumulating Audience Responses[2]

Media research is quantitative and qualitative: we count and conceptualize screen use. Qualitative active audience investigation is both consequent upon and criticizes structuralist study of responses to (principally) film. In structuralism's successor, reactions (positive or negative) to screen content are considered as creatively drawing on the viewer's culture, primarily as a gendered and socially located media user with a particular ethnicity and generation. This approach is generally regarded as initiated by Brunsdon and Morley in the early 1980s at the University of Birmingham UK Centre for Contemporary Cultural Studies. It can be named "active audience" theory by virtue of being understood as a reaction against 1970s structuralist accounts of screen narrative as wholly determining viewer response – as excluding significance for local negotiation of meaning.

Understanding Media Users discusses approaches to audiences which maintain that viewers actively interpret content, a perspective to be distinguished not only from structuralist media theory but from passive audience "effects studies." Effects studies consist of research conceptually articulated from a predominantly US behaviorist perspective. In these accounts, akin to "bullet" or "hypodermic needle" theory of media content's mechanically pushing viewers' behavior, events on screen are a two-dimensional cause of three-dimensional consequences. Media stimulate a passive response not mediated by viewer reflection.

Active audience theory has been consistently criticized as indeterminate (Roscoe et al., 1995). What do we mean when we (favorably) characterize an audience as "active"? In answering this question we can turn to the philosophical psychology of phenomenology and its literary offspring, reader reception theory. Here, interest focuses on the media user's activity of "reading" screen narrative. Research perceives the audience's making sense of content as a structured cognitive – sometimes very expressive – *process*. Emphasizing the viewer's achievement in making a program intelligible, such hermeneutic (Devereux, 2003: 96) media analysis asks the question: what are the enabling conditions of successfully coming to understand screen text? In answering we focus upon cross-cultural consumption of television or Internet.

Taking phenomenology on board, media user theory enables the multisite research exemplars set out in this book. We can integrate active audience theory's political emphasis on audience perceptions of their "positioning" by the screen and philosophy's account of the cognitive activity with which "readers" meet such alignment of viewers by texts. This reading process is hermeneutic – media users render cellphone and cyberspace narrative meaningful.

Active audience theory's silence (a discursive debit) on how viewers actually achieve understanding is addressed in phenomenology's thesis that perceiving screen content involves a structured process of thought, albeit often swift. In our "hermeneutical relationship" (Nyre, 2007: 29) with known media we anticipate and actualize meaning, seeking coherence.

Implicitly or explicitly, audience studies appropriate this philosophy of mind to develop a "genre-based theory of interpretation" (Radway, 1991: 10) in which texts are read as instantiating types.

We can ask sociological questions about the construction of media knowledge: how do people arrive at the cultural horizons from which program, phone, and web page content is conceptualized and concretized or read in particular ways? Why are these powerful conceptual perspectives sometimes contested, forming the focus of cultural struggle? Equally, we can raise psychological issues: how do those horizons of understanding constrain (Bird, 2003: 167) as well as creatively enable the process of understanding media? The goal pursued here will be integrating answers to these important questions in media user studies.

Mapping Media Understanding:
Using an Inductive or Interpretative Method?

As Morrison (2003: 124) and others have indicated, research arguing for widely applicable conclusions about TV or Internet use based on a limited number of responses to questionnaires (or inductive reasoning) can find it difficult to justify such generalization, "distinctive" or otherwise (Gauntlett and Hill, 1999: 11). Instead, seeking a universal cognitive core at the heart of media experience, *Understanding Media Users* discusses ways of interpreting people's reactions to content. Underlying variety we can locate a shared or cross-cultural process by reference to which we may account for emerging difference. For "qualitative reception analysis needs to be placed in a broader theoretical framework" (Ang, 1996: 137).

Far from responses to the screen being exclusively explicable in terms of the latter's content, active audience studies emphasize viewers' cultural and social experience as a constructive resource supporting discrete responses to TV program or web page. Conceptualizing reading as a meaning-making process, hermeneutics investigates how media users succeed in understanding narrative on TV and Internet often widely diverse in their cultural content.

Our inquiry into how we make sense of what we see on screen is guided by the insight from phenomenology that audience achievement of intelligibility requires cognitive activity: from the moment at which we commence viewing we entertain informed expectations or "projections" (Gadamer, 1975: 224) of textual meaning which our reading then shows to be accurate – or otherwise. For in media reception, viewers draw on their established "horizons of understanding" (ibid.: 217) or wider experience of narrative patterns as "media templates" (Kitzinger, 2000), positions of knowledgeable advantage allowing them to anticipate character development and events. The latter may or may not emerge as actually occurring.

This conceptual context of comprehension or "anticipation and retrospection" (Lury, 2005: 95) in looking at the screen sets the terms of media literacy (Livingstone, 2007a). Audiences seek (and sometimes fail) to integrate confirmed conjectural projections of television program or web page content in a synthesizing "hermeneutic circle of understanding" (Gadamer, 1975: 167), relating elements of a text to its perceived entirety. Likewise, consumers construct or "stitch" together (Ruddock, 2007: 130) coherent narratives of television or online marketing in their accounts of achieved anticipation.

Qualitative empirical research testing such communications or consumer reception theory is often conducted in focus groups whose participants discuss their responses to particular cellphone, television, or Internet narratives (e.g., adverts). Contributions confirm or contradict and frequently enrich an emerging philosophical psychology of media use – or media user theory.

Media user theory builds upon the insight from uses and gratifications analyses that people derive intrinsic and instrumental satisfaction[3] from their screen-related activity. Drawing on philosophically attuned reception psychology, the theory presented below holds that activity to be at its core an interpretative play-like (ludic) process integrating past, present, and future cultural moments. Instrumental media use constrains immersion in this "game" (although one of my students argued that a Google search could be a source of absorbing intrinsic pleasure). We note the emphasis on uses and gratifications theory in Chinese media studies journals over the last thirty years and the call to integrate this work with "reception analysis" (Zhou, 2006: 129).

Notes

1   Like Seiter in her guiding text *Television and New Media Audiences* (1999: 5) most of my examples will be drawn from projects I have conducted with others.
2   Barker calls for audience research to go "beyond accumulation" (2006) of studies to develop a theoretical model of our media response. Seeking the psychological structure of "understanding" as a continuing process focused on screen

content, *Understanding Media Users* addresses this project by drawing on Heideggerian and later hermeneutic phenomenology. This may not be the theory transcending the piecemeal study which Barker had in mind (and the mistakes are mine), but I am grateful that he signaled the need for a "fore-concept" of understanding "understanding."

3   A distinction between "intrinsic" and "instrumental" media use is made by others (e.g., Moyal, 1992: 53). In regard to phone use, the former (calls for pleasure) can include "all intimate discussion and exchange," while the latter (calls for a purpose) involves "calls of a functional nature" (ibid.). It is clear that a call can shift from the first to the second category (e.g., an intimate conversation which turns to resolving a "household crisis"). Likewise, a dutiful phone call may be continued for enjoyment. Media use is fundamentally immersive, analogous to a game in absorbing one in another space and time: functional media use remains tethered to here and now.

1

A Passive Audience?
Structuralist and Effects Studies

How do we respond to cellphone, film, Internet, television screens? Are there fundamental differences in our reactions to format and technology – or a core similarity? How do we cross cultures in understanding content? What is the relationship between the psychology of individual "readings" and the sociology of responses by groups, genders, generations? How can "scientific" audience research advance beyond accumulating data – what is "progress" in media user studies?

Addressing these questions throughout this volume, I begin with a short new media narrative of everyday cellphone use in a complex Southeast Asian city. Its content will be easily recognized by many among today's traveling academics and students (the few Australians in the large undergraduate and postgraduate classes I teach in Sydney are far outnumbered by those who have joined us from nations overseas). To others this story will seem more distantly located, though its moments of involved absorption and anticipation of screen text we shall argue are global. For the purpose of this brief book is to gain insight into the underlying universal structure of media use.

This short narrative was recounted to me and another researcher talking to people visiting a transnational telecommunications company customer support center at a vast shopping mall in central Kuala Lumpur, Malaysia's capital city. (The hybrid name of the center's location – Berjaya Times Square – signals the status which some have given Kuala Lumpur as the world's most global or postmodernist metropolis by virtue of its multi-cultural Asian-Western architecture, food, religious expression, and population). Many of these customers had come to the center to ask about their cellphone use or (as in the case of our story's source) to register their post-paid account in response to new legislation (see an extended description in chapter 6).

In this narrative a Chinese Malaysian middle-aged woman (or "aunt" in Malaysian English) tells us about the everyday but engaging pleasure she derives from the cellphone's ability to immerse her interest, with its incoming messages particularly distracting her from the tumultuous city through which she travels by bus. Let us call her (fictitiously) Ai Wei. Her times of passive absorption, of focusing on the phone, it is important to be aware, are simultaneously moments of active anticipation. Electronically engaged, she enthusiastically expects its narrative.

Never merely concentrated on the immediate present (caller numbers), Ai Wei's immersion in screen data is always also an informed future-focused concern with the associated call content she would receive by clicking on her cellphone pad. As the philosopher Heidegger might well have said had wireless communication existed in the last century, her absorption is continually *fore-structured* by anticipation or *fore-sight*: she has an always present *fore-concept* (1962) of messages from "familiar numbers" as "safe to access." Displaying an interpretative understanding of her digital-human environment, Ai Wei tells us in everyday words which need to be addressed by theory, "when I look at the number and I'm not familiar, normally I wouldn't pick it up" because unknown callers are likely to be "weird [people]" who "give you those noises."

In her cellphone use, this Malaysian Chinese aunt blurs the public-private distinction which has governed much media research conducted either outside or within the home (see Gauntlett and Hill, 1999: 4). For within the "architectonic structure" (García-Montes et al., 2006: 72) of the surrounding city Ai Wei links with domesticity, her (spatiotemporally) extended family. Receiving those calls or texts she chooses to hear or read, Ai Wei pursues (like their sender) a coherent meaning for their content. Absorbing rather than alienating her, a message can enlighten her life: "when I receive an SMS from my niece" who is able to use "all the short forms and even insert a picture," "it makes my day." Considering her subjective narrative in more abstract terms, we shall see in subsequent chapters that its underlying structure of *perception, prediction, positing,* and *pleasurable acquisition* of appropriate meaning characterizes audience activity widely. We need to confirm such theory (or at least fail to falsify it) by referring to everyday accounts of media use beyond questionnaires. Screen content can prompt painful responses.

Our Times Square interviewee ignores caller numbers she does not recognize: she resists responding, anticipating that she would hear "weird" sounds rather than comfortably familiar communication. Ai Wei reduces ("deconstructs") the former as dehumanized "noises" rather than meaningful messages and distances herself from such contact. However, as someone who herself writes SMS, she identifies with her niece's processing of communicative intent, evaluating her literacy favorably: "it makes my day." A less caring aunt could have displayed apathy.

Ai Wei has a complex response to her cellphone call and messaging content, appropriating some items, alienated by others. Appreciative but equally analytical, she resembles a fan of phoning, "moving fluidly" between "proximity and distance" from the material (Jenkins, 1992: 65).

Audiences actively interpret screen content. From a *sociological* point of view, using media across the world draws upon people's different cultural perspectives on events seen and heard. Muslim Malays characteristically do not regard television's religious images of Islamic practice in the same way as Caucasian Christians. We shall see Chinese New Year interpreted differently.

But the *psychological* process of our coming to understand stories has the same structure everywhere. Drawing on our background knowledge of media forms, patterns, or types, we identify narratives we hear or see unfolding: we anticipate and construct an account of their meaning. Program content confirms or upsets our preceding concepts (or stereotypes). This model of understanding we shall see is fundamental to integrating the study of media users.

In the pages which follow we trace the evolution of insights into media reception through the last thirty years of audience investigation – from European structuralism and North American effects studies to considering viewers as active, and from reader reception research to new media user theory. This is an important path to follow through communication studies linking "questions of signification" on screens to "questions of subjectivity" (MacCabe, 1985: 6) amidst audiences.

At different stages on this route we can look sideways and evaluate environmentally, weighing up from an "audience perspective" other aspects of media studies such as narrative theory or the political economy of content production. Moreover, at the conclusion of this discursive excursion, I shall show that knowing how we "read" media enables us to gain insight into a wide range of screen-using activity, from successfully advertising Coca-Cola on television in an Islamic majority nation to Asian tourists enjoyably engaged in reading Western websites.

So how do we draw on culture to construct an identity for screen content and self concept? I maintain throughout this book that we react to films, programs, or web pages in ways which are globally (psychologically) alike and locally (sociologically) particular. The cultural identity I am proposing for ourselves as media users is both fixed and fluid. The cognitive process at play in our "production of knowledge" (MacCabe, 1976: 10) from uncertain content on screen is structured mentally. We do not understand a program instantly, but rather aim at insight, gradually establishing it as a coherent story. But while this goal of comprehension is everywhere the same, the content with which we complete a media narrative draws its particular detail from the social context in which we achieve these acts of understanding.

Watching television, for instance, we universally anticipate events on screen or *project* (Gadamer, 1975: 224) narrative meaning ("they'll marry!," "they'll split up!"): subsequently, we check our speculation as the story develops. But we perceive or construct that meaning from particular cultural perspectives (for instance, secular and spiritual "readings" of a TV marriage are distinct). Living lives of disparate dimensions within a multitude of social circumstances, we draw upon different stocks of knowledge or conceptual *horizons of understanding* (ibid.: 217) in classifying (fore-structuring), considering as coherent and consequently comprehending content.

Our knowledge of media narratives is not immediate. San Francisco, Sarawak, and Sydney audience responses to television are psychological processes following a similar cognitive path of expecting and establishing content. Assisted by literary theory and philosophy, I shall later map this global activity conceptually. But drawing on our culturally local interpretations of what we see, we develop varying (and sometimes strongly evaluative) accounts of a program's events ("he's a real Casanova!"/"he's a real challenge to our Asian Values!"). In the chapters which follow, this global/ local model of media(ted) perception will be constructed, engaged with, and extended as a story of media use. It will be shown to support studies of cellphone experience and marketing as well as analyses of critical citizens and consensual consumers in their varying responses to online journalism and e-tourism. But we turn now to consider earlier theory, some "mass communications dinosaurs" (Ruddock, 2007: 3) in Europe and the United States: "techno-determinist" (Ferguson, 1992: 72) structuralism and early effects studies.

European Structuralism (1970s): Silent Subjects – Passive Audiences?

In structuralist media theory of the 1970s the conjunction of cinematic screen and spectator reaction was represented as wholly determining cause of an effect. Audience responses are constructed by the text. Passive audiences necessarily followed film politics. Spectators succumbed to ideology (or ideas serving the interests of the powerful): male chauvinist cinema effected sexist response. Structuralist study of the relationship between viewed and viewer reduced the latter to asocial atom acceding always to screen prescription: the "spectator must be placed in a position from which the image is regarded as primary" (MacCabe, 1976: 11).

Structuralist study of the visual and its effect on the viewer can be found in contemporary issues of the journal *Screen*, although as MacCabe noted the latter represented the voices of a "more general movement" (1985: 6) concerned with understanding signs and their communication of meaning. As we shall see, structuralist theory could never find a conceptual place for active media users: for these audiences did not merely absorb but rather independently evaluated screen narrative's political positioning of its viewers.

The structuralist narrative of the viewing subject or cinematic spectator excludes from its model of the media recipient the latter's past as a person in society. In this account, the "real reader is prefigured by, and coincides with, the ideal recipient the text posits for itself" (Robins, 1979: 363). That is, as mainstream film audiences, irrespective of our cultural background, we simply circulate the categories of worldly understanding to which we are "subjected" by the wide screen.

Structuralists evacuated from responses to media the spectator's conscious cognitive processing of content over time. Our expectation and establishing of narrative is eliminated. Instead, reception of screen images is regarded as immediate. According to this delusory philosophy, when engaged by/with audio-visual texts, we are no longer people endowed with a capacity for creative thought and criticism emerging from experience but become instead conduits of cinematic ideology – capitalist, patriarchal, or otherwise. Audiences purchase a pass/ticket whose true cost is constraint: apparently escaping the mundane, they merely reproduce the forms of sociopolitical understanding presented on screen. In the seductive space and leisure time of the cinema, the latter alone is efficacious in a "productivity of meanings" (McDonnell and Robins, 1980: 194) supporting the status quo.

The film's "structure," its particular inflection of ideology or political persuasion through storytelling, determines audience deliberation on its events. According to structuralists, we are passive recipients of cinematic imagery, the "loaded" representations of femininity and masculinity, ethnicity and social class with which its narratives allocate and deny power: the screen "puts in place an experience for a subject whom it includes"

(Heath, 1973: 11). While cinema narrates events, the unseen spectating "subject" in the dark of the auditorium is acknowledged and absorbed in the story's "articulation in which it is, in fact, defined" (MacCabe, 1974: 17). As attentive audience, playing its part, we wait and witness, acceding to film's sometimes spectacular address to those watching.

Structuralists argued, then, that cinema positioned spectators ideologically, passively and politically: audience cognition followed authored content. Acknowledging our place as (no more than) appropriate addressees of the screen text on display, we learn all we (should) wish to know. Acquiescing in this promised "supra-positional omniscience" (MacCabe, 1976: 18), we absorb an ideologically accredited insight, a ticketed totality of world view. The audience willingly adopts the cinema-defined philosophical and physical position of screen spectator. But, sinking into their seats, reduced to their role as cinema-defined viewers, people's wider experience is eliminated as a source of knowledge and understanding.

We become comfortable film enthusiasts: but the precondition of an easy and untroubled structuralist spectatorship is not only the purchase of a cinema ticket but our uncritical recruitment to the reactionary politics circulating on screen. As well behaved spectators we respond appropriately to movie narratives. But in our silent gaze and recognition of large screen authority we are appropriated by dominant cinema as spokespersons for the problematic, for concepts of the social world which are challengeable outside the doors of the movie theatre.

Considered within the structuralist account of being a spectator, when we listen to the detective Petersen in *Mildred Pierce*, we are nothing more or less than addressees of that patriarchal policeman on screen. With skeptical experience absent from our memory, our thought is taken into (his) custody. Now categorically unable to consider alternatives, we presume without question the authority of the police department: its status on screen is articulated in the film's visual privileging (e.g., through upward tilting camera shots) of Petersen as embodying justice and truth. Confronted by this dominant/dominating discourse of a powerful physique, the spectator is "fixed in his [sic] position securely by the reality of the image" (Brewster and MacCabe, 1974: 9). Construing the world in these cinematic terms of masculinity, our now absolute assumption of male authority underwrites our judgments about Mildred in particular and women more widely.

Science fiction movies primarily define this world rather than an alternative universe. When a story returns (us) safely to the "normality" of events in small town America after the vanquished Martian invasion, as structuralism's spectatorial "subjects" we unproblematically share that cinematic definition (delusion?) of security. From the analytical perspective of such *Screen* theory in the seventies, we are as an audience separated from individual (idiosyncratic?) memories which could suggest a different perception of rural tranquility.

In the cinema, we are said by structuralism to be "interpellated" as spectating subjects: a powerful "text ensures the position of the subject in a relation of dominant specularity" (MacCabe, 1974: 12) to film narrative. The camera both constructs and curtails our apparent omniscience as spectators knowledgeable of events on screen from motive to outcome. For with our own experience elided or forgotten in our position as textually "subjected" audience, we are entrapped. We see society simply from the film's ideological perspective, insulated from critical (e.g., socialist) alternatives.

Audiences are thereby fixed in a position of "pure specularity" (ibid.) while engaging with the "classic realist texts" of the mainstream movie house. These films "work hard to disguise the evidence of artifice" (Ruddock, 2007: 122) or technical construction. In our attending exclusively to the screen, its representing of extra-cinematic reality seems obviously valid. Where our messy mundane lives are absent, there can be no evidence for doubting a story's implicit politics.

Writ large on overpowering screens, an already socially dominant "symbolic system" is "*imposed on the human animal* in its construction into a subject" (Brewster, 1975: 6, emphasis in the original). At the door of the cinema we hand in any alternative conceptual currency we may possess – to be collected (if not forgotten) on the way out. In 1970s *Screen* analyses, cinema was separated from the society in which it was consumed. The viewer has no voice, becoming instead a silent subject. Theory of spectatorship was rendered autonomous from the actual audience: there is a neglect of historical specificity (McDonnell and Robins, 1980: 176–7, 202).

In this symbolic "petrification of the spectator" (MacCabe, 1974: 24) we are constrained to think the politics wherein cinema positions us: our speculative thoughts cannot move outside the categories or "mental machinery" of a mainstream consensus. Film incorporates "subject positions binding individuals into the production of certain forms of totality" (Brewster et al., 1976: 115). We look but lose sight of the progressive. Only radical Marxist film (known also as non-realist cinema) through presenting the audience with contradictory accounts of the social world is said to be able to prompt us to consider the tensions within capitalist ideology. When an "identification is broken, becomes difficult to hold," "we grasp in one and the same moment both the relations that determine that identity and our relation to its representation" (MacCabe, 1976: 25).

In 1976 MacCabe reconstructed his earlier structuralism [*Screen* 15(2) 1974] in which he "made the subject the effect of the structure (the subject is simply the sum of positions allocated to it)" (1976: 25). For all political intents and purposes, cinematic narration and consumption were identical. Instead, drawing on a linguistic model of the relationship between spectator and screen, he now no longer assimilates them. "Text and reader" are "separate" (1976: 25). In this turn to poststructuralist theory, MacCabe frees the audience from its subjection to a causally determining textual structure: reception does not replicate cinematic recitation of ideology. He looks to conceptually "focus on the position of the (active) speaking subject within the utterance" (1976: 12). As he later wrote in reference to his views, by "calling me a structuralist my opponents revealed their ignorance" (1985: 30).

> With discourse we become interested in the dialectical relation between speaker and language in which language always already offers a position to the speaker and yet, at the same time, the act of speaking may itself displace those positions. (MacCabe, 1976: 12)

Cinema's call to spectators to position themselves in "binding" (MacCabe, 1985: 10) identification with its representations can be resisted. Writing about an actively creative and critical audience capable of both alignment and antagonism towards politically "contradictory positions" (MacCabe, 1976: 12) in mainstream film texts now becomes possible within MacCabe's radically redesigned model of the media user. He concludes that is a "question of analyzing a film within a determinate social moment so that it is possible to determine what identifications will be made and by whom." Society comes to the cinema: "we have to consider the relation between reader and text in its historical specificity" (MacCabe, 1976: 25, 24).

The spectator's historical specificity – her or his culturally informed and informing experience – indeed needed to enter the abstract world of *Screen* structuralism. Avowedly Marxist, its high formalist theory circulated untouched by everyday reality. As Morley later remarked, the "problem with much of *Screen*'s work" is its theorists' "unjustifiable conflation" of the political position to which they perceive a film addressing its message with that of the actual "social subject" (1980: 159). Cinema's intended and real audiences are conflated. But many of us can think – for example – beyond the assumptions of patriarchal power to which much film subscribes as self-evident. Albeit mundane, everyday thought is not always contained within the profit-focused categories of the capitalist screen.

Film theorists may tease out of a mainstream text on screen a particular perception of "normal" behavior which many of its eventual spectators can share. Narrative cinema frequently presumes a successful heterosexual romance brings its assumed audience pleasure. But richly diverse three-dimensional human spectators will always "exceed" 1970s *Screen* contributors' reductive one-dimensional statement of their "political petrification" by film. Real media users must always be more than their abstract definition by structuralists as subscribers to suspicious ideology. Without a specific knowledge of signs signifying status they will not be able to recognize the ways in which the screen's address can "hail" them to serve the already powerful. If in our social capacity as spectators seated before the screen we are reduced to being merely one-dimensional ideological implants, how can we recognize from remembered experience the presence of police in a movie as an iconic imperative signaling the authoritative source of patriarchal pronouncements within whose terms we are required to think?

Recruitment to reactionary ideas requires that the conscript can understand the cultural signifiers of meaning – the local language – in which the message is encoded. The audience's acceding to film's furthering of a view of the masculine as overwhelmingly potent presumes their ability to recollect particular discursive ways in which cinema signals power (e.g., images of fast cars and fantastic residences). If she loses contact in the darkness of the movie house with earlier experience, the amnesiac addressee of film can no longer function to fulfill a "subject position."

Powerfully performing global ideology (ill-supported belief implicated in illicit power) requires supplementing by local knowledge. Spectators are conceptualized by structuralist analysis as no more than political positions, as without access to mundane memory when facing film. But deprived of their capacity to recall culturally specific experience, audiences lack a knowledge of signs enabling them to acquiesce in dominant cinema's audio-visual assertion of capitalist consumerism as "natural" or "normal," as constituting an everyday reality without alternative plausible possibility.

Cinema's ideological positioning of its audience requires particular memories from spectators, their recollecting culturally specific modes of conveying power. In *Mildred Pierce*, Petersen needs to be perceived as a detective if his performance is to accrue power for patriarchal structures of justice. If recognition rests upon remembering, we are necessarily always more than simply defined political addressees of those who seek and secure status on screen. As media users, we exceed their categories of service. Allowing audiences access to earlier experience must be written into accounting for their alignment by screen politics. Poststructuralism's argument (advanced below) is that memory, as well as allowing an audience's passive acquiescing in cinematic authority, can be a source of active protest.

Structuralism as excluding audience experience

Structuralism argued for a limited account of viewing pleasure: this derived from cinema's (alleged) capacity to resolve spectators' psychic conflicts. Watching film on a large screen, the audience uncritically adopted the cinematic text's apparently coherent view of the world and forgot its own contradictory and fragmented experience. "What is politically important about this textual organization is that it removes the spectator from the realm of contradiction" (MacCabe, 1976: 21). Here, enjoyment rested on amnesia.

Identifying with James Bond, male spectators displaced a "real life" disjunction between aspiration and actuality, between cultural "ought" and constrained capacity. As cinematic audiences, forgetting "constitutive contradictions" (ibid.: 27) they celebrated instant integration of masculine fantasy and fulfillment. Film accomplished a "fixation of the reader in (ideological) position as a unified and coherent subject, the apparent source (as narrative agent) of the text's meaning" (Robins, 1979: 367).

Fundamentally radical in rethinking response studies, the media user research which followed structuralism posited a distance between the cultural perspectives of audiences and those available on screen. From viewers' differing immersion in ethnic, gender, generational, and social class experience there emerges a wide range of interpretative insights – with media users "reading" narrative events in a variety of ways. For critical cultural theorists succeeding structuralism, where text conflicts with experience, the latter is not forgotten but used by an audience to forge an "interrogation" of content to the point of rejection.

Two concepts of "structure"

Structuralism, then, regarded media users as absorbing rather than actively responding to screen narrative's political proposition(ing). But as intellectual inquiry it had an additional deficiency. It focused on the structure of the product (the text), ignoring the equally structured process wherein audiences achieve understanding of narrative content in viewing. Structuralists concerned themselves with the storytelling forms of films or television programs. They argued that these narratives sought to resolve underlying social oppositions (e.g., conflicts between the benign and the bad, good and evil) or were covert conservative arguments for the status quo.

However, media use is also a cognitively structured process. The meaning of a program is developed by viewers as a particular "product of certain shared systems of signification" (Eagleton, 1983: 107). Audiences recognize a story as exemplifying a type or genre: they are thereby enabled to anticipate likely developments and seek confirmation of expectations. Watching television, accessing the web, we draw upon "frames of cultural assumption" (ibid.: 122) like a knowledge of narrative patterns and how they characteristically occur.

By which groups of media users is such cultural awareness held in common? How is it drawn upon by viewers to secure intelligibility for a particular screen content? What subjective – yet structured – processes occur when media users bring knowledge (e.g., of film genre) to bear upon a single text, seeing it from a wider aesthetic perspective or horizon of understanding?

When structuralist theory refers to "laws of the mind" (Eagleton, 1983: 109) its concern is not to posit patterns within an audience's pursuit of program meaning: for this process is regarded as "random, untheorizable" (ibid.: 114). Rather, these "laws" are to be found governing the product or conclusion of that mental event, as a less than explicit aspect of the established story. For instance, analyzing a narrative can yield the discovery that it has necessarily incorporated an (allegedly) universally occurring antagonism or opposition between agents of order (good) and disorder (evil).

Subsequent reader reception theory, on the other hand, seeks to "lay bare the very structures of consciousness": it asks about the shape of the media user's regular mental activity which makes understanding of texts possible "in the first place" (Eagleton, 1983: 56). Such philosophically sensitive psychology is concerned in studying audiences with discerning the intersubjective (or universal) structure of the informed thought *processes* through which media users make meaning. This patterned cognitive activity precedes (but is responsible for) the final *product* – an intelligible text on screen. Structuralism, on the other hand, ignores our understanding narrative, the "actual speaking, writing, listening and reading of concrete social individuals" (ibid.: 114).

US Media Effects Studies (1970):
Audiences as Observable and Measurable

US "mass communication research has been dominated by an effects-orientation." "This concern with media effects is guided by a one-way model of mass communication ... it fit [*sic*] well with the existing concerns of mass communication scholars." Studies of "media effects are empirical, quantitative social science investigations": one "cannot accuse these scholars of assuming that media effects are usually positive for the audience individuals under study" (Lowery and DeFleur, 1995: viii–ix).

The effects paradigm (or widely adopted theory) assumes media and their audiences are connected in a basic cause-and-effect scenario (Bryant and Thompson, 2002: 19). For instance, Bandura argues (with considerable intellectual intensity if not complete intelligibility) while presenting his social cognitive theory of mass communication that he is providing an account of media "determinants" operating in a "causal structure of factors" (2002: 139) in respect of their viewers. Both Bryant and Thompson (2002) and Lowery and DeFleur (1995) discuss in detail the developmental path followed by the effects model of media causing audience behavior: they provide major and widely available statements of the approach. I selectively cite their case studies in our critical focus on the theory.

In media effects research, strategies of investigation have been based on a model of inquiry adopted from physical science (Lowery and DeFleur, 1995: 2). However, the model against which this media research measures itself methodologically is only one possible account of scientific investigative activity. This *positivist* view of how inquiry is conducted defines the route to a successful research outcome as follows: when (1) events are *seen* and (2) highly correlated (ideally, constantly conjoined) *statistically* this is (3) *sufficient* to assert their *causal connection*.

Within this influential (but erroneous) account of scientific procedure which has for decades governed the effects program of exploring audiences, the focus of investigation must be observable. For instance, Lowery and DeFleur describe an experiment on cinema spectators in which electrodes and mechanical devices measured visible physiological changes (e.g., in breathing rates and sweating) as "indices of emotional arousal" (1995: 26). Preoccupied by studying events which can be seen (and heard), effects investigations are often of negative media content and (allegedly) consequent adverse audience behavior. Bandura's well-known research into this topic concluded that children who watched "physically aggressive actions" on screen later imitated the violence (see Bryant and Thompson, 2002: 74).

Bryant and Thompson (2002) consider four different methods of studying children's "fright reactions" to film and other media: (1) administering a questionnaire allowing one of four responses from "not at all scared" to "very, very scared"; (2) evaluating the child's facial expression from a videotape made while the child is watching the program; (3) attaching small sensors to the child's fingers allowing physiological data to be collected; (4) using "behavioral measures of fear" (181). Each focuses on observable, preferably quantifiable, signifiers of subjective fear.

Discussing the focus of effects research on the visible, Bryant and Thompson assert that numerous studies have found a causal link between the viewing of media violence and an increase in aggressive behavior. But this is established as a statistical rather than subjective relationship. They concede that in effects research no findings or theoretical formulations have explained why only a "few go out and imitate the actions they see on the screen" (2002: 3).

Fortunately, an alternative philosophical understanding of scientific activity known as *realism* (Harré, 1972) exists. (It is important to note that *this* realism has nothing to do with filmic "realism" or the careful editing of mainstream cinema images so that they transparently meet the spectator's desire to establish a coherent world on screen.)

Scientific realism has for many years emphasized the importance of attending to underlying processes or "mechanisms" by reference to which events in the observable world can be rendered intelligible (e.g., the kinetic theory's account of gas particles whose motion can account for pressure upon the walls of a container). The hidden mechanism through which visible causes give rise to effects which are seen and heard must never remain a "magic bullet" but instead be disclosed – or at least be examined indirectly (e.g., through a microscope). In the human sciences, focus groups and prolonged interviews can disclose subjective narrative data.

A realist study of human phenomena includes the unobservable as an appropriate topic for analysis (e.g., extended interpretations of television content which are presented both as rationally justified by audiences on the basis of stories seen on screen and as the reason for their subsequent action). But within positivism such a wide epistemological embrace – or focus of inquiry – is excluded as subjective and unscientific. (See chapter 5 for more on psychological realism in media user research.)

The positivist perception of acceptable research methodology identifies being "objective" with quantitative analysis (Lowery and DeFleur, 1995: 14). The questionnaire as a means of generating responses or data to be enumerated is assumed to be an unproblematic tool for investigating audiences. The idea that *what* is being counted (its meaning!) can be experienced and described in different ways – often profoundly contested – receives little enthusiasm from those who pursue a positivist approach to media analysis. Yet TV program or Internet page and responses by audiences are precisely of this indeterminate character. Together they can constitute a seemingly chaotic multiplicity of meanings at odds with the singularly focused "jargon" (or disciplinary discourse) of a positivist investigator. How does our mundane yet multicultural understanding of media use relate, for instance, to Bandura's theory-laden conception of an "agentic conceptual framework" involving "triadic reciprocal causation" (2002: 121) between program and person? It is important that otherwise enigmatic theory be related through definition to everyday thought.

Positivism rests on an account of human perception. For this erroneous reduction of scientific activity to focusing on the observable and quantifiable also claims that we see the world around us *immediately*. Irrespective of our diverging cultural histories, the same sensory impressions arrive instantly as conscious experience: we talk about perceiving compilations of these "sense-data" as seeing material objects. Language denotes or names these phenomena directly, excluding any reference to culture.

Phenomenology, on the other hand, has pursued the view that perception is *interpretative* activity, taking place over time. We do not passively receive a flood of sense-data, but rather actively fit present experience to pre-existing mental structure. At the core of seeing is synthesizing recognition, the preconscious matching of sensory data to cognitive template which results in successful perception. Looking at objects and people around us, we – slowly or swiftly – see them as instances of already known phenomena and respond to them accordingly. A friend approaching from a distance is recognized – gradually. The world is *mediated* through our cultural memories.

In short, for positivism there is no process in perception. Despite our manifestly different backgrounds and beliefs the world is held to be immediately impressed on all as identical. The view of media use presented in this volume rejects not only positivism but its adoption of this untenable *empiricism*. For seeing is an activity in which we come to recognize our environment, with people from culturally varying vantage points or horizons of understanding identifying where they are (their physical foregrounds) in divergent ways.

We shall pursue a scientifically realist approach in studying our perception of screen and sound, asserting it to be always engaged in the subjective activity of interpretation or *mediated* through thought. Looking is laden with assumptions. The bright disk in the sky has in the distant past been regarded as the sun revolving around the earth. In seeing, we assign meaning to events whether in our close environment or distantly located in a television program.

Often this process of interpreting is informed by cultural beliefs which vary substantially from one group of viewers to another across the world. Watching an imported US video, a Malaysian audience's "Asian values" can lead to a very different account of program events (e.g., as ethically problematic) from an American response. Because we are knowledgeable media users, our remembering past television supports our continually seeing new content as being of a certain type (from action drama to soap opera). Guided by memory our expectation and establishing of developments on screen is distinct from viewers located in other communities of cultural awareness (for instance, those who have never watched so-called "reality television").

Qualitative realist audience research focuses on *how* people come to see their media environment. Accurate description is as important here as correctly counting is to quantitative methods. Following a qualitative method is acknowledged to be possible but placed on the margins (and misunderstood) within media positivism as "exploratory" or "suggestive" (Lowery and DeFleur, 1995: 33). Analytical attention to listeners' or viewers' narratives of media consumption is reductively regarded as merely revealing radio or television's "subtle influences" (ibid.: xi) on people who otherwise perceive (passively record) the same stretch of narrative.

The empiricist story about our gaining knowledge is that seeing our surroundings involves receiving a flood of sense-data, of universally identical perceptions. Media users of varying cultural hues do not fundamentally interpret screen events distinctively, seeing different aspects from a range of perspectives or horizons of understanding. Rather, it is the same story on screen for all.

Empiricist discussion of watching television dismisses as merely subtle influence on the same (passive) response the centrally significant event of a program's culturally varying (active) interpretation. Yet this cognitive process generates a media user's observable quantifiable behavior. Positivism's investigative agenda does not include audience expectation and establishing of program narratives. Instead, it is determined to steer the researcher's attention away from the allegedly subjectively idiosyncratic and unscientific. Media investigation must construct a "dynamic discipline" of "generalizations, causal explanations, and theoretical predictions" (Lowery and DeFleur, 1995: xi–xiii) focused on human behavior – seen as identical by all.

Audience research was conducted on the movie *Birth of a Nation*, which "portrays blacks in negative terms and is considered an antiblack statement." This study of spectators seemed to show the film had a "substantial impact on the attitudes of its audience" (Lowery and DeFleur, 1995: 30). Exemplifying positivistic inquiry, the research focused upon two observable phenomena alleged to be related as cause and effect – negative movie images and antiblack answers in a multiple choice questionnaire. (Emphasizing the positivistic preference for enumerating visual evidence, measuring such participant responses can now be achieved by "automated instruments": Bryant and Thompson, 2002: 14.)

No reference is made in this investigation to the intervening process between cause and (alleged) effect, to the subjective experience of people interpreting *Birth of a Nation* as a negative ethnic statement. Qualitative research (using contributions from audience focus groups) could have recorded this activity. There is no room in this "striking" investigation for *seeing as* in plural ways – for a cultural diversity of media user backgrounds prompting variety in reading response (e.g., from both African and Caucasian American perspectives). Few of the subjects in the experiment had known or even seen an African American prior to watching the film (Lowery and DeFleur, 1995: 30).

Reflecting on a "one-time study" which has major methodological significance for us, Lowery and DeFleur cite work on the radio broadcasting of H. G. Wells' *War of the Worlds* story of a Martian invasion as a causal "trigger for panic behavior" (Lowery and DeFleur, 1995: 94, 55). Despite this positivist prelude to their account, in order to relate the media stimulus to its observable effect, the original research continues in realist mode: we are provided with a qualitative survey extensively exploring in narrative depth subjective listener interpretations of the broadcast.

These plural perspectives supported varying audience projections or anticipation of developments both on the radio program and in the world after the announcement of alien arrivals. Listeners classifying the broadcast as drama without material consequences remained calm. But media users designating radio as generally offering reliable access to reality (ibid.: 56) predicted disaster and panicked in the face of this Martian approach.

The meaning they perceived entailed imminent mayhem. In this research, permitting listeners' subjective interpretation and associated anticipation to be included (realism) renders observable data intelligible.

Media effects: uses and gratifications theory

Can effects studies be rescued from positivism? Lowery and DeFleur dismiss reducing the model of media response which informs these investigations to the "magic bullet idea" that people react to media messages "immediately and uniformly" as "merely passive receivers" (1995: 94–5). Adapting to a critical scholarly environment, effects studies developed a further informing guide to research in the form of uses and gratifications theory where media audiences are construed as more – or less – active. Under this broad banner of media inquiry, for instance, a qualitative study of US daytime serial listeners showed how subjective processes of audience identification with fictional characters are central to media users enjoying soap opera drama they had switched on to switch off from daily life. The gratification gained from viewing included "emotional release," "wishful thinking," and recognizing "valuable advice" (ibid.: 107–8).

But outside such enlightened investigation of mental activity the focus of research stimulated by effects studies engaging with uses and gratifications theory was still on what media are "doing to the people who regularly consumed its products" (ibid.: 96). Positivism's passive quantifiable percipients of media content continued to feature in research, for example, where people studied the "long term and additive" "effects of serials on their audiences" (ibid.: 97). In such effects studies' selective sight audience activity remained limited to visible viewing, to energetically engaging in observable channel choosing on domestic TV. The mental processes associated with media use occasionally featured on research menus (e.g., Perry's expectancy-value theory (2002: 77) refers to people anticipating the attributes of programs). But otherwise an audience's interpretative activity (whose successful achievement is presupposed by "gratification effects") is substantially beyond focus. Indeed recognizing its existence would be incompatible with continuing to talk of media *effects* – on a passive recipient of programs.

Media effects: two-step flow theory

In a subsequent makeover of media effects theory, Lowery and DeFleur argue for replacing the "hypothesis of powerful and immediate effects" with a "two-step flow idea": the "movement of information through interpersonal networks, from the media to people (opinion leaders) and from there to other people" (1995: 192). A further link is inserted here into the explanatory causal chain between screen and subsequent behavior. This extended model of media effects flowing from program to person subverts the earlier "stimulus-response framework" in which content had consequences with "little in between" them (ibid.: 209).

Belief in the immediacy of media effect yielded to the hierarchical conception of screen content descending from the heights of first-hand awareness (or creation) of information through opinion leaders to its lowly consumption. In this theory of postponed productivity, knowledge needs "two steps" in reaching audiences to have behavioral consequences (e.g., in voting). But the positivist guide to good methodology continued to inform the investigative agenda.

For instance, a research program on the creation of informed groups concluded that as opinion leaders, "better educated and more affluent" women are the "most influential," with the latter defined as having "many social contacts in the community" (ibid.: 208). As we have seen, arriving at such a conjunction of observable variables ("affluence," "education," and "influence"/"social contacts") is considered by positivists as being well on the way to recording their relationship as cause and effect. No attention is paid to the realist requirement that an underlying process of ratiocination be established to link these phenomena.

Media users subjectively form action-guiding opinion for which they can give reasons. But the mind is excluded from effects studies of listening or viewing experience. Investigating audience thinking was displaced by so-called "two-step flow" effects research which evaded the media user's subjective flow of ideas in coming to decisions. Positivist rather than realist in focus, these studies failed to elicit the trajectory of thought from media to audience action.

Media effects: agenda setting theory

In a further application of its "look and tell" approach, effects studies examined agenda setting – the capacity of newspapers and television to gain reader or audience consent to highlighted issues as important (or salient). Correlations were sought, for instance, between measurable media emphasis (e.g., the position of an item on a newspaper page) and voters' beliefs about the importance of a topic. Speculation about the subjective process involved in readers making these judgments is not substantiated through analyzing media user accounts of their experience. Instead, quantifiable observable evidence is regarded methodologically as adequate to justify the claim that there is a connection between textual and reader recognition of an item's significance. High correlation of media emphasis and viewer perception of topic importance is considered sufficient to establish a causal relationship between media and audience agenda.

In short, seeking scientific status, positivist media studies discount subjectivity. Research is limited to the seen and heard. Within this restricted methodological vision, the "thin" data of positive statistical correlation between observable phenomena (e.g., "social class background," "time spent viewing") showed explanatory connections: there was no need to provide "thick" narratives of subjective evidence (e.g., a variety of audience voices linking levels of social class and screen consumption).

Quantitative *counts* exclude qualitative *accounts*. The broad focus involved in a researcher's establishing the duration and frequency of a recurring phenomenon (e.g., watching television) is not compatible with her or his simultaneous attention to detailed data (e.g., specific stories about switching on favored programs). The realist imperative to secure and study audience narratives which could provide their reasons for varying time spent viewing different programs went unheard within positivist media science. Researchers speculated on reader subjectivity, but did not engage in appropriate qualitative study. In subsequent media analysis (see Baker and Ball, 1969) aligned with this abstracting and deficient vision, where a mechanism or process is proposed between cause and effect (e.g., violence on screen and in the streets), that connection is demonstrably observable (e.g., physiological arousal in viewers).

The effects model: edging towards reality?

The evidence needed to demonstrate a causal connection between phenomena has become systematically contested in social science. Has being required to justify claims about the causal role of media driven the effects model from purely observational quantitative positivism to the edge of a subjectivist qualitative realism? In other words – as researchers thinking about television's effects, do we need to consider the audience's thinking, the stories they tell about the complexities and consequences of watching programs? Are they persuaded – not pushed – to act by "stuff on screen"?

As we have seen (e.g., from Bryant and Thompson, 2002) positivism's methodological prescription is that researchers focus on audience response as the effect of forceful screen content. Here, thought follows text as an accumulated or cultivated necessary consequence: "regular exposure to mediated violence made [*sic*] viewers develop an exaggerated view of real-life dangers in society" (183). But this doctrinal assumption of media causality with audience behavior thereby *made* to happen has continued coupled with an account of viewers who *choose* to subjectively identify with media characters and hence learn to act in particular ways. For positivists also espouse a "social learning model" of television effects: "viewers may identify with television roles and thus learn certain of the behaviors depicted" (Lowery and DeFleur, 1995: x).

People identify with *people* where both occupy a similar role. If we *actively* align ourselves with others on screen, how can our resulting behavior be regarded as a *passive* effect of media? Watching television, we amend attitudes (e.g., towards an ethnic group) through freely furthering *rational* thought (perhaps because we find our previous views are incompatible with new evidence). Our outlook is not *caused* to change as an effect of events on screen. People's thinking is not pushed along by what they see on television.

Requirements for accuracy and consistency in our stories of subjective processes need to be satisfied. But there are additional difficulties for media effects theory seeking to incorporate audience alignment with others in causally accounting for the consequences of screen content. To assert that identification produces imitation and hence influence begs the question: imitation of *what*? Identification with a person terminating the life of a suffering partner in a television drama presupposes we view the action not as capricious cruelty but as charitable caring. Alignment assigns meaning which is then appropriated: identification actively interprets before it is influential. As media users we may engage in "behavior reenactment" or "modeling" (Bryant and Thompson, 2002: 70) of others' activity on screen, but only after first identifying with it in a favorable light. Imitation involves actively understanding content positively in the process of identifying.

More widely, audiences identify with characters or presenters (such as news readers) themselves always already engaged in the role of interpreting events on television. All seek sense. Media users align with those on screen in the *process* of establishing meaningful stories. But while this is a continuing shared focus of thought, may viewers not finally understand content differently from those persons seen on television also to be making sense of developments? Behavior regarded as the pursuit of justice by those "inhabiting" a program can be interpreted by media users in the last instance as disruptive. Identification in sense-seeking need not lead to imitation.

So, in summary, positivism faces two problems in seeing social learning as a media effect. First, in identifying with people on screen, *what* we learn to do is not a passive consequence but the result of our culturally informed continual active interpretation of content as worthwhile. Indeed Bryant and Thompson (inconsistently) acknowledge media user variation in "reading" content: "viewer perceptions and interpretations may conceivably render the most violent programs rather innocuous in their effects" (2002: 183). Second, identification is a complex process. While we can all align with characters (e.g., a detective) when we seek sense in events on screen, agreement may finally be absent on a concluding statement or *proposition* describing the result. One viewer's perception of "amoral violence" in a program can be another's diagnosis of "just retribution." Clearly, differing behavioral consequences are likely to follow.

Of course, even if a story's audience and narrative agents (characters) arrive at a shared perception of events in a program, they can disagree morally (or otherwise) over how to follow the latter's implications for action (or as effects theorists would say, on "abstract modeling"). Confronted by violence recounted in a complex narrative on television, just what constitutes the same behavior in real life? Audience alignment with those on screen, sharing the process and agreeing on the product of interpretation, need not lead to an identical implementing of insight off screen. Their consensus that someone's activity is courageous can be continued by viewers in different ways.

In short, Lowery and DeFleur argue that "people attend to, interpret, and respond to the content of mass communications selectively in ways influenced by their group memberships and social ties" (1995: 399). But it is difficult to see how the complex process of active audience interpretation and identification can be accommodated within effects studies' positivist model of media use. For fundamentally the latter is centered on perceiving viewer response as a passive effect of content exclusively described by the researcher.

Conclusion

We started this chapter with an account of an active media user. Our Chinese Malaysian urban dweller selectively attended to and appropriated cellphone content from a family member: "it makes my day." We hear her "integrating" media meaning into her "world-view" (Dahlgren, 1988: 287). She was critically alienated by other calls, perceiving them as irritating impositions of (probably patriarchal) power. Fundamentally challenging to theories of the "dominant text" (Abercrombie, 1996: 200), she is neither structuralism's nor effects studies' passive recipient of meaning. Listening to her, in chapter 2 we consider active media users as speaking subjects.

2

The Active Audience:
Speaking Subjects

In chapter 1 we discussed the screen as potential cause of audience behavior. While structuralists were explicitly political in their thinking, positivist effects analysts focused on establishing statistical correlations between observable screen content and audience data. For both structuralist and effects theory, in their very different accounts, viewers are passive consumers of media meaning. But as our Southeast Asian cellphone user demonstrated at the outset of the first chapter, audiences are active: research participants articulate long sentences worth hearing. We turn now to the second "broad tradition" (Gillespie, 2006: 2) of media user studies.

UK *Nationwide* After Structuralism (1980):
Active Audiences – Speaking Subjects

Poststructuralists are sharply at odds with positivists. Unlike the latter, they would not regard a statistical correlation between observable events on screen and human behavior as ever sufficient to warrant asserting their causal connection. In poststructuralist communication studies the relationship between media and their users fundamentally involves audiences interpreting narrative content. So our response is not a *passive* effect of events shown in television programs or on web pages. Rather, in a mental process of reading we *actively* assign meaning to heard and perceived content. The psychological narrative or subjective story (of our constructing narrative) has a beginning, middle, and end on each of which we shall focus in turn.

Media statistics count the responses of people watching television or using the Internet as well as events on screen (the "stimulus"). Research with such a quantitative dimension is important. But in fully accredited positivism these reactions are classified and coded (or represented) from the point of view of investigators, not from an audience perspective. Media users can be asked to record their responses by selecting from a limited set of possibilities drawn up by a psychologist as a multiple choice question-naire. But if we follow this research route, we reduce audience reactions emerging from their rich subjective capacity for interpretative reading to quantifiable (dis)agreement with assertions from an "objective" investigator.

Potentially recordable *thick* narratives of response to complexity of TV or Internet content are lost by focusing upon *thin* observable data – by counting a form-filling audience's evaluation of a program from 1 to 10. This objectifying enumeration of their reactions renders viewers almost as silent as the phenomena investigated by physical science, despite our being subjects who in watching television or going online create substantial meaning from screen narrative. Instead, in studies of speaking subjects, respondents' "conceptual frameworks" (Morley, 1992: 177) are to be taken as the epistemological bedrock (or basis for developing categories) sup-porting researchers' diverse analyses of media use – both qualitative *and* quantitative.

While statistical investigation of people's responses to media is clearly crucial, it is equally important that we consider *what* we are counting in communication studies. How does an audience whose media behavior we are investigating *themselves* classify screen content and how have they arrived cognitively at their conclusions? How is their interpretative focus related to our own as students of media use? Ignoring these issues of con-ceptual interrelationship "substitutes the (researchers') logic of statistical correlations for the (audience's) situated logic of actual responses" (Morley, 1992: 31).

As audiences we can contest an investigator's account of what takes place on screen. Our dispute is likely to be particularly fierce where we think that a methodologically misguided researcher is denying morally or politically significant difference. Employing quantitative methods of content analysis, investigators count the recurrence of an event (e.g., violence) across televi-sion or the Internet in "calculable categories": as a condition of doing so, they need to ignore or "suppress" contextually specific narrative features, the characteristics which make each occurrence of that event distinct (Morley, 1992: 175). They can appear resolutely blind to qualitative distinc-tions which as members of an audience we wish to insist are ethically important (e.g., between two instances of violence on television, one of which we would regard as justified retribution and the other as unprovoked assault).

Likewise in research on people's responses to media marketing, categories or classes of content can be established by investigators. For instance, they may ascribe a national identity to products advertised in television commercials during a survey of consumer attitudes. This formulation should be consistent with their research participants' perceptions of meaning on screen – in this case, consumers' classification by country of those possible purchases or their "logics in use" (Morley, 1992: 31).

Viewers' construction of a screen's situational logic (their conception of media content as comprehensible narrative) can be explored and established in focus groups. Research is able to record how they are identifying instances of aggression or altruism and subsequently responding: the audience's classification of content and consequences then provides the conceptual groundwork establishing the "meaningful components" referred to and summarized by a survey's "aggregated statistical results" (Morley, 1992: 177). Numbers must count the screen user's – not the student's – reading of content. Basically, the "atoms" of media analysis belong to the audience.

Effects studies connect human actions as stimulus and response: for instance, the former can be said to initiate imitation. Violence on screen (as defined by the researcher and her associates) is asserted to bring about a similar performance in real life. But, we noted earlier, the decision both as to whether events seen *are* violent (does verbal chastising constitute "violence"?) and just what subsequent behavior constitutes copycat activity is open to debate, not least by the audience. Content is not a causal "stimulus which may or may not produce a response (effect) at the level of attitudinal change": it is a conjunction of signs carrying meaning to be "decoded" (Morley, 1992: 30).

As we have seen, effects studies rely on the statistically significant constant conjunction of events to impute a cause-effect relationship between them. Suppressing subjective differences (as merely idiosyncratic?) in responses to violent action is a condition of counting these reactions as instantiating the *same* quantifiable phenomenon (e.g., alleged copycat behavior). Down-playing local participant perception maintains unchallenged a global investigator's numerical account of observable events. But it equally halts research into the particular cognitive process during which viewers develop their specific response to the screen. Without knowing the shape of the narrative path followed by this psychological series of events, we cannot come to understand media use.

For poststructuralists, meaning resists attempts to anchor it in definition (to finally "fix" it). The sense we make of a text will at no point be consensually singular, acceptable to all. Rather it is continually plural, emerging from an "endless play of signifiers which can never be finally nailed down to a single centre, essence or meaning" (Eagleton, 1983: 138). Viewers are versatile in understanding content: they can see progressive ideas in reactionary texts (Fiske, 1987).

Media user studies perceive meaning to be produced by an audience's experientially informed cognitive "play" in responding to pre-existing screen signifiers. From our distinct perspectives as viewers we speculate upon and subsequently substantiate alternative versions of events viewed. Reading is "fore-structured" (Heidegger, 1962), shaped by the view from the cultural horizon we occupy. Different social classes, for example, can focus upon varying aspects of a single program, constructing significantly discrete accounts of its content. This interpretative model of media use finds a place for audiences to vigorously disagree over program narrative. Television's value judgments on events it represents on screen can be political statements invoking audience understanding and alignment. Such evaluations are prescriptions for behavior to which resistance by media users is also an appropriate response.

Understanding as a cognitive product (or proposition)

People watch television. While doing so, they draw on their half-conscious, semi-articulated awareness of "definitional frameworks" (Morley, 1980: 8) or settled social meanings (most obviously that news is said to deal with fact, drama with fiction). These circulating "structures of reception" (ibid.: 9) or forms of cultural classification ("fore-concepts": Heidegger, 1962) are patterns of meaning which we mentally import or recollect while viewing: they support our perception of what we are watching as instantiating defining types of content.

Screen content is "read" by audiences as exemplifying one or more formats ranging from the most general categories of "television program" and "web page" to the more specific genres of "soap opera," "talk show," "portal," and so on (probably *ad infinitum*). Consequently, during any given form of viewing, we expect a particular shape of narrative. In this way, media users place the items they are responding to within definitional frameworks or cognitive horizons of understanding which are more or less specifically culturally located. Audiences must undertake a "kind of 'work' in order to read meaningfully what is transmitted" (Morley, 1980: 11). But paradoxically our "work" of enlisting memory to establish likely media content can be said to set program meaning in "play."

In his pathbreaking work after structuralism on television audiences watching the UK current affairs show *Nationwide* (1980), Morley's cultural-sociological account of media users interpreting the program makes little reference to the time-taking (though often swift) cognitive *processes* of comprehension. These are the audience's goal-directed narratives of psychological projection and provision of textual meaning. We anticipate and (customarily) achieve intelligible content. Instead, Morley focuses on the relatively unchanging but necessary cultural horizons of that understanding from which people look at TV and Internet. Remembered types of people and programs constitute frameworks of vision. So we shall first attend to these forms of understanding (fore-concepts) which position us mentally (with expectations) when using media.

In Morley's innovative and influential study (1980) of nationwide current affairs television, perception of programs by both audiences and those who analyze them is from a political perspective. The cultural ideas guiding his viewers' media comprehension are considered or fore-grounded in preference to the path of their psychological use. Reading within particular frameworks of interpretation is said to constitute a conceptual competency acquired by virtue of one's social position and the knowledge to which one thereby has access. Morley asks: "What is the nature of the 'fit' between class, socio-economic or educational position and cultural or interpretative competencies/discourses/codes?" (1980: 25). Through what "educational" route does one acquire the conceptual tokens enabling one to construct a particular political sense for current affairs television? From which cultural horizons of understanding can perception secure meaning for these programs?

In contributing to a Marxist sociology of media knowledge, Morley wanted to at least outline the extent to which basic socio-demographic factors of class and education can be seen to "structure and pattern, if not straightforwardly determine" people's "access to the second level of cultural and ideological frameworks" (ibid.: 26). For, as we have just noted, it is to these cultural frameworks or "codes" which we refer in our different ways while interpreting a program to bring meaning to our screens. How do we arrive at our television screens educationally equipped to resolve their enigmas? What information from a recent past enables present insight, which background supports an audience's political focus on programs now?

Morley wished to establish how television's texts prompt a range of "readings" by different sections of their audience identified in terms of their social class or "structural position." His question was: why do people interpret programs from varying perspectives? How do they come to occupy their distinct political viewpoints or horizons of understanding when watching television – with agreement, apathy, or animosity towards the medium? His answer focused on the social genesis of cultural perspective, leaving the generation of meaning as a cognitive process to be studied by reader response theorists (see chapter 4).

Importantly, as Morley indicates, his account does not establish a direct relationship (a path necessarily followed) between viewers occupying a social class and their subsequently finding reasons to speak critically of (or in consensus with) a program. Instead, Morley's explanation has two stages. First, he devises a theoretical framework which he systematically relates to the actual political perspectives or horizons of interpretative understanding from which viewers regard *Nationwide*'s current affairs narratives of a "united kingdom." Audiences themselves classify the program in complex ways. He outlines three ideal-types or broad political categories of possible response to the program's accounts of the nation in the texts on which he focuses during this early phase of his audience research:

(a) where the audience interprets the message in terms of the same (dominant ideological) code employed by the transmitter ...

(b) where the audience employs a "negotiated" version of the (dominant ideological) code employed by the transmitter ...

(c) where the audience employs an "oppositional" code to interpret the message. (Morley, 1980: 23)

Secondly, Morley investigates the social (rather than psychological) production of this variation in political response, establishing a sociology of knowing about media. Looking at how we arrive at our cultural horizons of viewing content, he traces an informational route between:

1   "dominant," "negotiated," and "oppositional" focus group perceptions of *Nationwide* and
2   the source of these "decodings" in a *conjunction* of viewers belonging to a social class and their educational access to particular interpretative

frameworks (or "discourse"): "it is always a question of how social position *plus* particular discourse positions produce specific readings": "social position in no way directly correlates with decodings" (1980: 134, 137).

Occupying different class positions enables audiences – after their varying experience of education – to take up alternative if not also opposing perspectives on society (or employ diverse forms of social understanding). However, there is no necessary route between class and consumption of a particular educational "package": for instance, individuals from a range of social groups may join the same political party.

Morley's research shows that interpretative response to his chosen television programs is mediated through a person's political position, but a single social class can appropriate and operate a range of political perspectives on media content. He argues on the basis of his *Nationwide* focus groups that even those occupying the same social stratum (the apprentices and shop stewards) but "educated" in different discourses and institutions (e.g., of "mainstream working-class populism" or Labour Party politics) can make contrary dominant and oppositional readings of a program. The apprentice group "inhabits a populist 'damn-all-politicians' ideology comparable to that of the program" (1980: 135), while the trade unionists dismiss *Nationwide*'s politics as a "bloody sweeping statement" (ibid.: 108). Conversely, those occupying different class positions (the apprentices and bank managers) nevertheless can make the same dominant reading of a program. In short, Morley concluded that the groundwork in studying audiences is not established by the positivist's constant conjunction of numbers but by focusing upon the conjunction of normative discourses from which we draw in responding to TV and Internet.

Audiences read complex texts which are themselves syntheses of multiple components. A program's view of the world can advance the interests of a particular social class but is always inflected (or mediated) through distinctive types of aesthetic discourse. Television's content takes the narrative shape of serials (as in soap operas) or series (like current affairs shows investigating a single topic) yet can combine aspects of both formats. Unlike the customary relationship between film and its spectators, program presenters engage in a direct "mode of address" from the screen, appearing to look at audiences. So when analyzing television's underwriting a reactionary *status quo*, one must recognize a specific formulation of ideology articulated through a particular program discourse and mode of audience address (Morley, 1980: 134).

Understanding as a cognitive process (or projection)

In exploring the degree to which "different sections of the audience did interpret the messages in different ways," Morley asks "to what extent they projected freely onto the message meanings they would want to find there" (1980: 23). When viewers project or anticipate narrative content this subjective process is continually constrained or shaped (fore-structured) by the frameworks of understanding (fore-concepts) within which their expectation occurs. Knowing the customary format of television journalism, we don't anticipate a news presenter will engage in activity appropriate to a game show.

Media users identify a program and persons within its unfolding space as instances of a type likely to evolve in characteristic ways (e.g., the stereotypical gossip on the soap opera street). Constructing a likely story, we watch, checking anticipation for accuracy. Morley wants to show how varying accounts of screen content are "generated" (1980: 23) by viewers. However, his research on responses to current affairs television reveals little about an audience's *projecting* program meaning from a horizon of understanding where we continually engage in a generative process of generic recognition, remembering, and rendition of anticipated media narrative.

In his extended work on audiences responding to the BBC (British Broadcasting Corporation) early evening program *Nationwide*, Morley complains that the subjective "level at which the decoding operates is not explored" (1992: 30) in effects studies. But this is a major criticism which can be directed at his own work. For his account of how media audiences make meaning (the process wherein they form their understanding of a text) remained at the sociological level. He does not engage with the psychological activity implied by his view of media response as interpretation. Reflecting on the discussions he facilitated, Morley analyzes not people's subjective cognitive purchase on a text but the shared "collective" process in focus groups through which "understandings and decodings" are produced by their contributors considered as members of "critically significant groupings" (ibid.) in society.

Morley writes of textual forms as "internal structures" (1992: 75) and it is viewers' memories of these which guide their subjective process of reading (e.g., expecting a soap opera episode to remain enigmatic at its ending). But a knowledge of these "cultural frameworks" does not function by causally "determining individual interpretations" (ibid.). Rather, as we have noted, the media user's awareness of genre and other aesthetic forms defines the range of her or his anticipation and possible readings of content. These limiting horizons of an audience's textual understanding are said by Morley to be "conceptual frameworks," "definitional frameworks," or "interpretative frameworks" (ibid.: 80). When we watch television, we clothe or fill a program framework with perceived content. But our expectation of further narrative development eventually ends. From a media user perspective, a program's wholly "answering" our anticipation (our completed or fully formed understanding of its content) can then be regarded as "closure." For we hold

> a "now more-inclusive knowledge – in the enclosing, framing, gathering-together plenitude of our 'sense of a sufficient and necessary ending'", a "retrospective-circumscribing 'over-look' of the item: what it *all* means …," a "completed, circumscribed understanding (what the item was *really* all about)." (Brunsdon and Morley, 1978: 65, emphasis in the original)

In short, audience responses are structured psychologically as well as sociologically. Drawing on media memories, we construct the meaning of a text by setting "discourses in play," our "cultural competences in play" (Morley, 1992: 119, 127). Equally, they can be said to play upon *us* as the horizons of our understanding, creatively resourcing or curbing cognitive capacity. Morley (1992: 174) cites Hammersley and Atkinson's work on ethnography to the effect that a theory must "include reference to mechanisms or processes by which the relationship among the variables identified is generated" (1983: 20). Nevertheless he did not develop an account of the psychological process defining media reception – of the structured cognitive play in our responding to programs.

Morley considers *Nationwide*'s political positioning of media users (successfully or otherwise). Unlike reception theorists in France or Germany (see chapter 4), he has little to say about the process of interpretation through which audiences come to understand the textual focus of their response. In his analyses, the television viewer has always already arrived at her or his conception of program meaning, a personal response to be subsequently discussed in a public focus group. However, his later work reflectively expresses appropriate concern about using a model of media user "decoding" which "would seem to blur" or confuse the activity of comprehension with the achievement of consensus or criticism:

> "what is involved [in 'decoding'] is a *set* of processes – of attentiveness, recognition of relevance, of comprehension, and of interpretation and response – *all*

of which may be involved for a single audience member in front of the screen." The "model [of 'decoding'] as it stands would seem to blur the axis of comprehension/incomprehension of signs with that of agreement/disagreement with forms of propositional meaning generated from these signs." (Morley, 1992: 121, emphases in the original)

Participating with a presenter in the "axis" or process of "comprehension/ incomprehension" during which we establish the meaning of television programs is to be distinguished from acceding to the propositional beliefs which we conclude are being asserted in these texts. Sharing emerging understanding of a narrative does not necessarily mean evaluative consensus on content.

One can align with a presenter's activity in comprehension, in making a meaningful identification *of* a story. This is distinct from identifying *with* the result of that cognitive undertaking. One's absorption in her processing meaning through question and answer is not the same as alignment with her conclusion. Trade unionists found *Nationwide* narratives intelligible but did not share its judgment of industrial disputes.

Audience alignment: varieties of identification

Watching television, we construct narrative to be known. We recognize a program type and consequently anticipate or project its likely content. Talk shows, for instance, mostly expose the private to the public. Expecting and establishing events on screen we gain answers to our question, "What's going on?" Through this creative play of ideas, their cognitive pursuit of sense, media users come to understand television and Internet narrative. Interpretation precedes and can be the focus for identification. While involved in discerning the content of drama, viewers can position themselves with those seen on screen also intent on making sense of their surroundings.

A final discussion of Morley's inflection after structuralism of 1980s emerging media user studies will assist us in distinguishing between the principal modes of audience alignment with narrative agents and presenters which issue from the viewer's cognitive activity of interpreting a text. Going all the way from enabling the process wherein viewers make identification$_1$ *of* content to encouraging their identification$_2$ *with* the views of its characters, a program's attracting audience-consumers can be slowly seductive.

Recognizing a story as "relevant" to (or instantiating) a type of narrative is fundamental to its comprehension: realizing its format we can anticipate and establish its development. Knowledge of genres is being aware of "sets of rules for the production of meaning" (Morley, 1992: 127) by viewers. Our wider cultural awareness when watching soap opera, for instance, gives us the "ability to predict the range of possible consequences attendant upon actions in the spheres of the domestic/familial" (ibid.: 129). Subsequently, we confirm consequences and construct program meaning.

Establishing the content and identity of narratives on television or Internet positions us as media users with those on screen in search of similar insight. Realizing that would-be knowledgeable audiences and current affairs narrative presenters engage in parallel projection or assemblage of stories is fundamental to answering Morley's questions about why we accede to these presenters information gathering on our behalf: "How far do the different presenters secure the popular identification to which they (implicitly) lay claim?" "To what extent do different sections of the audience identify with an interviewer and feel that they are 'lending' him/her their authority to interrogate figures in public life on their behalf?" (1980: 24).

People are able to amicably agree with presenters' perspectives. Aligning oneself with those engaged in identification$_1$ of narrative events on screen (a *process* of asking "what's happening?") can lead to identifying$_2$ with the *proposition* which establishes the answer. Presenters become "'points of identification' within the message" and consequently "transmit the preferred reading to the audience" (Morley, 1980: 11, 10). Positioning ourselves with Oprah Winfrey in the process of coming to understand her talk show contributors, we are encouraged to share her concluding ideological proposition that they are praiseworthy in resolving their own problems rather than seeking social change. Both knowledgeable audience and narrative agent can thereby succeed in comprehending a participant's circumstances. Sharing the sense of a story, we are led to secure a politically nuanced solution: and screen-related practices "reinforce" (Pauwels, 2005: 605) real life.

But media users may resist the proposition arrived at by those viewed or agree only partly or in private (Wilson, 2001). Outside *Oprah* ideology, don't people's personal domestic difficulties ever have public debatable causes (can fiscal policy lead to family breakdown)?

In understanding media users it is important to consider an audience's consensus with (or criticism of) a program's conclusions. But it is also necessary to focus on the cultural conditions of narrative comprehension – of media users making sense of a story on screen. Unintelligible narratives prompt not speculation on their content but a reader's silence. Issues of insight and identification do not arise: under such circumstances, they are simply marginal to media use.

An audience's epistemological environment (accustomed cultural conditions) of sense-making in everyday life can be quite different from those on screen. In a significant discussion which deserves further thought, Morley notes how a focus group of black British students "refuse to read" (1980: 134). Unable or unwilling to share the process of comprehension played out within the text, they cannot "make identifications with any of the positions or persons offered through the program": nor do they engage in criticism for "they fail, or refuse, to engage with the discourse of the program enough to deconstruct or redefine it" (ibid.: 142–3).

A number of mainly West Indian or African young women with a working-class English background likewise conveyed a discursive "disjunction between their cultural world and that of *Nationwide*" (ibid.: 72). Consequently they could not meet the terms of understanding the text: they were unable to comprehend, consider stories to be of a certain type, and thus anticipate or align with narrative. "I don't understand it, that's why I don't like it." "I couldn't understand a thing he was saying" (ibid.). Substantive political criticism is simply impossible. Eight years later Bobo's study of black women as cultural readers comprehending in different ways is important since they did make "types of oppositional readings" (1988: 103).

Focus group contributors who expressed their alienation from *Nationwide* because they "don't understand" concepts and consequently content represent one negative response. Clearly, where media users deny the very possibility of interpreting a text, aligning with the presenter's process of making an identification$_1$ of content to secure the goal of comprehension is immediately excluded. Two other types of reaction which we place on the agenda here do not dismiss the program as failing to cross cultures, as illiterate in its address to "others." Instead, in refusing to identify$_2$ with its perspective on current affairs they evaluate its particular focus and politics as illegitimate.

Some research participants distanced themselves not from the very activity of asking questions in the program but from the particular topics it chose for inquiry. Perceiving themselves as readers from a different generational culture, they could not identify with the program's (implicit) evaluation that these issues were worthy of attention. A group of working-class West Indian young women students saw *Nationwide*'s focus as being appropriate for a "different audience": "older people – like you (the interviewer)," "middle-class people …," "parents who've come in from work, especially fathers who've got nothing to eat yet" (Morley, 1980: 88). Interestingly, other West Indian and white young women students with a working-class background did align themselves with the program's selection of current affairs stories:

> Question. "So is there a bit of *Nationwide* that feels like it's for you?"
>
> "Yeah, about the students, about the lion …"
>
> "The fact that they're trying to do it on their own …"
>
> "Yeah … that was really good …" (Ibid.: 92)

A capable program presenter and culturally appropriate audience can align, projecting meaning with a similar focus. Enjoying this parallel process of seeking understanding, each asks a set of questions about events on screen: they secure information which allows them to engage in the process of identifying$_1$ a *Nationwide* story. Here anticipation and actualizing meaning leads to a shared evaluative perspective on the narrative: these viewers identify$_2$ in their judgment of it as a "really good" story.

But, as we have noted, for writers after structuralism like Morley who are critical of social disparities in power it is important to emphasize that judgments by media users can be at odds politically, evoking distanced criticism of presenters rather than close identification with their position. While *Nationwide* announced that "well, there we are, most people seem agreed the tax system is too severe …," an all-male audience of working-class white trade union officials of varied ages asserted in response:

> "That's a bloody sweeping statement, isn't it? … from four bloody edited interviews!"
>
> Program: "… and of course the lower paid workers will benefit … from … er … the … er …"
>
> (Unionists): "Extra crumbs falling from the table!" (Ibid.: 108)

We engage like presenters in anticipating and actualizing narrative knowledge. But there can be a political distance between the evaluative perspectives or horizon of understanding from which accounts are constructed by people on screen and those from which viewers assemble content. *Nationwide* positions us audio-visually with a presenter: "we 'see' from an absent but marked position, which is where the presenter's *voice* appears to come from: 'this mysterious clicking noise …'" (Brunsdon and Morley, 1978: 64) (emphasis in the original). But clearly our moral or political judgment of seen content can differ from the voiceover: spatial and political positioning are distinct.

In short, we "need to ask to what extent the audience identifies with the (mirror) image of itself" coming to understand which it can perceive in the program presenter's own activity of constructing meaning. Being able to associate oneself with that image of mentally *processing* a report does not entail agreement with the political perspective advanced in the text (or what I have called "*propositional* identification") – that the "audience will then take over the frameworks of understanding within which the presenters encapsulate the reports" (Morley, 1992: 85).

Where the audience does express its consensual agreement or identification with a presenter's political position this announcement of faith can be regarded as its assent to the "preferred reading" of a program suggested by the text's "framing and linking discourse" (ibid.: 84) around issues. As we have seen, identification *with* a program's preferred reading of a narrative fundamentally presupposes our cultural capacity to achieve an identification *of* the latter's content.

Anticipating media user theory: audiences constructing texts

We have moved in this chapter from one theory to a diametrically opposing point of view. Our discussion began by considering the structuralist account of audiences (see also chapter 1), where the latter's response is constructed by the text. We conclude by anticipating media user theory in which sense is synthesized by those seeing the screen. Meaning is not passively absorbed but actively achieved.

Viewing checks the cash value of a program as promissory note. A cognitive psychology of audiences (open to testing in focus groups) emphasizes three inseparable aspects or "moments" of media use as projection and positing meaning on page or program. Viewing always involves audiences in (1) immediately forming fore-concepts or tacitly classifying perceptions of TV programs and web pages (e.g., as chat show or chat room) and consequently (2) constructing or fore-structuring our anticipation of content (3) which we subsequently confirm (or otherwise).

Media use is contextually framed or informed by the statable cultural horizons from which content is accessed (or guided by a knowledge of *genera*), allowing the identification of text as instance of a type. Limiting cases will involve film, television, and Internet which fall within the category of incomprehensibly foreign content. Identification supports the anticipatory cognitive processes of projecting content. In reading we check conjecture.

Barker's recent work (2004) on cinema audiences provides a brief concluding example of research consistent with (if not incorporating) media user theory. Movie goers interpret events on screen within frameworks of comprehending content ("that sort of stuff"), categories for classifying consumption of artifacts they know to the point of familiarity. Cinema buffs may talk of a "bog standard Hollywood Action epic," a "drive-in movie type film," "cerebral film," "trash movies" vs. "worthy films" (Barker and Brooks, 1998: 75). Two-dimensional action on screen can meet an audience's three-dimensional anticipation. People buy tickets on this basis: our fore-concept of content generates cash for the cinema. Spectators expect to view stories which can be recognized and understood drawing upon a well rehearsed and much repeated awareness of signifying practices (associated with action epic or awesome entertainment) marking out conceptual horizons of cinematic insight. In doing so they culturally orientate their gaze, often presupposing that they will enjoy (or otherwise) particular perceptions of stars (or stereotypes).

Beyond cinema walls, media users engage more widely in these "prefigurative processes" (Barker, 2004). Manifesting varying degrees of self-awareness, they draw on background information to classify particular acts of screen consumption: in doing so they construct or "live out" informed expectations of story development. Through this cognitive "interplay between (institutional) generators of prefigurative materials and audiences" (ibid.) prior knowledge shapes anticipation of action. Audiences establish expectations (project potential storylines) and interpret narrative according to preceding awareness of format. Media use is everywhere placed in context by commentary and concept, aligning audiences in anticipation, prioritizing some points of view and marginalizing others.

In "prefigurative talk" (Barker, 2004) amongst spectators one can hear that, for some, "there's nothing more annoying than a predictable film" (contributor, Barker and Brooks, 1998: 60). Stories predictably confirming audience anticipation may equally bring easy enjoyment: "there is nothing amiss in enjoying two-dimensional films." On the other hand, many spectators' projections of probable pleasure in watching narrative development apparently are regularly subverted by skepticism. Expectation is knowingly, regretfully, restrained with movie goers "getting ready to be disappointed" (Barker and Brooks, 1998: 58, 59).

On the recurrent occasions to which these sad cynics refer, they look forward from cognitive horizons bearing conflicting information. Audience anticipation (prefigurative projection) is inconsistent: it draws on contradictory memories. Spectators entertain side-by-side both high hopes prompted by the "prefigurative publicity" (Barker, 2005: 360) of narrative images outside the cinema and low expectations arising from their repeated viewing of films as less than advertised. Explicitly or implicitly, prefigurative items (ibid.: 354) in text and talk guide media users projecting potential narrative – rejoicing in celebratory anticipation or restrained by skeptical realism.

Conclusion

To conclude, philosophically inspired studies of screen users converge in media user theory. Structuralists "liquidated" the human subject, reducing her or him to an "impersonal structure" occupying an implicit presence within the cinema, a textual addressee (Eagleton, 1983: 112–13). Writers after structuralism re-equip an audience with active employment of their cultural and social knowledge in reading, an awareness supporting a range of responses to recognized content. This theoretical endeavor emphasizes a "proactive" (Taylor, 2005: 627) percipient of programs rather than the passive media response presumed in effects studies and structuralism.

However, a philosophical psychology of understanding is required to flesh out the reception process wherein an audience actively constitutes a content for television and Internet, constructing and checking its accounts of screen narrative. By drawing upon the "micro-narratives and micro-histories" (Kuhn, 1994: 202) of media use, a phenomenology of reading can establish the unchanging structure of that play-like subjective process of engaging with the screen which nonetheless results in contrasting audience perceptions of textual content.

Writing of moments in realizing a meaning, media researchers share – to a greater or lesser degree – phenomenology's conceptual focus. Its concern is to carefully elicit the temporal form of human awareness, a shared structure embedded in the subjective activity of rendering textual content intelligible. In other words, recognizing how we think alike in media use is as important as celebrating variety in response.

Hermeneutics focuses on the "space where the reader meets text" (Freeman, 2007: 926), where the "event of understanding" (ibid.) occurs, the "performance of understanding" (ibid.: 942). Such audience study necessarily has a historical dimension. In coming to understand narrative on television screens, we remember a previous sequence somewhere, at some time, alike in one or more respects to the present program. Consequently we are always anticipating similar events emerging, projecting a parallel story. Our activity is likewise with other media.

At the outset of chapter 1 we saw how a Chinese Malaysian cellphone user's responses to the phone numbers of incoming messages were fore-structured by her conceptualization of those which were "familiar" as not likely to bear "weird" content – her looking from a horizon of expectation. When meaning flows in understanding – our anticipation is confirmed – we do not question the text's identity. But "questions occur when something about the text creates dissonance" (Freeman, 2007: 934).

Textual knowledge is arrived at by media users setting "tacit assumptions" (Eagleton, 1983: 62) in play to be subsequently checked against events on screen. These beliefs constitute a socially shared (Straubhaar, 2007: 227) memory of previously viewed content (e.g., of television narrative as generic). From these cultural horizons of understanding, more or less consciously, audiences project meaning on a program – whose narrative then may not advance as anticipated.

3

Perceiving is Believing:
From Phenomenology to Media
User Theory

Reception studies after structuralism emphasize the variety of readings which can emerge in responses to film or television. Media users from different ethnic groups, generations or social classes, female and male audiences, perceive programs in varying ways. Stereotypical images can be seen by some as "truth" and by others as distorting oppression. The interpretative "angle" or horizon of understanding from which a Hollywood film is watched can be aesthetic or ethical, political or pleasure-seeking. Some media users resist a program's view of the world, others rejoice in recognizing its familiar powerful perspective. The cultural categories in play during media consumption are diverse.

But beyond this enunciation of audience perspectives within a "pluralist tradition" (Curran, 1996: 270), what have reception studies achieved? From the late 1970s onwards, an increasing "exasperation" has been expressed towards response studies simply celebrating media users' proliferating "acts of interpretation" (King, 2000: 211). So what? In this chapter we seek to integrate these diverse readings by showing them to emerge from a single (or transcultural) psychological process of assigning meaning in which viewers actively engage everywhere. We examine how different interpretative frameworks inform people's participation in this process, particularly where it occurs cross-culturally. Understanding media users presupposes that we understand their "understanding."

Poststructuralism + Phenomenology =
Media User Theory

We shall look at the accounts people provide of interpreting pages and programs to discern the underlying subjective – but similar – pattern of their anticipating and achieving meaning. This universal (if not always immediately evident) activity of making sense constitutes the necessary mental processing wherein readers generate a variety of meanings from a given text. We saw in chapter 2 that television theorists like Morley focus on the *sociological* structuring (e.g., by social class) of screen responses. Poststructuralists emphasize that people arrive from varying backgrounds to assert different beliefs about content. Drawing on phenomenology, media user studies nonetheless seek a shared *psychological* structure for the cognitive process in which we move towards comprehending narrative on television or Internet in our distinctive ways.

Though he does not claim phenomenology as his inspiration, Couldry writes that "large-scale patterns can be found in empirical evidence of people's reflections on their encounters with the media process" (2001: 171). We shall entertain the presumption that these encounters have the structure of absorbing goal-seeking activity, of a teleological immersion in making sense of text.

A succession of writers have conceptualized this structure as the audience's future-orientated projection of meaning: we can trace the philosophical genesis of the idea in phenomenology to its subsequent appearance in literary reception theory and understanding media users. In "schematic processing" (Machill et al., 2007: 200) of stories we anticipate narrative from a generic horizon of understanding. *Projection* is the fundamental link between spectator and screen: it is the (in)formed cognitive process in which audiences "grasping" (ibid.: 194) connections draw on the context of their viewing to respond to events. Our perception of narrative content is mediated through cultural memory (Sturken, 2008).

Morley wrote in 1992 that his interests had increasingly come to focus on the "*how* of television watching," on understanding "how the process of television viewing is done as an activity" (133, emphasis in the original). But this emerges as a sociological focus on the changing family environment of viewing, not on subjective activity. The mental – cognitive – structure of media use is invariant.

The British Birmingham Centre for Contemporary Cultural Studies inspired much discussion of media audience responses towards a program's perceived *political proposition*. What do viewers think of *Nationwide*'s ideological purchase on industrial conflict? Nevertheless debate did not move towards significant integration with wider European discussion focused on *psychological process* – exploring how viewers come to understand (if at all) the narrative meaning within which a program's politics of representing the world is contained. Yet the audience's interpretative path through exploring and establishing meaning is as powerfully resonant as any conclusion regarding its "bias." From what political perspective (horizon) are we coming to understand content? "Reading" television is temporally as well as socially structured.

Understanding a story takes time: insight is not instant. Establishing textual meaning is "temporal or sequential rather than spatial" (Seung, 1982: 185–6). We speculate on content, conclusively discarding one possibility, then constructively developing another probable path we consider narrative action will follow in a program. As we saw in the last chapter, cinema theorists who engage in analyzing spectator responses have called for a psychological (cognitive and emotion-recognizing) account of screen use as a *process* of establishing meaning. Viewers anticipate and attempt to achieve apparently coherent content.

Developing a wide-ranging model of the audience's interpretative thought, whether in the cinema or domestic circumstances, should integrate a multiplicity of psychological reactions. It would show how spectators follow a parallel path of speculating and substantiating meaning: although they do so within different horizons of understanding to make distinct readings of a text's discourse.

Thinking about screen use as occurring *from* a cultural horizon assists in remembering that it always involves looking from a perspective, emphasizing or fore-grounding an aspect of the text. But screen narratives are also viewed as located *within* a cultural horizon: they are continually responded to as instantiating media formats and genres. "Horizon designates comprehensiveness albeit constituted from an angle of perception" (Iser, 2006: 37). Looking is both located and normative.

Media users draw on varying cultural maps of screen knowledge to constructively project narrative or form an unfolding story. In this way, the "freeplay" of meaning is "limited" by the "given and existing" (Derrida, 1970: 264). These semi-articulated general guides to assembling media content embrace the conceptual or philosophical (ranging from our awareness that every event on screen must have a cause to our accepting that under patriarchal conditions of popular cultural production the latter is more likely to be male than female). Or we can be assisted in setting out a story by our memory of genre and its types of possible narrative – to one or more of which the tale before us conforms. Looking from plural perspectives while always anticipating a story's meaning, readers everywhere conjecture: our informed imagination plays with possible developments and outcomes, seeking narrative integrity in a text.

The thesis of projection provides a necessary *psychological* rather than sociological framework within which we can understand the "particularity of individual responses to different types of programming" (Morley, 1992: 134). In projecting we draw upon cognitive horizons of understanding textual content, a "cultural repertoire of resources" (ibid.: 136) supporting interpretation. In one of Morley's focus groups an interviewee's narrative assertion that "police are no angels" (ibid.: 135) underwrites their anticipation of television content. But from time to time, a reader's cultural horizons of comprehending the world are so distant from the text's that the former responds with silence.

The philosophical investigation of human consciousness known as phenomenology is one source for a mental narrative of reading as a subjective activity of forming textual meaning or "temporal theory of meaning-experience" (Seung, 1982: 188). Phenomenology abstracts (or abducts) from people's concrete accounts of responding to texts to determine the essential cognitive process which must be accomplished for the latter's comprehension. This is equally a conceptual and empirical inquiry (reporting both on the nature and experience of understanding). Listening to participants discussing books in focus groups, for example, we are able to consider how they posit narrative meaning: we can establish a core process at the heart of their understanding. Does each anticipate on the basis of remembering similar storylines? What is their concept of succeeding in "comprehension"? We can abstract from their discursive contributions to discern how they anticipate developments on a page (or in a program) in accordance with their assumptions about its type. Thus we devise a phenomenology of psychological projection.

Such philosophical analysis of subjective experience answers the question: what is the structured and similar thought process presupposed by *any* accomplishment of understanding? Yet phenomenology as a route to interpreting media audiences was summarily dismissed by MacCabe as solipsistic – as implausibly excluding reference to society from any account of how we gain knowledge. Warning us against this philosophy, he informs us that in this approach to understanding "understanding," the isolated "subject is seen as the founding source of meanings" (1981: 226) (see Wilson, 1993).

How can such a philosophy of separate existence be relevant to interpreting reading when making sense of book or screen content involves relating it to prior knowledge (e.g., of linguistic meaning or locations) invariably acquired from others? We shall see that where phenomenology does acknowledge that viewing is necessarily informed by wider cultural and social awareness, it can illuminate the route whereby textual meaning is constituted by the reader's "interpretative synthesis" (Seung, 1982: 189) of shared and personal understanding.

To illustrate this rather abstract philosophical model or paradigm of audiences interpreting a text, we shall draw on a (hopefully!) straightforward exemplar. This cross-cultural reception study (March and August 2005) of screen mediated political communication considered responses to National Day television advertisements sponsored by the Malaysian oil company (Petronas) "selling" the necessity of inter-ethnic harmony. We shall focus on the first of these marketing narratives. "The Bush" (44 secs) shows a hedge being trimmed and we hear an Indian Tamil song: the gardener is hidden, for at first we see only the top of the cutting shears. As the male singer slowly rises from behind the "bush" his identity is revealed to be Chinese. To this visual surprise the final shot adds a question and attributes corporate ownership: "'Don't you just love this country?' *Selamat Hari Kebangsaan* (Have a Good National Day) Petronas."

Constructing Textual Meaning: Projecting Coherent Narrative

For structuralists of the last century – to paint a picture inattentive to detail – the cinematic screen centrally determined spectator reaction. As we noted in the first chapter, these theorists of media reception argued that from two-dimensional cause emerged three-dimensional consequence, invariably a passive audience following of reactionary film politics. Powerful ideology positioned percipient: sexist film effected sexist response. Global structuralist study of the relationship between the reader and read excluded local subjective process, falling into the "hypodermic needle" fallacy of seeing communication effects as direct and immediate (Schroder et al., 2003: 109).

Poststructuralist opposition to the very idea of passively perceived media argued for active television viewers. The latter were considered as relatively freely reacting to, sometimes rejecting, screen narrative. During the 1990s, celebrating the variety of screen response was in vogue – the "heterogeneous distribution of meanings" (Arnould and Thompson, 2005: 869) or multicultural reception. Yet positivism (ignoring the unobservable) lingered. Viewer perceptions of screen content were presented in research not as cognitive *processes* establishing textual meaning but as propositional *conclusions* at which audiences had always already arrived.[1]

Nevertheless, within the emerging alternative European tradition of reader reception theory, hermeneutics as an account of how we make sense of books did consider understanding texts as an *event*. In a "search for invariants" or "trans-individual" activity (Merquior, 1986: 108, 131) its philosophical partner, phenomenology, sought to anchor users' pluralistic response to books in a universal (or essential) psychological process: for it argued that reading involved a speculative anticipation and actualizing of meaning to be modeled as cognitive *play*.

Generating a new paradigm (Kuhn, 1962) of audience-text interaction, hermeneutic phenomenology insisted on the "event-character" of understanding which Gadamer analyses with his own concept of "play" as an (active/passive) "being taken" (Grondin, 2002). "Play" refers here to the cognitive events wherein readers concurrently recollect and speculate, absorbing past and articulating future meaning – in ludic moments or aspects of media use. Recognizing screen romance, we anticipate (and find) emotion: we are actively/passively absorbed in understanding.

Hermeneutics, in short, resists the view that we are immediately, knowledgeably aware of the world: rather, we assemble and arrive at a meaning for pages and programs. As a poststructuralist, Tulloch argues that a subject's "locus" in a societal formation structures her or his range of access to discourses and ideological codes (2000: 182). Our social class forms a conduit through which we acquire knowledge. Nevertheless, we need to establish the recurring reading process wherein looking from varying cultural horizons of understanding we "receive" an individual text (Casebier (1991: 21–5) illuminates this use of "horizons").

Understanding is a patterned process of remembering and rendering meaning. How does recollection, the source of narrative expectation, relate to establishing knowledge? We need to foreground a necessary public exploration of audience subjectivity, the "processes through which people actualize media meanings" (Schroder et al., 2003: 122).

Recognizing content by reference to familiar frameworks for ordered understanding of texts – such as viewers' awareness of program format, generic formulae, and stories articulating stereotypes – enables audiences to constitute TV or Internet narrative from perceived events. Our knowledge of talk shows supports our seeking and synthesizing participant stories. Drawing on our cultural experience of characteristic narrative development (or "portfolios of interpretation": Hill, 1997), we project meaning on cognitively playable pages, expecting and establishing a story's sequence.

Reading produces difference shaped by familiarity. Drawing on the "plenitude" of our cultural past we interpret specific texts as particular inflections of general types: content is perceived to instantiate codes. Understanding is always fore-structured by fore-concepts.

> Subjectivity is a plenary image, with which I may be thought to encumber the text, but whose deceptive plenitude is merely the wake of all the codes which constitute me, so that my subjectivity has ultimately the generality of stereotypes. (Barthes, 1974: 10)

But from time to time we cannot recognize or identify a narrative: we consider it "strange," realizing we are unable to see it as instantiating a known type. We become aware there are limits to our horizons of understanding: audience projection or speculating on that story's meaning fails. After watching the Petronas National Day television advertisement (noted above) with its Tamil song, a male Chinese viewer responded to a question about its content: "I don't know the language.... I have no idea." Instead, he offered an interpretation of the sequence as visual event only. His *seeing* the event *as* narrative is coherent but constrained by cultural background:

> "What I see is that it's about the Malaysian simple life." In Malaysia "you have time to cut your own bush and sing at the same time. That's the idea behind the advertisement lah." "Maybe [it] has other extra meanings, but I couldn't get it."

In projecting meaning – whether successfully or otherwise – viewers identify the direction of events on screen. This philosophical psychology of the media user emphasizes understanding as a process. Here audience analysis regards as pivotal such viewer experience of narrative as a female Chinese contributor in the National Day reception research records below: "I took time over understanding" the story. Comprehension is a time-structured construction of meaning moving from fore-concept to establishing content. Realizing this underwrites the investigator's focus on an audience's perception of textual significance as the same process across cultures – though there are wide-ranging differences (and sometimes difficulties) in the understanding which emerges.

Taking time, our female Chinese respondent indicated her early narrative projection of the advertisement's ("first") meaning was revised in the face of events: "you think it's an Indian guy singing, then you see a Chinese man." Her fore-structured understanding of content was not confirmed by the text. With the singer no longer considered to be Indian, aspects of the story require reconciling in a hermeneutic circle of "to and fro" understanding, her re-presenting the whole narrative as consistent: "so I guess it makes sense, lah." "I took time over understanding it."

> "At first, before they showed the visual of the Chinese guy cutting, before he came up, at first I thought it was maybe a hidden guy standing up. So in that way it made sense, in that part, but when he came upright, at first I said 'is it?' You know, 'what is it?'" [intense indecipherable speech and group laughter] "I thought 'Oh. OK.' But I think normal, lah ... but not many Chinese can sing [Tamil] so fluently.... So I guess it makes sense, lah. OK. And I took *time* over understanding it." (Female, Chinese, speaker's emphasis) For her friend, the story is "not really a surprise because Malaysia is a multi-cultural country." (Female Chinese)

Understanding is a process resulting when successful in an interpretative statement.

In outlining reactions to this narrative of enigma and resolution, one can distinguish (as a female Chinese contributor did) between audience projections of advertisement "action" and readers realizing therein a propositional "message." In this time for identification, viewers may agree with the latter or assert their distance. The Chinese respondent concluded by signaling alignment with her proposed multicultural propositional meaning ("message") for the narrative as audio-visual event ("action").

> Actually it's good because, that guy, I think he's a Chinese and then he's singing a Tamil song ... so it's across the race, the language. It's good because Malaysia [has] got different races, cultures. (Female Chinese)

Hearing an Indian song we think we will shortly, if not immediately, see an Indian person on screen. Drawing upon the schemata of hermeneutic reception theory, we can say that our cultural horizons of understanding constitute or in(form) our "fore-conceptions" (Heidegger, 1962) of narrative.[2] Recollecting these foundational "frames of reference" (Barker, 2001: 28), that is, directs our anticipation and identification of stories on screen. Our projection of narrative meaning plays on the "juke-boxes of memory" (Van Dijck, 2005: 311), selecting informative horizons of textual understanding within which to interpret particular content.

More prosaically, we presume that detectives customarily provide the resolution of enigma on screen and "read" them accordingly. Access to such cultural assumptions allows us to anticipate and (where our expectations are confirmed by events) achieve meaningful narrative. The operation of these frameworks guiding interpretation can be discerned through experiential investigation (e.g., in focus groups). Projecting meaning is precisely play-like because it focuses on that which does not (yet) exist.

Informed media users develop "patterns of expectation" (Barker and Petley, 2001: 8), confirmed to a varying extent in understanding different texts. Some programs show our anticipation to be accurate, others surprise. Responding to an individual screen from this wider perspective, we interpret its content "as" a particular type of story (or classify it within an "as-structure" of perception: Heidegger, 1962).

In a (to and fro) movement of cognitive play, we repeatedly relate text to its context (our knowledge of format, gender, or genre): this placing in perspective allows us to identify, anticipate, and actualize a page's or program's emerging narrative sketches as instantiating a pattern of story-telling. Guided by our expectation of e-journalism as menu driven, going online to access news content we first focus on text headlines rather than pictures or graphics (Chan and Leung, 2005: 358). In media use, we project and process particular narrative meaning within wider conceptual horizons of understanding: knowledgeably watching stories unfold, we anticipate and achieve insight (Wilson et al., 2003: Wilson and Tan, 2005).

Perception is cognitively, often expressively, interactive. Audiences assemble screen narrative in a ludic reception process both past (retensive) and future-orientated (protensive). In the first place, their thought can be characterized as retrodictive play, moving back and forth between cultural horizon (remembered aesthetic type) and identifying events on program or page (as typically presented instance of a news story and so on). From memory emerges expectation, to be subsequently established as confirmed or contradicted, valid or vanquished.

But secondly, in a "blurring of the boundary" between the remembered and the real (Lee, 2005: 48), readers not only flexibly refocus from known context to indeterminate content: they also participate in the construction of narratives with the aim of making sense. Media users engage in a hermeneutic circle of understanding – completing stories. Relating part to whole, reflecting to and fro, we build book content. Continually integrating anticipated narrative and actual program (or page) detail, reading a text is ludic in its cognitively play-like pursuit of holistic content as a goal – "for-the-sake-of-which" (Heidegger, 1962) we keep looking.

This hermeneutic phenomenology of understanding contributes to a philosophically resourced psychology. We can learn *how* we learn. Screen reception study is culturally connected epistemology. It is concerned with lifting the mist from memory, making clear conceptually an audience's horizons of interpreting their own viewing experience. These typifying frameworks of comprehension are repeatedly discerned throughout focus groups in contributors' discussion of their specific responses to television (e.g., perceiving advertising as a persuasive "message").

Of course reference to readers' interpretative "horizons," frameworks of knowledge to which they refer in understanding media narrative, is metaphorical. We can share a horizon of understanding a text but be located at different points upon it (for instance, agree to interpreting a book from the point of view of what it says about gender, but understand "gender" differently). The term "horizon" is intended here as heuristic or helpful imagery to guide our thinking about people's responses to screen content in terms of them always looking from a cultural perspective. Focusing on the contours of constructing meaning as horizons of understanding allows an emphasis on the varying political dimension of the process. Brunette (2000) invoked a similar analytical reliance on analogy with "'frame' of understanding" (e.g., a set of cinematic conventions for viewing) that "both allows and constrains meaning" (92).

In summary, habituated perception flows so rapidly that we regard as "brute facts" data that are actually the creative results of our routinely employing "interpretive conventions" (Tompkins, 1980: xviii). Looking is temporal or future-orientated. Projecting – or anticipating – narrative events is an aspect of reading or media use everywhere. This universal cognitive play between the audience's expectation of content and establishing that which actually occurs on screen draws on the media user's cultural knowledge of categories for classifying content (e.g., as instantiating a soap opera serial rather than situation comedy series). Such speculation and substantiation of stories results in a varying cultural play of meaning across the many interactions between indeterminate text and interpreting readers. Correlatively, one is bored when "one cannot produce the text, open it out, *set it going*" (Barthes, 1977: 163) (emphasis in the original).

Understanding Perception:
Phenomenology's Criticism of Positivism

Heidegger's account in *Being and Time* (1962) of the fundamentally inter-pretative dimension of understanding (188–95) is a profound criticism of the positivism we discussed in chapter 1. As we have seen, his phenomenology of "interpretation" as the "working-out of possibilities projected in understanding" (189) is appropriately applied to the process of media users "articulating" (190) the meaning of screen narrative. Contrary to positivism, the process of interpretation is at the core of observation. Through emotions we see and make sense. We need in the following pages to investigate this cognitive activity both conceptually and experientially.

Perception or understanding *always* interprets the identity of that which is seen *as* instantiating a known type. "Anything interpreted, as some-thing interpreted, has the 'as'-structure as its own" (ibid.). "In the project-ing of the understanding, entities are disclosed in their possibility. The character of the possibility corresponds, on each occasion, with the kind of Being of the entity which is understood" (192). Otherwise no meaning can be found.

Prior to interpretation – "fore-having" (191) the unknown in front of us – we are in a pre-predicative or pre-conceptual phase. When we emerge from varying cultural backgrounds "in advance" (ibid.) of understanding we have not yet identified the "entity which is understood." But we look in our distinctive ways from discrete horizons of knowledge. Hence we neces-sarily perceive or constitute content differently from the first moment of interpretative looking.

Perception of textual identity then is continually future-orientated: it has a temporal "fore-structure" (192). Understanding, we have noted, is a process of reconciling anticipation with actuality: it is never instanta-neous. Our projection ("fore-sight") of possibility is fleshed out through measuring our "fore-conceptions" against content (191). "This fore-sight 'takes the first cut' out of what has been taken into our fore-having, and it does so with a view to a definite way in which this can be interpreted" (ibid.) – establishing a conception of narrative.

Anything understood which is held in our fore-having and towards which we set our sights "foresightedly," becomes conceptualizable through the interpretation. In such an interpretation, the way in which the entity we are interpreting is to be conceived can be drawn from the entity itself, or the interpretation can force the entity into concepts to which it is opposed in its manner of Being. In either case, the interpretation has already decided for a definite way of conceiving it, either with finality or with reservations; it is grounded in *something we grasp in advance – in a fore-conception.*" (Ibid., emphasis in the original)

"Fore-having" her cellphone in front of her, our Chinese Malaysian traveler in chapter 1 regards it with the insight ("fore-sight") that some content may be unpleasant. Culturally experienced in this wireless communication, her fundamental fore-conception of unfamiliar callers is that they are likely to be "weird." She refrains from checking this projection of meaning.

Notes

1 For a critique of lingering positivism (or empiricism) one can turn to a phenomenology of perception such as that clearly articulated, for instance, by Errol Harris in his *Hypothesis and Perception* (London: Allen and Unwin, 1970). "'The fact' is saturated with prior knowledge" (288). He argues that every "act of perception" involves an "essential element of interpretation" (244) establishing the identity of the phenomenon before us. Seeing is a "process of forming and testing hypotheses" (251) or conjectures as to meaning.

Interpretation draws upon a "structured background" (286) of knowledge. "Thus every perception takes place within a 'horizon,' or against a background, of accompanying and acquired knowledge, without which perception is hardly possible" (285). Such knowledge would be, for instance, our awareness of types of action and aesthetic forms on the basis of which we speculatively interpret (or "project") perceptual content as constituting an instance. Moreover, incorporating the hermeneutic circle of understanding with its presumption of being able to secure coherence, "perceptual activity is constantly one of integrating impressions whether successive or co-temporaneously spread out in space" (254).

Perception, therefore, "must be understood as the activity of referring a present sense-content to the systematically structured background knowledge of the world" (288): understanding involves the "corroboration of cues" (289).

2 Heideggerian hermeneutics could be said to regard audience reception as "fore-structural" in multiple respects, structuring the processual ludic reading of a screen. Drawing on cognitive frameworks or the cultural horizons of our always located understanding, we direct a constructive point of view (or *fore-sight* – Vorsicht) towards our surroundings. In regard to the latter we are already

positioned in *fore-having* (Vorhabe) them before us. Fore-seeing screen content, we project an interpretative *fore-conception* (Vorgriff) of a text's narrative possibility, perceiving its events as emerging story. We engage, that is, in the "seeing as" which hermeneutics seeks to explicate as the construction of meaning, our delineating a fore-conception of TV program or web page.

Projecting a fore-structure of understanding (a *fore-ward* looking formation of textual content), in other words, we anticipate in reading, forming a fore-conception of stories. In doing so, we draw on (are in-formed by) "stocks" (Harré, 1984: 8) of generic narrative knowledge abstracted *be-fore*, from past experience, forming a horizon of understanding beyond which thought cannot (logically) occur. "Minds are structured and stocked from a social and interpersonal reality" (ibid.).

4

Meanings Are Ours:
Reader Response and Audience Studies

We saw in chapter 3 that phenomenology prompted a focus on understanding as an interpretative process. This emphasis on making sense as a time-structured occurrence was shared and developed by reader response theorists who promoted the "reader as a sense-maker" (Littau, 2006: 104) mentally constructing meaning rather than consuming it as product.

Among the "assumptions (about reading) to which I stand opposed" is that "there is a sense, that it is embedded or encoded in the text, and that it can be taken in at a single glance" (Fish, 1980: 172). Readers, rather, arrive at a text from many horizons of cultural understanding. Consequently they anticipate and achieve a variety of textual interpretations in a *structured process* of meaning construction. It is the "structure of the reader's experience rather than any structures available on the page that should be the object of description" (ibid.: 167).

Reader Response Theory:
Conceptualizing Consuming Books

Media user theory was anticipated not only by those considering film and television audiences but by those engaged in analyzing the productive process of reading books. This wide range of scholars has argued for a quarter of a century (albeit to sometimes unconvinced if not also uncomprehending audiences) that "meaning has no effective existence outside of its realization in the mind of a reader" (Tompkins, 1980: ix). Reading, they assert, produces meaning from writing, merging audience and textual conceptions or horizons of understanding the world.

Reader response theory shares poststructuralism's finding in media studies that perception of meaning is a consequence of being in a particular situation in the world (Tompkins, 1980: xxv). For instance, it is a function of the knowledge to which one has access in one's social position. Or as Holland writes, celebrating a certain discursive democracy, "all kinds of people from different eras and cultures" can "replenish" a text by "infinitely various additions" (1980: 118).

However, response theory also seeks to discern people's shared "interpretative strategies" for establishing a text's meaning. First, as we have noted, readers universally anticipate (project) narrative developments (which may or may not take place). Second, this cognitive process of comprehending a text can apply (more or less) shared conventions for assigning significance. Rules common to an "interpretive community" (Fish, 1980: 182) such as those which govern how readers should understand signs (words, phrases, sentences) form the cultural circumstances or horizon within which they establish the meaning of pages in a book. Codes enable our agreement on meaning.

To illustrate the continuing focus on the interpretative process from earlier reader response to media user theory we shall consider an inventory of ideas common to these interdisciplinary studies. (Illustrative use of such centrifugal core concepts can be found in the essays edited by J. P. Tompkins (1980) as *Reader-Response Criticism From Formalism to Post-Structuralism*.)

Presupposed in one's narrating a tale is the listener's or *narratee's* capacity to find it intelligible. Our word selection must allow sense to be constructed by assumed audiences. For otherwise, there is no point in telling a story. The hermeneutic phenomenology of reading establishes essential conditions for such understanding to emerge. These define the necessary or minimum process in which the "zero-degree narratee" (Prince, 1980: 9–11) must engage to construct a meaningful story, whether the role of narratee is filled by fictional or real readers.

Successful narratees project and position a series of events on the pages of a book as a coherent story: its construction necessarily occurs within or is shaped by their horizons of understanding or knowledge of narrative formation. At the most abstract level they draw upon a schema of interpretation or set of epistemological assumptions which Prince defines as being that "narrative possesses a temporal dimension and that it necessitates relations of causality" (1980: 10). For the cause and effect sequence through time is the fundamental framework or mold into which readers must pour their perceptions of text to produce intelligible content.

Mobilizing our memory of narrative, we engage in the construction of stories. Recognizing the romance genre being fleshed out on the pages before us, we project or predict a particular novel's developments. Riffaterre's key terms of "predictability and unpredictability" are derived from his picturing the reading process as significantly temporal: texts arouse certain expectations which they then either fulfill or frustrate (Tompkins, 1980: xiii). His account has a place for events not predicted but nonetheless emerging and perceived: "where predictability increases, so does the effect of an unpredicted element" (Riffaterre, 1966: 204). Unpredictability challenges the reader's projection.

This temporal model of reading prefigures (or anticipates) media user theory where audiences aware of genre are represented as constructing (projecting) and checking anticipated program narrative. Riffaterre's model encapsulates a process whose achievement shows the reader finding a text intelligible, establishing an interpretation.

Iser brings a phenomenology of the reading process to fruition. For he argues that in book use we become co-creators of content along with the author(s): we supplement stories, adding events and environment which are only implied (e.g., the murky details of a murder). Authorial hints prompt an audience's hermeneutic activity.

During this "concretization" of a text the "reader's imagination comes into play" (Tompkins, 1980: xiv–xv). Iser, in short, considers that books arrive at their readers incomplete or indeterminate and are subsequently filled out in a determinate cognitive process of narrative construction. Thus a text presents imperfectly at the point of consumption: people engage in the process of "consistency-building" (Iser, 1978: 16) or providing it with coherent meaning through addition of content.

We fill out elliptical narratives, projecting and positioning a chain of connecting events between cause and distant effect. Where the location of a city is left unspecified, it can be supplied by the assumed audience. A reader produces a rounded narrative from a repertoire or knowledge of textual convention (e.g., her or his awareness that shadows on a face can signal turmoil within the person). Media texts characterized by indeterminacy of information provision, "absences" (Schroder, 1999: 24) or "blanks" (Iser, 1974: 113), depend on their users to provide closure. Audiences can ensure that stories are completed in ways appropriate to their genre.

Active within reading's cognitive "field of play" we establish a "work" from an indeterminate text (Iser, 1974: 274–5). We "bring into play our own faculty for establishing connections – for filling in the gaps left by the text itself" (ibid.: 280). "What is missing ... stimulates the reader into filling the blanks with projections" (Iser, 1978: 168). "Whenever the reader bridges a gap, communication begins. ... Blanks indicate that the different segments and patterns of the text are to be connected even though the text itself does not say so" (Iser, 2006: 64, 65). But as in the space and time of games, we can also build new aspects of our identity (e.g., as critical consumers).

This theory of reading (or "actions involved in responding" (Iser, 1980: 50) to a book) is clearly close to reception accounts of the media user's projection of meaning. Her or his educated capacity to form a coherent story reduces absent content. The text "does not flow into indeterminacy in my vision" (Sobchack, 1992: 185).

Recognition prompts projection of meaning. Iser's phenomenology of reading as a temporal process focuses like Riffaterre on expectation generated by our perception of text as narrative type and subsequently pursued to the point of establishing a specific story. In doing so, where we are confronted by events not anticipated ("negations": Iser, 1978: 131), we revise our projection of content to attain a consistent story – an ambition thwarted only by a book's contradictions. Where people surprise us we amend our assessment of their personality: their earlier action may be re-evaluated as prompted by caring, not corruption. There is a "retrospective effect on what has already been read" (Iser, 1974: 278). This process of "continual modification" (ibid.: 281) or rereading extends to our own lives.

Establishing a psychology of audience response which owes much to earlier phenomenology, Iser argues that the "reader's mind" works on the "raw material of the text" ("sentences, statements, information") producing narrative "connections." This process of "anticipation and retrospection" does not "develop in a smooth flow," for it involves a "sort of kaleidoscope of perspectives, preintentions, recollections" (Iser, 1974: 279). Where the "flow is interrupted" by the unexpected we have a particular opportunity to synthesize a story. "While expectations may be continually modified" and "images continually expanded," the "reader will still strive, even if unconsciously, to fit everything together in a consistent pattern" (ibid.: 283). In a reading "process (which is) virtually hermeneutic," the "text provokes certain expectations which in turn we project onto the text in such a way that we reduce the polysemantic possibilities to a single interpretation in keeping with the expectations aroused, thus extracting an individual, configurative meaning" (1974: 285).

Sharing Iser's intensive focus on the process of establishing meaning across the pages of a book, Fish refers to this cognitive activity as the reader's "anticipatory adjustment to his [*sic*] projection" (1972). Consistent with his place in reception theory inspired by a phenomenology of understanding,

Fish "rivets attention" on the "sequence of decisions, revisions, anticipations, reversals, and recoveries that the reader performs as he [*sic*] negotiates the text" (Tompkins, 1980: xvi). In doing so he can provide a precise psychological narrative to define consumption of texts as requiring our actively mediating presence interpreting content. We continually engage with a story as we anticipate and adjust projected narrative to accommodate actual textual event. The sense of a text is not a "fixed object of attention" but a "sequence of events that unfold within the reader's mind" (Tompkins, 1980: xvi–xvii). In reading we repeatedly revise. Meaning, in short, takes time.

The reader's activities

> include the making and revising of assumptions, the rendering and regretting of judgments, the coming to and abandoning of conclusions, the giving and withdrawing of approval, the specifying of causes, the asking of questions, the supplying of answers, the solving of puzzles. (Fish, 1980: 172)

Establishing a text's intelligibility through prediction and revision draws upon the linguistic and literary competence of the reader: for the subjective or private process in which meaning is produced requires our knowing public conventions. The reader's wider awareness of character and narrative type, of literary "genre, style, or form" (Jauss, 1982b: 24), constitutes a broader horizon of cultural understanding, of informed looking: equipped with such knowledge, he or she is able to recognize events, predict developments, and subsequently establish a story. We anticipate confirming different expectations when reading a novel from those realized in consuming a textbook: we put into play awareness of other conventions for expressing content.

Fish depicts the passage of subjective time for someone engrossed in a book as the "*temporal* flow of the reading experience" (emphasis in the original): the "reader responds in terms of that flow" (1972: 388) "monitored and structured by everything the reader brings with him [*sic*], by his competences" (ibid.: 404). During the "developing of those responses" our knowledge of cultural and literary convention interacts with the "temporal left to right reception of the verbal string" enabling us to generate an account of the text – "project *the* developing response" (ibid.: 404, emphasis in the original). Guided by this philosophical psychology of reception, when investigating the process of media user meaning construction Fish claims the ability to "*slow down* the reading experience so that 'events' one does not notice in normal time, but which do occur, are brought before our analytical attentions" (ibid.: 389, emphasis in the original).

Fish focuses on "*meaning as an event*," on seeing the "reader's actualizing participation in that process." He dissents fundamentally from the structuralist view that meaning is "located (presumed to be imbedded) *in* the utterance" with the "apprehension of meaning" an "act of extraction" (1972: 389, emphasis in the original). We comprehend "in terms of a *relationship* between the unfolding, in time, of the surface structure and a continual checking of it against our projection" (ibid.: 406, emphasis in the original). Meaning is formed, not found. Like Iser, Fish maintains that books where readers' narrative expectations are continually upset, prompting them to focus inquisitively on their features as unpredictable texts, promote reflective reading.

Reader response theory, in summary, asserts that meaning is enunciated or emerges from the process of interaction between texts and their attentive users. But creativity has necessary conditions: we make sense of a novel or poem only if we have access to a set of conventions for reading such texts. Knowledge of genres informs "sets of expectations" (Culler, 1975: 129). One can test (through discussion, interview, or focus group) the validity of one's hypothesis or speculation about the public knowledge a reader has drawn upon to produce intelligibility. As we have seen, these shared conventions, codes, or correspondences between word and idea constitute the horizons of cultural understanding from which we regard a book. They are literary (if not literal) limits to our thought.

Yet sometimes texts resist the interpretative gaze of those who engage with them: constructing a coherent story seems impossible. Becoming concerned and contemplative, readers turn their attention away from content to the conventions they have employed in seeking a book's meaning. They question their own mode of determining sense in a text. Is this continually error-prone detective in the novel to be correctly construed as a source of *knowledge*? Realizing one's assumptions and goals when reading allows insight into a text's "refusal to comply with one's expectations" (Culler, 1975: 129).

We have considered a series of response theorists who follow Gadamer in arguing that a book's meaning is *everywhere* achieved through the cognitive play of the reader's shifting, refocusing attention. Barthes (1977) regards this "projection of the reader into the work" (162) as an appropriate account of audiences seeking to understand particular "Texts" which, rather than appearing to offer access to reality, draw attention to their own construction (a filmic instance would be Godard's *Tout Va Bien*). Denying the possibility of straightforward reading, these Texts "play" (162) with meaning. They are characterized by their "infinite deferment of the signified" (158) or "ludic" inscription (161), prompting a parallel plural interpretation – the audience's "playing the Text as one plays a game" (162). In these particular instances of reading, Barthes argues that understanding "plays" but does not conclude in a goal, a story's comprehension.

Hermeneutics argues, on the other hand, that reading *is* (normally) ludic. In continually expecting and establishing narrative, we are oriented teleologically towards texts: reader responses, in other words, are structured by their achievable goal of furthering understanding. Our viewing texts is cognitively mobile, perpetually in play, remembering and recognizing content to establish coherent narrative. Meanings are ours.

Reader response and media user theory are underwritten by an agreed account (or epistemological philosophy) of how knowledge is formed. Perceptions of narrative are fundamentally perspectival: constructions of content occur from an audience point of view. As we have seen, they emerge from the reader's interpretative strategy. This is a universal cognitive process of projecting narrative which nonetheless draws upon memories of a particular cultural past: the experience of reading is an "in-gathering and in-mixing" (Holland, 1980: 130) of situated self and text.

Globally, acquiring knowledge is locally shaped and informed (Chitty, 2005: 557): different expectations of a program arise from varying frameworks of anticipation. Reading texts from distant cultures entails people negotiating between distinct conceptual horizons of understanding the world. Lacking a border crossing between interpretations, audiences fall silent.

The response theory which we have been discussing rejects epistemological dualism, an account of knowledge which argues that *who* we are and *what* we see are independent. That positivist philosophical analysis of audience awareness claims that the cultural context of looking has no bearing on the content of perception. Identical meaning is accessible to all regardless of historical and social perspective: but determining it may require elimination of bias, the "splitting of the knower from the known" (Holland, 1980: 130). Instead, media user theory maintains that seeing is always inflected or informed by the cultural horizons within which we perceive texts. The "mechanics of perception" take place "not through data impinging on the human mind, as the stimulus-and-response theory had it, but by projecting the mind itself onto the world outside" (Iser, 2006: 43).

"Identification" in Response Theory: (Sub)merging the Self?

In early response theory, the reader's identification with characters is restrained. We can share their concern to understand events, but not their criticism or celebration of actions. Prince's zero-degree narratee (or audience assumed in writing) exists in a "cultural vacuum" dispossessed of values and consequently unable to make judgments (Tompkins, 1980: xii). Should the role be filled by a real reader, the latter will have the capacity to identify with narrative agents in the process of elucidating events taking place: yet he or she neither aligns with nor is adverse to a book's prescriptive implication. In subsequent theory of a text's reception, now enjoying an ability to evaluate, media users can move from consensus with characters to critical attention, distancing themselves morally or politically from the latter in belief or behavior.

Reader response and media user theory acknowledge that audiences immerse themselves enthusiastically in texts. Initially perceiving a narrative's unfolding from outside (extra-diegetically), we can subsequently share an intense concern with those participating to make sense of its events. Significantly, this is not argued to induce passivity or total absorption of the psyche. The positioning or identification of our "wandering viewpoint" (Iser, 1978: 108–9) with those in a story is considered to be a process predicated upon our continuing to actively construct its meaning.

In thus aligning we nonetheless retain a separate identity. Media consumers and characters "build" text in parallel ways, encouraging epistemological empathy: we engage like them in resolving enigma in the same story. However, while narrative agents seek answers internally to a story, as audiences we do so bringing to bear knowledge (e.g., of genre) unlikely to be used by those in a drama or novel. In this sense we retain our external perspective (Mackenzie, 2006: 7). Identifying with another in a similar process of making sense we unavoidably exert difference.

Yet analyses of "identification" do not always conclude that aligned audiences are active. Gibson argues for the idea of a "mock reader" as a role that the real reader is "invited to play" (Tompkins, 1980: xi) when identifying with a "speaker" in a novel. Accepting the invitation, immersed in a book, readers become "controlled," "remote from the chaotic self of daily life" (Gibson, 1980: 1). Consent is constraint. On the other hand, opening a "bad book," "we discover a person we refuse to become, a mask we refuse to put on, a role we will not play" (ibid.: 5). A separate self continues: we distance ourselves from the text.

Where responses are considered within Poulet's conceptual framework, absorption in a book is more clearly the annihilation of self. The reader is said to forget, "foregoing himself [*sic*]; dying, so to speak, in order that the text may live … allowing (his) consciousness to be invaded by the consciousness of another" (Tompkins, 1980: xiv–xv). Identifying, we become passive. As Poulet puts it: "I deliver myself, bound hand and foot, to the omnipotence of fiction."

> In the "act of reading," "I am thinking the thoughts of another." "I am on loan to another, and this other thinks, feels, suffers and acts within me." "When I am absorbed in reading, a second self takes over, a self which thinks and feels for me." "[From] the moment I become a prey to what I read, I begin to share the use of my consciousness with this being … the conscious subject ensconced at the heart of the work." (Poulet, 1970: 58, 59–61, 63)

Here, identification with those in a text involves transparent loss of self identity: when we align with characters they construct our psychological processes. At the heart of our reading experience we accede to passivity: we are absorbed by others, immersed in the flow of the text as the vessel of their views.

Poulet's discussion is wholly opposed to phenomenology's account of the reader retaining her or his separate role, anticipating and achieving a developing story throughout the experience of engaging with a novel. This cognitive activity may run parallel to a narrative agent's making sense of life but is never psychologically the same process. Media user theory argues that when immersed in books we are able to identify *with*, but are at no point identical *to* the characters we enjoy on their pages. More widely, in aligning with a presenter's views we can simultaneously assert their implications for our separate self: Oprah Winfrey may be regarded as educative. Television helps people "navigate their lives" (Cronin, 2004: 363).

Audiences think similarly to narrative agents in constructing accounts of events on pages or in programs. Poststructuralists argue that cultural context fundamentally informs these processes of comprehension. Drawing on the broadly informative horizons of our sought-for understanding (guided often by awareness of genre and its instances), our subjective reception of literature is asserted by reception theorists of a phenomenological persuasion to be a structured cognitive, sometimes expressive, process in which we aim at producing meaningful text. As Eco indicates, every "reception of a work of art is both an interpretation and a performance of it" (1981: 49). The reader's past-informed projections-in-play – or contextualized assumptions about content – are subsequently confirmed (or otherwise) by an unfolding narrative.

Philosophically aware, Iser (influenced by phenomenology) and Jauss (knowledgeable of hermeneutics) developed reception theory (Holub,

1984: 83). Iser, as we have seen, argues that the reader's projection of narrative meaning overcomes "indeterminacies" or uncertainties in textual content. Coherent stories are constructed. In this context, the idea that cultural consumers' awareness of aesthetic form and genre establishes an interpersonal framework or "horizon of what is expected" (Jauss, 1982a: 17) is a useful conceptual tool. It allows reception studies to analyze our awareness of books as a knowledge of past narrative patterns supporting the psychological play of anticipation and correction in the reader's interpreting stories. Subjective responses to texts draw on knowledge shared by hermeneutic interpretive communities.

Understanding events in a story is a process participated in simultaneously by knowledge-able audiences and narrative agents alike. We have argued that this common focus is a continuing point of alignment allowing identification between the subject reading and the subjects "read": audiences recognize in the text their own structured process of reaction. Someone engaged on screen in resolving a story's enigma thereby invites audience alignment with this activity. Texts can be construed as making "offers of identification" (Jauss, 1982a: 93), allowing consumers and characters to share in achieving intelligible narrative. Positioned alike in the process of establishing sense, those reading and those read may also identify ideologically (see Willett, 1979). Politics – like meaning – can be shared.

Investigating Media Use Beyond Books: Crossing Horizons of Understanding

Reception theory can be recruited in understanding media use. Here meaning is not found, but made (Bordwell, 1989: 3). On the one hand, as we have seen, phenomenology emphasizes universal aspects of the process (e.g., the audience's activity in projecting meaning, with their cognitive play through responding to a text constituting the definitive structure of comprehending content). On the other, poststructuralism argues for the media user's understanding of programs as a "free play" (Brunette, 2000: 90) of meaning drawing on the cultural resources available to her or him as a socially situated self. Both these ever-present and varying "moments" in the production of textual sense need to be addressed and integrated within media theory.

For instance, Bordwell argues that cinema audiences construct meaning out of "textual cues" everywhere (King, 2000: 212) while simultaneously drawing upon an institutionally located local interpretative knowledge.

The projecting spectator always makes sense *in* narrative, applying "knowledge structures to cues which she identifies," "conceptual schemes to data picked out in the film" (Bordwell, 1989: 3–4). Echoing response theory, Bordwell asserts that "in following a narrative, we make assumptions and draw on schemata and routines in order to arrive at conclusions about the world of the story" (ibid.: 269–70).

In the powerful play of meaning between the individual and the institutional, organizations engaged in film scholarship such as universities establish cultural horizons of understanding which shape and inform people's varied readings of textual cues. They regulate producing novelty in interpretation or engage in the "taming of the new" (Bordwell, 1989: 256). *Film noir*, for instance, receives accredited readings. Critics necessarily refer in understanding cinema to an always already established framework of legitimate possibility in undertaking interpretation. Institutions allow and restrict readings (both culturally and physically).

The screen user's speculative expectation of developments is substantiated through reading. Accessing electronic content such as an e-journalism menu of stories can appear to be immediate, near intuitive, without intellectual deduction. But like the smooth functioning of invisibly supporting software, it is a subjective, time-structured activity wherein readers expect and establish understanding. We gain no instant experiential awareness of our surroundings: perception does not occur without process. Screen meaning is not preformed for participant consumption, prepackaged rather than requiring assembly. To assert that media users immediately understand content excludes study of the structured interpretative activity which accounts for the "active audience's" pluralist rendering of sense on screen. As we saw – all seeing is seeing as. Even the simplest act of perceptual recognition is "interpretive" (Bordwell, 1989: 2).

Understanding stories is temporal: it has both a synchronic (relatively static) and diachronic (swiftly moving) aspect. We respond to television and Internet within conceptual horizons of media awareness which shape our thought, making use of a substantially unchanging "schematic," "culturally shared" (Markova, 2000: 434) knowledge. Drawing upon these familiar if far from frequently considered frameworks (schemas) of understanding (a knowledge of web page and television program types), we project a particular narrative's likely emerging content as an instance of a genre. Such classification of stories alters slowly. But our speculating on storyline is subsequently tested against events on screen in the rapid process of watching television or making use of the Internet. Confirmed anticipation yields audience pleasure, while the "cognitive dissonance" (Schroder, 1987: 9) of expectations contradicted evokes dismay. What's happening?

Such cognitive-expressive anticipating and actualizing of "episodic" meaning is "constructive" (Valsiner, 2000: 497). Transferring a phrase from reception studies, theorists of media use write that we watch the screen within a "horizon of expectation" (Jauss, 1982b: 23) cognitively *in play* (Huizinga, 1970) between past and future, projecting meaning. Coming to view sports events we anticipate television's *liveness* (Davis, 2007). We transcend the present in drawing upon memory to speculate upon and substantiate narrative development. "The new text evokes for the reader (listener) the horizon of expectations and rules familiar from earlier texts, which are then varied, corrected, altered, or even just reproduced" (Jauss, 1982b: 23).

Meaningful texts in time and space on screen emerge from our audience activity. As subjects-in-play, we are ourselves embodied stories formed by developing projects: the "literary experience of the reader enters into the horizon of expectations of his [*sic*] lived praxis, preforms his understanding of the world, and thereby also has an effect on his social behavior" (Jauss, 1982b: 39). "Nuanced" reception studies responsive to reader reports are needed of our new media use (Selwyn et al., 2005) focused upon its continuing construction of sense in our lives.

Consumption of screen stories, then, whether those of information-bearing news or imaginative drama, is characterized by their offline/online readers' capacity for crafting meaning. While television program and web page narratives are understood in global "panhuman" (Berry et al., 1996: xiii, in Smolka: 2000) cognitive-expressive processes, they emerge interpreted by their viewer-users in differentiated local detail. The audience's hermeneutic anticipation or projection of textual event to be subsequently established is universal, a mental prerequisite of forming any meaningful narrative. Yet the process is shaped by always varying cultural horizons of understanding supporting heterogeneous reader perception of page or program.

Media user theory articulates a constructivist epistemology (Murphy, 1997) in which descriptions of the reading subject and the object (or text) read (Coffey et al., 1996) are inseparable. Accounts of viewing are necessarily *of* stories: content is invariably enunciated *from* a perspective. Regarded from such a horizon of understanding, audiences engaging with television or the Internet are seen to be informed by their pre-existing knowledge of culturally relative formats for interpreting programs or pages (e.g., as transnational news websites).[1]

Enabled by their wider awareness of screen narratives as instances of types, viewers speculatively constitute textual content in always occurring cognitive-expressive processes (often an emotionally colored anticipation of likely stories, falsifiable by emerging events on screen). Enigma (the "hermeneutic code" of questions: Barthes, 1974) characterizes the fate of an uncertain audience projection, their securing only an indeterminate program narrative.

Analogous to constructivism in film theory (see Sweeney, n.d.), media hermeneutics argues that what's happening on television or the Internet is decided in the last instance by the audience producing (projecting and substantiating) a varied "heterogeneity" of stories on screen (Poster, 2003: 283). Anticipating and finding narrative actualized, conjecturing and confirming accounts, we make meaning. We shall explore in subsequent chapters the ways in which representations of media content from cellphone to television and Internet are developed. Considered as aesthetic processes, the screen's narrative properties accrue from the audience's interpretative frameworks and negotiations of content (Brey, 1997). The "reality" of the text emerges from dialectical interaction between viewer and program or page (Lye, 1996), with the reader, not the author, privileged as the "grounding centre" of knowledge (Ryder, 1995). Attaining and anchoring meaning, audiences secure cognitive pleasure, "psychic reward" (Plantinga, n.d.).[2]

Analyses of media use are able to underwrite a political economy of television program and Internet page production. For one can see how the continual "successful" reception of new media's narrowcast ("post-broadcast": Hartley, 2004: 7) content congeals into profit (Eischen, 2003: 76) expropriated from narrative-constituting niche audience-consumers (Smith-Shomade, 2004) of pay channels on Internet or TV. In the absence of political criticism, this process can be hegemonic, accommodating and advancing the powerful cause of the privileged.

Capitalism's cultural cunning is programmed across the screen. But ethnic privileging can also be alleged by audiences. The Malaysian National Day advertisements discussed earlier were shown in March 2005 to a small group of mental hospital patients. "The Bush" encouraged an audience member to align himself with an environmental reading of its hedge trimming: "they want to beautify our environment" to "induce (in) us and our youngsters a sense of belonging ... to this nation we love. And we want to live in peace and harmony" (male Chinese). But a female Chinese patient distanced herself politically from this marketing promotion's prompting to commitment ("Don't you just love this country?"). "In this country ... everything is for the Bumiputra (Malay) people. Not fair!" (she laughs).

"Where is the Audience Going?"

Discussing the "nexus between cyberspace identities and real space identities" (Krishna, 2003: 132), the Director of the Pew Internet and American Life Project (a Washington, DC research center) argued that the immediate future of Internet studies was in "qualitative, context sensitive" research answering "deeper questions" about how people are shaping and being shaped by the Internet (Rainie and Bell, 2004: 51). Media theory drawing on reader reception studies posits that in her or his cyber-shaping, the web user is primarily at play, projecting, putting meaning into place. Positivist preoccupation with standardized surveys quantifying media responses needs to recognize the latter as always informed by interactive understanding productive of sometimes challenging interpretation (Potter, 2003).

We have seen in this chapter that reading is structured by anticipation. Indeed Culler claims that this insight characterizes structuralism. Literary works "achieve their effects" by resisting or complying with readers' expectations: these emanate from the role of audiences as "repository of conventions" and "agent of their application" or "citational play" (1983: 81, 85). But in reader response studies we see a firmer focus on the structure of meaning construction.

We have considered reception and media theory's account of the cognitive and sometimes emotion-bearing process wherein readers and screen users interpret narrative in books, television, and Internet. From this discussion has emerged a philosophically informed narrative of the "projecting spectator" engaged in the creative hermeneutic activity of establishing intelligibility. Reading printed books and using programmed media have both diachronic and synchronic aspects or moments: we anticipate particular stories, drawing on a wider knowledge of characteristic developments, our cultural horizons of understanding.

Audiences continually entertain a fore-concept of emerging content. Thereby informed, screen responses are goal-directed or teleologically fore-structured – aiming at sense. This play-like assemblage of meaning is instantiated by "readers'" forward looking expectation of likely events enabling them to establish a narrative: media users seek (to and fro) integration of textual detail to the point of a story's completion. We shall discuss how knowledgeable audiences identify processually with narrative agents in articulating a coherent development of events – whose normative implications can also form a focus for propositional alignment by real life people with those virtually on screen. Radway (1984) considers how reading romance rekindles lives: audiences appropriate drama. In short, projecting meaning links consumer with content.

Conclusion

Hermeneutically, audiences are "hungry to bring order to chaos" (Rehak, 2003: 485). Virtual narrative is never entirely new: audiences respond to pages or programs as instances of types, with consequent tentative expectations of the latter tested in subsequent reading. A story's detail is interconnected through the process of a reader's holistic hermeneutic circle of understanding content: we relate part to page or program considered as generic whole (e.g., journalism site or soap opera). Watching programs, visiting web pages, people engage in their understanding – a face to interface assigning of meaning to narrative content. When focused upon this activity, the "analytic lens" (Mehra et al., 2004: 783) of hermeneutic literary and philosophical theory can discern the details of our screen cognitive-expressive reception. The following pages consider media use in its differing instantiation across TV, cellphone, and web.

Notes

1 Drawing on conceptual frameworks or horizons of understanding, screen users identify narratives as instances of types or genres. However, audiences can themselves be productively responsible for a new genre's development (e.g., by frequent cinema attendance). Equally signaling viewers as creatively active is their ability to perceive a single narrative as occupying several genres (e.g., to possess characteristics of both investigative and melodrama media forms).
2 Recent work discussing "interface theory" (Silver, 2004: 62) provides a similar discourse psychology of people generating narrative through television and Internet screen reception.

5

The Projecting Audience:
From Cinema to Cellphone

So how do we make sense of making sense? Research on audiences lacks awareness of *how* as media users we come to make claims about screen narrative content. Accessing the Internet, grasping a cellphone, that is, requires grounding in a theory of knowledge – or epistemology. While recognizing variations in modes of program delivery and consequent responses, reception analysis needs at its core an account of media users processing their perceptions of screen stories – the interactive *play of understanding*. Only then can our critical protest or consensual positioning with programs be placed in a properly cognitive context.

Audience studies require philosophical underwriting. We need to justify the route taken and conclusions reached in scientific or testable studies of viewer subjectivity – the "patterned complexities" (Barker and Petley, 2001: 3) defining screen response. Investigators of media use should hear their audiences in complex ways (ibid.:16). Yet media researchers can be found to engage in *ad hoc* theorizing of empirical data, a piecemeal placing of findings in categories lacking further support in a philosophically attuned psychology.

Research methodologies make implicit assumptions (see Olson, n.d.) about the construction of knowledge by both investigator and investigated – about the forming of their respective "subjectivities." When investigating the media's consequences for audiences and consumers, *we* need validated knowledge of how *they* view – justified insight into their (so-called) "emic" categories and processing of programs therein. Media theorists' earlier use of phenomenology in reception study suggests a conceptual path to such a goal.

Play as a Powerful Theoretical Tool:
Media Use – Towards a Philosophical Psychology

The "notion of *play*," wrote the late Roger Silverstone, is a "powerful" "tool for the analysis of the media experience" (1999: 59, emphasis in the original). Both audience membership and games involve – somewhat paradoxically – "escape and engagement" (ibid.: 66). Like media use, play is mostly mundane but equally "set apart" from a tiresome turn of events here and now (Buckingham, 2006: 7). Accessing screen content is "essentially a separate occupation, carefully isolated from the rest of life" (Caillois, 1961: 6). Internet use, like sport, is "circumscribed within limits of space and time" (ibid.: 9) elsewhere than our immediate material circumstances.

Being an audience, engaging in play, stands outside "ordinary" life (Huizinga, 1970: 32): often "intensely and utterly" (ibid.) involved, we forget the daily self. Viewers take aim at achieving sense in a mediated story: they anticipate and actualize textual meaning as goal. Like games, accessing the screen is a "stepping out" of "real" life into a "temporary sphere of activity with a disposition all of its own" (ibid.: 26), an "intermezzo," an "interlude" (ibid.: 27). This is the pleasurable distracting/extracting "fun" (ibid.: 43) associated with television or Internet surfing. Messaging on a cellphone screen, our concentration looks beyond our material location.

Watching television or accessing the Internet can be comprehended as play-like in emotions expressed as well as cognitively. Those engaging with dramatized events on screen characteristically enjoy their distraction: the experience functions as a passing escape akin to offline/online tourism. This release, while temporary, can be evaluated against substantial aesthetic criteria and at its height considered quasi-religious. Such for some people is the pleasure of their involvement with televised sport – focusing in tunnel vision on football.

Media use displays a cross-platform identity in audience processing. Our regarding this identity as play-like emphasizes a concern with underlying "universals" in how people regard screen use or "latent aspects of human communication that run deep and are pervasive" (Campbell, 2007: 359). In establishing these moments of media use our research procedure is not *inductive* (generalizing from instances) but rather *abductive* (abstracting from instances). Do particular discursive interviews provide evidence of underlying universal or abstract aspects of media experience? Short auto-biographical narratives (such as that from our Chinese Malaysian bus traveler we shall discuss in detail) are of centrifugal significance to this method.

Our media involvement is pervasive and distracting. Drawing on other studies of games and screen enjoyment we shall propose that everywhere throughout such experience are four aspects of employing media which also characterize play: our active *absorption, anticipation, articulation,* and *appropriation* of content (or *perception, projection, positing,* and *positioning* of meaning more widely). Rather than appropriating or learning from an experience of media use/play, some can find it (fifthly) *alienating* and distance themselves in a cognitive "reorganization of power and identity" (Chow-White, 2006: 885). Often, but not always, perceptions of texts as constructed (deconstruction) accompany criticism of content (Michelle, 2007: 191).

These are experiential moments in media reception occurring either simultaneously (e.g., as absorption-anticipation of narrative) or successively as we look at the screen. They can occur once or repeatedly in response to a media text. But their description also signals a series of *a priori* conditions for understanding, aspects of a psychological process logically presupposed by a claim to comprehend. We cannot articulate content to constitute a story in the absence of initial or prior speculation on the identity of those events (anticipation). Likewise, appropriation of meaning from cellphone, Internet, or television to inform our lives presupposes our satisfactory articulation of coherent content on screen.

The culturally substantial process of screen use instantiates a single structure. Our hypothesis that responses to media are characterized by ubiquitous play-like processing would be falsified if these alleged abstract aspects of their use could not be discerned as thoroughly imbricated in experiential reports of screen-centered communication technology. Audiences must refer to them – albeit not constantly nor always completely. Importantly, invoking these moments in our media gaze can provide a much sought after "analytical framework" (Michelle, 2007: 182) for thinking about screen use in its many and differing manifestations.

The philosophical psychology of the ludic (Caillois, 1961; Hans, 1981; Huizinga, 1970) has shown how the extended experience of playing features multiple defining moments of being immersive, goal-oriented, and identity-forming. In this chapter, after reflecting upon other phenomenological approaches more widely, we shall consider such ludology or theory of games as a "critical location" (Simon, 2006: 62) for understanding media use, particularly interactive cellphones (Wolf, 2006). Reading the screen employs a ludic literacy.

Following Silverstone's lead we shall explore the idea that play can be used as a metaphor of media involvement – as a model of the audience's projected goal-oriented expectation and establishing screen content. Appealing to multiple aspects of ludic experience allows us to consider and conceptualize (to recognize) both shared cognitive processes and separating differences in the many forms of handphone, watching television, and Internet consumption.

Narrative images online (e.g., a news report) support audience escapism previously associated with a cinema-outing or watching television. Yet, as in a game or "temporary world circumscribed by play" (Huizinga, 1970: 30), ludic or playful involvement on the web is rule-governed and is thereby "very serious indeed" (ibid.: 24). Groups considering their experience of the Internet construct guides to "correct" procedures believed to enable success in accessing web content. Play is performed with the "most perfect seriousness": constituting serious fun the "rules of a game are absolutely binding and allow no doubt" (ibid.: 37, 30).

Play and media use may be evaluated aesthetically: they can be judged as constructing personality, distributing power, evoking well-being. Mundane media content constrains our cognitive play. These electronic forms of digital departure from daily immediacy may be profound: though they can also yield to a more instrumental interest in using screen "data" which limits one's ludic escape. *Absorption* may be abbreviated. Reading emails is not infrequently on the cusp of freedom. Where this is the case, duty (the leash on the ludic) can call one back to the "pragmatics of everyday life" (Gergen, 2002: 235).

Readers' fore-structured cognitive play in consuming media texts is in constant motion between *anticipating* information ("projection") and verifying speculation (their hermeneutic hypotheses). Coming to understand a set of web pages linked by hypertext and integrating their ideas requires a cognitive comparison of content, an energetic to and fro *articulating* movement of the mind in furthering meaning. Our oscillation back and forth can find a physical parallel in many games. Likewise, to aim at a coherent account of an online text is to set oneself a goal, particularly where confronted with indeterminate content. Anticipation is challenged by uncertainty. Although clearly not the only enjoyment to be found in surfing the worldwide web, the pleasures of insight, of finally comprehending content, are comparable to those of success in sport. In both, celebration is consequent upon conforming to rules, seriously satisfying protocol, securing expectation.

Absorbing screen content from a perspective informed by earlier experience, we *anticipate*: our gaze is future-oriented. Play is purposeful, with media use inherently projecting meaning to be realized: "the beginning of play is always necessarily connected to a foreproject" (Hans, 1981: 10). Ludic and online, people drive themselves forward (sometimes compulsively) to further involvement in content, exerting themselves to attain the creative goal of finally knowing. Seeking a determinate meaning, the player "wants something to 'go,' to 'come off'; he [*sic*] wants to 'succeed' by his own exertions" (Huizinga, 1970: 29). This teleological (purposive) aspect of media response imports an "element of tension" to reading, "a striving to decide the issue and so end it" pleasurably (ibid.). Yet constantly available hyperlinks to further information mean that wholly integrated insights on the Internet are continually subverted. Our *articulating* meaning is always open to addition: complete comprehension is deferred, undermined.

Playing a game is essentially unpredictable in its result, as are the epistemological consequences of going online to access limitless hypertext. Phenomenologists long ago pointed out the indeterminate logic of the ludic. "An outcome known in advance, with no possibility of error or surprise, clearly leading to an inescapable result, is incompatible with the nature of play" (Caillois, 1961: 7). People accessing Internet content, prompted by ever-present hyperlinks, are required to exercise an "openness," a "willingness to let the conversation go where it will" (Hans, 1981: 12). Such openness on the part of those voyaging online implies "risk," defined by Hans as a "willingness to forego one's own territory" (ibid.). "The primary criterion for play" is "openness," though "openness does not mean a lack of orientation – it only means a willingness to put that orientation into question" (ibid.). The Internet interrogates; IT stimulates self-questioning.

We have noted how ludic media *absorption* is limited or constrained by instrumental tasking, its pursuit for offline obligatory or other purpose. On such occasions our goal-oriented cognitive activity of *anticipating* and *articulating* meaning on screen continues. We remain liminally ludic, the mind is maintained "in play," creatively. In multiple respects, doing one's duty (e.g., answering email) should not be opposed to game-like behavior, particularly where both are now supported on the same cellphone or website.

Being instrumentally online can productively be analyzed as structurally analogous to ludic activity. But while such media use is motivated by requirement, playing "is not obligatory": "if it were, it would at once lose its attractive and joyous quality as diversion" (Caillois, 1961: 9). Diversion differs as escape from duty. Where we go freely online, escape can be celebrated energetically by engaging in the "most absorbing, exhausting game in order to find diversion, escape from responsibility and routine" (ibid.: 6). Instrumental media use limits ludic immersion.

Drawing on phenomenological method, then, emphasizes establishing modes of subjective apprehension as essential to studying media use: understanding cellphone and television narrative is similar but significantly distinct. Play is basic human behavior, here articulated cognitively in variously focusing upon a screen. Viewers anticipate that distinct types of television will support a range of reactions. Likewise, Internet genres encourage particular modes of story construction in an audience's play-like engagement with their content. Smart phone formats (data download, email, messages, texts – increasingly hybrid multimedia compilations) prompt our ludic looking away from "here" and "now," connecting us "elsewhere."

The Projection Process: Theory of "Throwing" Meaning – From Ludic to Ludology

According to Krzywinska in the definitive journal *Games and Culture*, serious games studies are "grounded in phenomenology" (2006: 121). While distinct, the focus of cellphone study in particular and investigating the processual concept of "understanding" in media use more widely can likewise be sharpened by philosophical consideration of reception and response as playful activity. Generating meaning is game-like.

Screen-focused "sense-making structures" (Mayra, 2006: 103) of thought are play-like: they are goal-driven in creating meaning according to rules. In generating sense we are gamers, achievement oriented in actualizing content. Handphone use is immersive: it detaches us from present surroundings, as if we had relocated within a game's separate space and time. Meeting uncertainty (will the connection hold?) we nonetheless anticipate achieving the goal of receiving an intelligible call or text: we interpret, drawing upon a framework ("horizon") of expectations established as soon as we recognize familiar content. Thinking to and fro like flexible players on a football field, we articulate content in its context, allowing us to substantiate narrative along with appropriating its implications.

The Malaysian Chinese woman with whose experiences we began this brief book on multicultural media indicated that cellphone use distracted her pleasurably from bus journeys. She remained "inserted in personal networks while traveling" (May and Hearn, 2005: 201). A familiar number supported her anticipation of particular content; and thinking holistically she achieved a wider understanding of her call (it "makes my day").

More often at home than on buses, audiences watch television teleologically: we seek sense. We are ambitious to achieve understanding. Among the media theorists I discuss in chapter 5, future-oriented, goal-directed, rule-informed play – escaping from everyday life to a separate space and time – is invoked as a research productive metaphor. We have seen that it can function as a model of our purposive orientation towards attaining intelligibility (projection) during viewing. In our immersive screen reception, we expect and establish meaning structured by format (e.g., the half hour news bulletin): informed anticipation shapes our response to different types of pages or programs (Wakeford, 2004: 131). Our goal is one of understanding.

Play, indeed, is a "key concept for understanding the interaction of users with new media" (Kerr et al., 2006: 69). Listening to research participants' linguistically articulated reception of media (their accounts of being an audience) enriches the assertion that multiple aspects of the ludic characterize viewing. Active audiences are similar to "avid gamers" (Consalvo, 2003: 327).

Central to this philosophically inspired interpretation of the screen's reception, we have claimed, is the idea of people "projecting" narrative meaning – assuming and aiming at textual intelligibility. For phenomenology, such playful speculation is a constant companion to reading (Friesen, 2002). This future-directed anticipation of developments is (in)formed by media users' pre-existing cognitive "horizons" (Husserl, 1973: 42) of awareness that texts are instances of types. Expectation of likely events on screen (e.g., an episode closing in enigma) can rest on an audience realizing that the television drama they are watching conforms to serial format. Media reception occurs over time (Rentschler and Kaes, n.d.) with viewers remembering earlier program structures and applying that knowledge to productive engagement with the instance before them. In everyday gossip and focus groups, audience talk about television signals such recognition and subsequent realization of meaning. They frame (Williams, 2003: 526) particulars, placing them in patterns.

The cognitive play in which viewers engage to interpret content involves repetition (remembering formats, genres, types) coupled with integrating future-distinguishing difference – projection of a new screen narrative.

We saw in the last chapter that Iser's reader reception theory informs the language of media user studies. Moving skillfully from *genera* to given instance, the viewer's project in constructing (and subsequently checking) her or his anticipated narrative chain of events is to understand – to constitute coherent story content. We place meaning in the gaps or lacunae left by the text itself (Iser, 1978: 171–2). Lacking explicit information in the program (e.g., as to a developing relationship between two characters), readers render determinate the indeterminate, measuring the accuracy of their hypothetical interpretations against an unfolding narrative (for a discussion, see Brehony, 1996). Researching audiences interpreting news stories about developing countries, one writer notes how they fill in the gaps with post-colonial beliefs about Africa and supposed innate faults of Africans.

One of the more thorough accounts of media reception theory inspired by hermeneutic phenomenology underwrites the research methodology in Buckingham's book *Public Secrets* (1987) on the BBC's *EastEnders*. He draws attention to the subjective processes in which an audience overcomes indeterminacies of meaning in the television program. Appropriating Iser's phenomenology of reading (see chapter 4), he shows how using their generic knowledge of soap opera, viewers "'fill the gaps' between scenes" and assemble coherent stories "out of the series of fragments they are shown" (1987).

Speculating upon and substantiating a program's stories, an audience's response to the screen forms the hermeneutic play of understanding, the ludic comprehension of a visual text, a "guessing game" (Joyce, 2004: 80). Likewise, the viewer's purposeful to and fro gaze or looking (Chandler, 1998) at an image instantiates in time through "concentric circles the unity of the understood meaning" (Gadamer, 1975: 259). Discussion may integrate details seen to shape the audience's holistic comprehension of visual content.

In these processes of perception, sense on screen is anticipated and invariably achieved. "We read for closure and coherence" (Woodlief and Cornis-Pope, n.d.). Television's linear texts where program narratives have a single spatiotemporal reference point (e.g., the soap opera community located around a street) are easily represented as meaningfully unified. Much more difficult to render intelligibly integrated are the multi-linear texts formed by a web page and its hyperlinks to stories occupying distinct locations in space and time (Hima, 2001). Our perceptions of coherence need a focus.

Media theorists have sought to draw up a phenomenology (or investigate the experiential structure) of the screen user's embodied gaze/glance at mediated events as the ludic construction of narrative meaning. This activity may take different forms, from the momentary to the more prolonged. Looking back and forth across a filmic scene in comprehending relationships between characters is accomplished more swiftly than viewing a further episode of a television serial to check one's anticipation of story developments. Investigating either, hermeneutic analysis places an "emphasis on flux, becoming and subjective perspectives" (Di Tommaso, 2004).

The concept of "identification," writes Buckingham, is "rather imprecise" (1987: 82). Two forms of identification have been distinguished: (1) aligning with others in thinking and (2) agreeing on the intellectual product of that process. Through interpretative play with the text, we come to see the "self" in programs. Our *processual* alignment/identification is with those on screen "like us," individuals authorially developing a coherent understanding of events just as we project an intelligible narrative, the "descriptive identification" (Phillips, 2004: 700) of content. The serial audience's cognitive, frequently expressive, interpretative activity parallels BBC *EastEnder* characters establishing meaning in their lives, supporting media user alignment with those on screen. With the Simpsons in the US, we try to make sense of life. And – perhaps – as people watching we also agree with *personae* on television about a *propositional* perception or statement of these activities' normative implications (frequently supporting heterosexual romance or the health of capitalism). We can share the program's values as well as its meaning.

Associated with media use, then, is a psychology and politics of interacting with the screen (Miller, 1995). Viewers and viewed align in the *process* of accomplishing narrative understanding – as distinct from agreeing on the ethical or political *proposition* which may be implicit in a story engaging viewers in screen-related "judging acts" (Kamir, 2005: 269).

Possibilities for propositional alignment will be circumscribed by appropriation or use of the text for work or play. Being motivated by extraneous duty in reading excludes audiences from declaring that they share characters' pleasurable absorption in events (on the other hand, duties to others online can heighten the experience of escape). In seeking to supplement a poststructuralist focus on viewers' responses with phenomenological accounts of screen user subjectivity, we are integrating propositional and processual aspects of identification. Both *subject* and *subjective process* of agreement can be studied.

Processually aligned, audiences identify with a narrative agent engaged in similarly seeking to comprehend events: while the former focuses on a live screen, the latter regards a life-world. An enigma requiring imaginative resolution thereby involves viewers, generating both their "being in" the text and continually coming to know. "Moments of absorption are *simultaneously* moments of reflection, and also moments of preparation, recollection-in-advance, account-building, and role-management" (Barker, 2005: 357, his emphasis) in comprehending a story.[1] It is precisely these activities which align us with the narrative agents we see engaged in understanding their own lives. On the other hand, when watching reality television "unravel" we can identify with people failing like us under stress to make sense of surroundings (Ruddock 2007: 126, citing Hill, 2005).

Despite arguments to the contrary (see Wilson, 2004) it can hardly be the case that identification involves "audiences losing self-awareness" (Barker, 2005: 357). Instead, moments of biographies in current affairs and drama are likely to be appropriated, informing audience lives. Identities for both the read and the reader emerge from resolving "imaginative uncertainties" on screen (Tulloch, 2000: 229). Diasporic media consumption within a shared cultural tradition can lead to the "reinvention" of particular selves (Georgiou, 2006: 72).

One impediment to insight may be the reader's erroneous identification *of* screen content, her or his positioning or locating the emerging story within the wrong horizons of interpretative understanding (e.g., viewing it as fictional drama rather than documented narrative, thereby excluding information of assistance in establishing it as intelligible). But reading a text from within alternative aesthetic or ethical-cultural frameworks of comprehension can result in imaginative interpretation (e.g., perception of a sex comedy as supporting family values).

A critical theory of subjectivity acknowledges that textual displays of (individual or institutional) power to build screen narratives can be thereby potentially hegemonic in also underwriting an audience's subjective self-understanding (Koegler, n.d.). We identify with both construction and content. Television advertisements offer selective sense of our lives. Where negative in their "processual power" (Mansell, 2004: 97), such dominant metaprescriptives (Gane, 2003: 438) need to be resisted, their reception marked by recalcitrant response.

The study of a text's address to audiences (or poetics) should recognize, in other words, that the former may be seeking a preferred reading or evaluative response from viewers. An advertisement, of course, can readily be interpreted as aligning intended audiences with purchasing the promoted product – or propositional identification with that "message." To understand why a particular "positioning" of media users occurs it may be necessary to adopt the analytical perspective associated with the political economy of meaning (e.g., to elucidate the nature of the profit sought with the text's production).

Media propose, audiences dispose. The defining qualities of contemporary information culture are "power and play" (Lunenfeld, 2004: 68). Watching television, negotiating their way through indeterminate narratives, people construct coherent accounts of those on screen, stories projected and tested in an audience's ludic adjustment to discursive schemes (Koegler, n.d.). Actions established as emancipatory (Kahn and Kellner, 2004) can lead to us reinterpreting our mundane selves. Identity is a reflective (and reflexive) project (Bennett, 2003: 146).[2]

Everyday Expectations of the "Ordinary Effect": The Phenomenology of Familiar Television

Scannell's study of media use is quintessentially phenomenological in focus. As is characteristic of this approach more widely (see Moores, 2006), his interest is in accounting for the experience of familiarity: we find the "usual programs on the usual channels at the usual times" (Scannell, 1996: 6). Why do television programs seem so frequently recognizable? He sets out to explain "this ordinariness, this obviousness" (ibid.; see also Scannell, 2007: 8). In the routine life-world of cellphone use, everyday media unproblematically "measure up" (Scannell, 1996: 12) to our expectations. Familiarity of content is not only a condition of comprehending media, but a consequence.[3]

Buckingham also notes how "texts invite readers to read them in familiar ways" (Buckingham, 1987: 35). His definitive study of the London-based BBC soap opera *EastEnders* emphasizes the guiding light of familiarity. Television flows repeatedly in narrative types known to intended audiences.[4] Gazing or glancing at the screen from the same cultural horizon, viewers enjoying prior shared awareness of these program forms generate meaning of a closely parallel kind. Focusing on the familiar, people project: we expect and establish *EastEnders'* enigmatic ending at each episode.

Yet people are inevitably also variously informed. They respond to their own perceptions of indeterminacy in a text – to their own awareness of narrative gaps inviting completion (Buckingham, 1987: 77). Conceivably, each can discern a distinct enigma. Soporific viewers may see none: their "absence" renders them oblivious to a program's passing puzzles.

When they do focus on a long-running twice-weekly drama (soap opera) from different horizons of understanding (informed by varying assumptions), audiences fill in a story's moments of silence in alternative ways. Looking at content from a range of perspectives, distinct aspects are emphasized or appear marginal. While people recognize that a program is generic or follows the pattern of a media type, they also project a multitude of readings developing its narrative detail. Confronted with an "extraordinary degree of fragmentation," viewers "assemble the different narrative strands" into a "meaningful pattern": they build a "stable and coherent concept" of character (Buckingham, 1987: 60, 76).

Television narratives are *open* to differing interpretations, enabled by the addition of distinct knowledge. A soap opera's "relative indeterminacy" can produce a "range of actualizations" (Allen, 1985: 63). A program also may be *open* in its values, with an ambivalent political perspective on the world, prompting a range of ideological responses or perceptions of how it defines the powerful. On the other hand, presenters can strive to position viewers on a particular horizon of understanding events, a point of view which necessarily excludes others. Audience members may align with attitudes (in a fusion of horizons) or distance themselves. But watching *EastEnders* all can enjoy the same politics of celebrating a community on screen.

Buckingham provides a detailed account of responses to the soap opera where "retension" refers to the "process whereby viewers are given cues which invite them to recall past events" (1987: 50). Likewise, "protension" describes the "process whereby viewers are given cues which invite them to project into the future and to speculate about coming events" (ibid.). But this is to reduce psychological phenomena to features of a text, the audience's active understanding to its passively acquiring prompts to conjecture.

Cognition is not to be confused with code. Buckingham conflates (or occludes) Gadamer's hermeneutics of the reader's thought with Barthes's hermeneutics of the text. The former points to the psychological phenomenon of projection (or anticipation continually implicit within present perception): focused on securing the goal of coherent meaning, projection we have noted to be cognitively play-like. Barthes's concern, however, is with that textual "element of narrative" (Buckingham, 1987: 61) establishing enigma.

Consciousness is not to be identified with cues for thinking. Rather, retension involves remembering the character and textual types which constitute one's horizons of understanding.[5] In protension one projects meaning guided by these cognitive structures underwriting everyday expectation, a constant aspect of the audience's continuing engagement with a

television program or web page. The informed audience's protensive projection of anticipated story occurs by virtue of the former's memory or
retension of narrative pattern (with events viewed on screen regarded as
fleshing out this form). In short, protension and retension are not "common
features in all narratives" (Buckingham, 1987: 54). Instead, these are cognitive activities undertaken in response to verbal or visual texts on the
audience's horizons of understanding. In this "dialectic of protension and
retension" (Allen, 1985: 76) we comprehend, we conjecture, we confirm.

Cognition as Interaction: Putting-Into-Play, Projecting, Positing, Positioning Meaning

The phenomenology of television and Internet use contributes to epistemology (Westphal, 1999: 417) an account of media knowledge. It posits
people's coming to understand a program or page as a to and fro process of
being cognitively *in play* which, while drawing on past retention (the
memory of previous television or websites), is at the same time projected
towards the future (protention or anticipation of developments). Remembering, we think we recognize a storyline. Our awareness of present
events always already classifies experience in known categories (fore-
concepts), allowing us to continually anticipate or fore-structure the future.
Such play is productive (Pearce, 2006: 17). Cognition is interaction
(Steinkuehler, 2006: 97).

Reception of content as comprehensible is not passively given, but actively
generated through an audience's playing – epistemologically – between
their (past-oriented) awareness of story type and (future-oriented) establishing a particular narrative instance. Equipped with generic knowledge of
television texts (Nutt and Railton, 2003: 580) as situation comedy or soap
opera, viewers "anticipate the coming of meaning" (Amerika, 2004: 72).
Where programs are perceived to belong simultaneously to different types
(e.g., romance and science fiction), anticipation will be complex. While
acknowledging that media use is routine (centered on the everyday process
of projection), hermeneutics as the study of how we understand narrative
emphasizes creativity in response as establishing the particular shape of
expected events.

Hermeneutics is implicit within active audience media theory. The latter
resists accounts of people merely absorbing screen content, denying that
television transmits "prepackaged bits and pieces of culture to increasingly

passive spectators" (Goldman, 1982). Instead, drawing on a "meaning-constitutive background" (Koegler, n.d.) of presuppositions or "cognitive frames" (Phillips, 2004: 703), such as their knowledge of the sorts of serials there are, viewers actively anticipate and achieve understanding of media narrative. Watching a soap opera, they are cognizant that entertaining pessimistic expectations can be appropriate. Hermeneutics argues audiences view from a horizon of existing awareness where they make meaning "under conditions which are not of their own choosing" (Buckingham, 1993: 14).

We formulate and fit together stories synthesizing screen content. Media users' tacit knowledge of their constituting meaning from a text is disclosed (Chan and Garrick, 2003: 291) in focus groups where the process can be closely analyzed through the investigator's qualitative "conceptual lens" (Boczkowski, 2004: 145).[6] Researchers listen to accounts of others making sense. While differing culturally, audiences engage in the same process of constructing meaning (Buckingham, 1993: 15).

Following a conversational route (Lewis, 1991: 81), researchers can employ the close empirical scrutiny enabled by focus groups or "depth-interviews" (Lo, 2002: 77) to map viewers' hermeneutic processing of content through their cognitive-expressive activities of media consumption. Recording the recipient's point of view, we form an emic or participant perspective (see Love, 1994). Listening to contributors, their tacit thematizing of preferred values may be discerned (Aronson, 1994) (e.g., that news should draw on plural perspectives).

Interpretative accounts of people's reading local and global programs, we have noted, can draw productively upon Gadamer's (1975) literary hermeneutics, theory thoroughly imbued with the philosophical phenomenology of Husserl (1973; see also Gurwitsch, 1966). Media content is only accessible to us in terms of how we understand it (Ross, 2002). Hermeneutics investigates viewers' declared achievement of comprehension through the "lens of language" (Bovenizer, 2000) – their talk (and writing) about the meaning of texts.

The phenomenology of play (the ludic) considers it to be a structured cognitive-expressive experience of absence from the mundane – time "taken out." We shall see that the game can function as heuristic source of ideas appropriate to scrutinizing focus group audience claims about the process of their responding to the screen (projecting from past to future).[7] Both, for instance, are shaped by participants seeking goals. In such research, viewing emerges as complex and absorbing ("serious fun"), resolving enigma and realizing emotion.

Employing a different set of categories from positivist science's quantitative studies of the world, qualitative scientific description of watching television aims to make explicit essential structures implicit in media experience as lived (De Mul, 2003: 262). Audience accounts of screen use form the focus of attention. For such a phenomenology of perception, one is already in the situation of which one is attempting to "take the measure" (Connor, n.d.). We need to understand the screen's interpretative reception using philosophically resourced theory which can "speak" (Thompson et al., 1994: 447) to stories of media comprehension expressed by "us," the present users. The language of close analytical scrutiny must connect to viewers' concepts. For otherwise, "prefabricated questionnaires" force media users to consider their experience through "categories that may deviate ... from their lifeworld" (Schroder, 1999: 28).

Fundamental to hermeneutic theory is the conviction that a cognitive play of/in projecting meaning (Sutton-Smith, 1997) pervades our perception of pages or programs. In this narrative of watching, we construct the watched. Audiences always anticipate, activating and achieving understanding. From our wider awareness of ludic experience can be derived a model of media reception which allows a "fusion of horizons" (Gadamer, 1975: 273) between psychology and personal experience: it bridges the semantic distance between high theory and the lowly audience's own perception of its responses to television program or web page. Play provides a mediating image of media consumption.

Seeking an account of subjectivity in-between audience and screen, media user theory argues for hermeneutic phenomenology as a resource. It conceptualizes people's screen reception as a culturally located cognitive, often expressive, *fore-structured projecting* (expecting and establishing) potential narrative on radio or screen. Viewers engage in a play-like – or ludic – production of meaning, a memory-informed textual inscription whose aspects (or "moments") are here considered. *Time* should be foregrounded in television and Internet studies with reception theory derived from realizing the structure of perception as process. Screen user *intentionality* – or construction of on-air/online content to form meaningful narrative – needs to be explored.

In narratives of "in-between subjectivity,"[8] media users interpret a text's events, projecting or "throwing" meaning on screen. "Well-managed" audience research should open up how they "live out their prefigured encounters" (Barker, 2004) with content. Media use is never a "predominantly passive" (Taylor, 2005: 627) response.

Testing the Model of Actively Absorbing Play:
Narratives of Media Use

How people read, respond, and react to proliferating information sources are questions that inform empirical investigation of screen use (Nettleton et al., 2004: 535). As I have shown, hermeneutic theory of media users as ludic answers that they become actively absorbed in stories told on screen, drawing on the fore-structure of their understanding or "patterned prior expectations" (Barker, 2004) in projection of textual meaning. On these occasions, seeing has an as-structure in which content is perceived *as* narrative.

Moreover, this cognitive-expressive process is at the heart of theorizing audience alignment. It is in projecting a probable story that audiences draw on prefigurative material (such as their awareness that the text conforms to a genre) to resolve its uncertainties. Dealing with enigmatic events positions "us" as audiences with "them" as characters in a story. Empathy is indeed cognitive at its core.

Our interpreting a story plays back and forth, tracing a hermeneutic circle between abstract frameworks and anticipatory fore-understanding – our temporal referring elsewhere in order to recognize the present and resolve enigma. Viewing is teleologically undertaken, a patterned "relating meaning as preinterpretively understood to meaning as more explicitly articulated" (Smythe, 1992). We engage in comprehension, drawing upon the culturally preceding, provisionally positing events. Reference to such processual "looking forward" is necessary in explaining and exploring patterns of discourse in audience response to media. Analyzing these readings, we look for discursive signs of a story's emerging production.

Reception studies require a realist scientific method (Harré and Secord, 1972) which focuses on establishing narratives of subjective participant response (see chapter 1). We have disputed research constructing generalizations about relationships between observable causal events on screen and alleged audience behavioral effects. As we have argued, even in much post-positivist reception study, attention is directed to contributor conclusions about content rather than the cognitive and often expressive reading process through which the response is constructed. Failure to engage with the latter results in an "absence of attention to the decision-making process" (Malaviya et al., 2001: 118) of interpreting a screen text.

Investigation of audiences should follow a falsificationist (Popper, 1963) scientific method, seeking "resistant materials," asking what further research

The Projecting Audience

might "test the nature of the claims" (Barker, 2003: 332, 331) to knowledge of media use. Interviews and focus groups provide access to test material in the form of participants' performative discourse narrating their cognitive-expressive response to screen texts.

An inductivist approach attempting to generalize such particular contributions as evidence for a thesis emphasizes homogeneity, marginalizing participant construction of alterity or subjective difference. (See, for instance, claims about the "generalizability of the stories" involving domestic computer use in Selwyn, 2004.) Concrete qualitative detail is effaced by abstract enumeration. On the other hand, a falsificationist methodology for reception studies not only can accommodate varying audience narratives, but actively searches for "qualitative diversity" (Schroder et al., 2003: 159) as a means of testing hypothetical assumptions about reader response (Malaviya et al., 2001: 116). Do people project meaning drawing on memories of media forms? If so, how do they differ in subjective speculation?

Qualitative research should follow a realist falsificationist approach to scientific audience studies which sees each individual as a unique being (Oatey, 1999). This methodology emphasizes in testing cognitive hypotheses a continual reference to readers' narratives of reception accomplishing meaning. Theory surviving attempted falsification by reference to people's actual processing of content is thereby extended by confirming empirical instance – while the former's "lens of concepts" (Barker, 2003: 327) brings the latter into focus within a framework of interpretation.

(In)formed by the cultural horizons of their understanding (not least the assumption that stories occur within time), audience anticipation or projection of narrative meaning is the experiential core of reading, a fore-structuring of program comprehension. With their contributors addressing "sense-making questions," focus groups and interviewees selected for "maximum diversity" (Schroder et al., 2003: 148, 160) can attain participant perceptions of actual success – and sometimes failure – in rendering a given text meaningful. Contributors engage in "storied sense-making" (Edwards, 1997: 270). Speech makes explicit their implicit awareness of anticipating narrative. Viewers projecting a story "thrown" on indeterminate cellphone, Internet, or TV items support the experimenter's hypothesis that concrete screen sense is continually subject to audience conjecture, with expected developments confirmed or refuted in media use. Meaning-making is a cognitive, expressive process occurring within a framework of understanding – readers knowing the forms and genres of customary screen content.

Reader reception theory's constructionist (Willmott, 1994) emphasis on individual audience members' projective processing of media content within shared horizons of interpretation is echoed by discourse or narrative psychology (Edwards, 1997: 288). A person's cognitive activity is structured by public or collective concepts to which talk refers. Seeing involves mental processing during which, while subjectively we anticipate meaning, we actualize a shared horizon of perception. Our knowing the world is not immediate, but a time-structured testing of interpretative frameworks against events – an activity foregrounded in audience discussion. We agree we are watching a soap opera.

Yet marking out horizons of understanding content can constitute a politically "contested ontology" (Nissenbaum, 2004: 195). Humor shared by some can be seen as reactionary by others. Necessarily seeing screen events within varying "cultural frames" (Tulloch, 2000: 212), people reading narrative nonetheless align epistemologically in similar cognitive-expressive play. Moving mentally back and forth in a hermeneutic circle to draw upon a wider tradition to interpret the particular text, they speculatively anticipate and subsequently ascertain sequential content for stories. Assessing moral or political propositions therein, they identify with or are indignant at narrative agents similarly seeking sense. Aligning with those online, Internet users can imaginatively morph in chat room "identity experiments" (Valkenburg et al. 2005: 383). On the other hand, capitalism colonizes concepts: uncritical citizens are reconstituted, naturalized as passive consumers (on technology as a "contested domain," see Salter, 2005: 292). Alienated audiences distrust, deconstruct, and distance themselves.

Conclusion

We can set this chapter in context by citing philosophically comparable analyses of media use. Research attempts to declare "enabling conditions" (Harré, 1998: 45) of reading a screen. These include the semi-selfconscious projection of a potential story within cultural horizons of "interpretative flexibility" (Lenert, 2004: 235), a "tacit condition of meaning" (Smythe, 1992). We test hypotheses that audiences anticipate particular content drawing continually upon a broader generic frame of reference in processing a radio and TV program or Internet page. "Memory and anticipation become our only access to time outside our own" (Williamson, 1978: 155).

Cultural horizons of understanding content enabling identification of narrative can be effaced or evident. They are "critical variables" (Kluver and

Banerjee, 2005: 31), constricting or creatively liberating. For "much like a game where individuals improvise within the constraints of rules ..., consumers' horizons of conceivable action, feeling, and thought [make] certain patterns of behaviour and sense-making interpretations more likely than others" (Arnould and Thompson, 2005: 869).

"We've been going around in hermeneutic circles for a while now" (Westphal, 1999: 422). In chapter 6, we explore people realizing meaning, their epistemologically expressive play and protest in response to the screen's "cultural shaping of subjectivities" (Ortner, 2005: 46) in cellphone use. The Chinese texter and traveler of earlier chapters re-enters to take center stage.

Notes

1   I am grateful to Martin Barker who commented on an earlier version of this chapter: his conceptual map of "identification" includes in that process audience "self-awareness" (Barker, 2005: 357). See also Wilson (2004: ch. 4, sc. 4.4). Viewer identification is continually "in play," a flowing realization that in processing meaning and subscription to propositions we are similar to or distant from other people. Audience alignment in constructing an intentional object of belief presupposes memory, not suppression of the reader's past.

2   Empirical research towards a hermeneutics of the audience's projecting meaning would be referred to by Murphy and Kraidy as "quasi-ethnographic research" (2003: 305). See also Wakeford (2003a: 237) on ethnography.

3   Scannell's phenomenological study of "familiarity" (1996: 6–21) opens his volume on *Radio, Television and Modern Life*. Recognition of a program rests on its conformity to our prior, often *public* knowledge. Here Scannell writes not only of the "intentions of the program-makers" (16) but of our "intentionality" (ibid.) as "common ground" or "shared knowledges and understandings." More commonly in phenomenology "intentional objects" as the constant content of consciousness form the focus of an *individual's* subjective knowledge. So, for instance, Stecker defines "intentional" as the "property of aboutness had by our thoughts" (2003: 3). The latter interpretation of the concept generates the question of how we can come to share knowledge where the isolated "subject is seen as the founding source of meanings" (MacCabe, 1985: 46).

4   There can clearly be debate about media formats and types. For instance, television news may include popular current affairs programs and even talk shows which bear information to a wide public. News should "embrace more popular, entertaining formats that will enable it to engage more directly with private or personal concerns" (Buckingham, 2000: 21).

5 Following Husserl, the phrase "horizons of understanding" needs to be used in reception theory to denote our interpretative knowledge of phenomenal types, conceptual awareness allowing one to engage in the projection of meaning, rather than to refer to "textual codes" (Allen, 1985: 86).

6 During news or documentary television, a textual interpretation can be offered by the program itself (e.g., in voiceover) on behalf of a presumed audience (Hassanpour, n.d.).

7 "Hermeneutics or interpretation is concerned with the generation, transmission, and acceptance of meaning within the life-world" (Heelan, 1997). This definition of hermeneutics relates comprehension to an idea at the heart of phenomenology, that of "life-world."

8 Yu Shi writes about the "in-between subjectivity" of the Chinese diaspora in the United States (2005: 56). My use of the phrase denotes rather an interactive process, the projection of meaning occurring "between" an audience's cultural horizons of understanding and a particular text.

6

A Phenomenology of Phone Use: Pervasive Play and the Ludification of Culture

Continuing and accelerating development of digital technologies (from cellphones to personal computers) has led to the "ludification of culture" (Raessens, 2006) or "gaming of cultures" (Boellstorff, 2006: 33). Translucent two-dimensional screens with their accompanying texts and tunes pervade everyday life, drawing us from the three-dimensionally material. Our intermittent "absence" from immediate surroundings as if suddenly caught up in a game elsewhere is frequent and found everywhere: absorption in new communication technology is easy. Phones ring and engage us in a different agenda: during these times of ludic listening or looking we play away from driving, sitting at the café, walking on the street.

Callers and text senders focus purposefully elsewhere, continually linking to another's networked place – albeit with local disturbance to this distant distraction. Sharing a moment visually (Villi, 2006), we can immediately transmit photographs of our spatiotemporally "present" surroundings from which we are subjectively "absent." Owning and operating a phone enables us to initiate culturally nuanced meaning which is both "here" (e.g., in decorating or "dressing" the technology) and not "here" (e.g., in messages received by a faraway partner). Supporting "co-present communication" (Moores, 2000: 108) with someone elsewhere, cellphones complicate the spatial and temporal positioning of communication.

In this "surging expansion of absent presence" (Gergen, 2002: 231) the screen's pervasive distracting capacity to render culture ludic means that a definitive boundary between the play-like and dutiful work can no longer be drawn (Yee, 2006). The "solid architectonic distinction" (García-Montes et al., 2006: 72) between private and public place has vanished: every day people send and receive personal calls in work settings (Gant and Kiesler, 2002: 129). Digital opportunities to "chat" on office computers continually tempt the otherwise employed from the tedious. Tasks offer a "threshold"

(Lie, 2003: 123) or gateway to play: at one's desk dealing routinely with daily employment duties one can escape on screen. A contributor to Jensen's writing on Internet use may "log out of [his] work life" "by reading a private email or checking out a website that [his] girlfriend suggested that [he] look at." Both worlds coexist (2005: 20). Many websites (such as Yahoo!) offer concurrent opportunities for laborious and ludic activity.

From a hermeneutic perspective in which arriving at understanding involves the flexible to and fro construction and checking of content, work is liminal. While driven by obligation, as interpretative activity it is play-like in creating meaning, presence from absence. The ludic and the laborious approximate each other, moreover, in rule-governed structure and the production of human identity. We are our delights and duties.

In summary, engaging in games offers an appropriate analytical model for interpreting the media engrossed – particularly those using cellphones. We are a "dispersed audience" (Couldry, 2005: 189) or "mobile public" (Drotner, 2005: 187). Reflecting upon the cognitive processes associated with play allows us to develop an understanding of making and receiving calls, messages, and texts (Myers, 2006: 48). The interactive study of "call" and "cognitive" permits each to inform the other – the empirical ground of our research to be related to (and in turn illuminate) theory (McMillin, 2007: 139).

Five Universal Moments in Cellphone Use: Absorbing-Anticipating; Articulating; Appropriating/Alienation by Mediated Meaning

Seeking to gain insight into the "magnitude of mobile phone adoption" (Campbell, 2007: 343), much may be learned by focusing for the moment on Malaysia, with its diasporic people drawn from several Asian regions. We can "connect the specific with the universal" (Qiu and Thompson, 2007). The nation's three numerically larger cultural groups of Malays, Chinese, and Indians are complemented in the east of the country by a variety of "peoples" (Bidayuh, Iban, Kadazan, and others). Throughout this diversity, an ethnic pluralism of personal experience in creating a new communication culture can (in)form global theory. We recognize varying social patterns of "cellphone," "hand phone," or "mobile phone" use.[1] In this chapter, these phrases are synonymous in referring to an increasingly "hybrid ensemble" (Farnsworth and Austrin, 2005: 14) of communication tools within a relatively tiny device.

As noted earlier, our research method does not involve *inductive* generalizing from a sample of users. Rather, drawing upon the preceding philosophical psychology of play, we argue *abductively* that there is an underlying ludic structural similarity in reception and response to these emerging small media. Our abstract analysis of cellphone users' understanding-in-use is then tested against concrete contributions in focus groups or interviews. Hearing a participant's hermeneutic processing of calls signals a corroborating case (as in the narrative exemplar below), a subjective instantiation of structure.

Our research commenced in Kuching, Sarawak, East Malaysia (Saturday 23rd and Monday 25th September, 2006). It continued in Kuala Lumpur, West Malaysia (Saturday 25th November, 2006). We conducted interviews at customer support walk-in centers operated at malls and other areas of major consumption by a northern hemisphere transnational telecommunications company with a southern presence in Malaysia.

Cellphone manufacturers are "creating many, many functions but nobody knows how to use them.... We are trying our best to *learn* also and to teach our customers" (female CSP, Chinese-KL, emphasis in the original).[2] Consumer support "shops" constitute an advisory interface in media use. "Before customers walk in, they will call to our contact centre first": they then visit to supplement guidance given at that earlier stage (female CSP, Chinese-K). Along with roadshows, an associated website, and displays in newspapers as well as on television, these "channels to educate the customer" (FT) seem to us to fill an important informative role: "every time the new technology [is] coming in, we have to teach them" (male CSP, Malay-KL). Brightly decorated in corporate colors, with innovative interiors, the shops provide a welcoming source of support to consumers seeking a face-to-face resolution of issues in handphone use (and, indeed, researchers were also welcome).[3]

We were interested in exploring differences and similarities in customers and their cellphone use, encouraging participant classification of variation to emerge: "How do you see the differences? How do you categorize them?" (FT-K). In doing so we sought to negotiate a research path within contributors' conceptual horizons of understanding. Customers and service personnel, of course, could have conflicting perspectives on issues. We needed to mediate through *our* investigative "perceptions" how *they* "see" handphone use. During discussion, facilitators moved swiftly to rephrase questions participants found difficult:

> "What is your perception of customers' use of cellphones, SMS [short message service], or GPRS [general packet radio service] accessing?" (FT-K)

"My perception? ..." (female CSP, Malay-K)

"How do you see their use of phones in that way?" (FT-K)

Cross-culturally, handphone use is cognitively shaped. Like other electronic communication (e.g., dial up Internet) it is guided by "audience" anticipation and purpose, with consequences for the identity of those sending messages. In Malaysia, as elsewhere, people congregate publicly and socially in cafés only to sit privately and separately in front of their laptops (Ito, 2007). We shall see that parallel to media use more widely (Wilson 2004, 2007), engaging with cellphone content is akin to the "immersive experience" of goal-directed, future-oriented play, focused other than on the here and now (Kerr et al., 2006). *Locally*, mobile media are interpreted by callers within their cultural horizons of understanding technology and text. In our play-like (or ludic) use of cellphones (whether work-oriented or otherwise) we absorb, anticipate, articulate, and appropriate – or are alienated by – meaning.

A Hermeneutics of Handphones: Narrative Exemplar

Cellphone, Internet, and television prompt an identical structure of inferential response to their varying formats – for which play is able to function as a heuristic or useful model. We can illustrate this with a Malaysian instance of "technosocial tethering" (Ito, 2005) to which we shall give further attention subsequently. In this narrative the Chinese woman whom we considered in chapter 1 speaks of her satisfaction with the mobile phone's capacity to absorb her in a segment of separated space and time, to carry her away metaphorically from present circumstances, to distract and connect her elsewhere in a "personalization and privatization" (Okabe et al., 2005) of subjectivity. Detached from her immediate context, she forms a mediated hermeneutic circle of close contact with another of the phone-embracing "networked public" (Ito, 2007).

We learn that surrounded by a cacophonous city, her interest is in constructing digital intimacy, immersing herself in a "telecocoon" (Habuchi, 2005): "no matter where you are, you're on a bus or you're traveling, you have the phone there and you can SMS anybody." We shall refer to such passing of time as an *absorbing* moment of media use.

While her outgoing phone communication could be to "anybody," this woman only answered incoming calls when she recognized the source: "when I look at the number and I'm not familiar, normally I wouldn't pick it up." Her selectivity was prompted by anticipating that unfamiliar callers would be "weird [people]" who "give you those noises." In hermeneutic terms (chapter 3), our fore-conceptualizing emerging content supports expectation: in perceiving, we project likely events. We shall call this the *anticipatory* moment of media use. Our understanding of narrative is fore-structured, an always future-oriented interpreting of signs.

The Chinese interviewee continued by telling us that "when I receive an SMS from my niece … I'm *amused* that she's able to, you know, put all the short forms and even insert a picture" (emphasis in the original). We shall refer to her niece's practice as sender and her own capacity as recipient to "put [together]" coherent multimedia content as *articulating* meaning.

Finally, our female respondent tells us about the pleasurable significance of this particular – recognized and responded to – multimedia messaging from her niece: "it makes my day." Media use constructs the mundane. She *appropriates* (Gadamer, 1975) content to inform or shed light on the wider context of its reception, positioning for us her perception of the call's contribution to her familiar life-world. On the other hand, unfamiliar callers are considered likely to be "weird" and hence profoundly *alienating*: they are dismissively condemned to remain at a distance.

Telephone talk can produce enriching eudaemonic effects (the consumer's "well-being"): cellphone consequences for health, like those of sport, have been much discussed. Here, new technology supports rather than subverts the extended family.

In considering them to be play-like, we are looking at whether cellphone use and media enjoyment more generally are characterized by multiple aspects of absorbing, anticipating, articulating, and appropriating meaning – or alienation from content. Do these moments manifest themselves within interviewee discourse? Can we distinguish between such aspects of contributions in people's narratives of cellphone reception and response? Are they global features of Caucasian, Chinese, Indian, Malay stories?

A Philosophical Psychology of Cellphone Use as Ludic

Absorbing/absorbed by mediated meaning

Cellphone communication is "delocating" (Caronia and Caron, 2004: 30) or detaching from immediate surroundings. In a "doubling of place" (Moores, 2005: 102) using the handphone we absorb ourselves cognitively and often with enjoyment in the mediated spatiotemporal life-world of others elsewhere – just as being on the sports field extracts one from everyday life. Immersion is seen as one of the "key pleasures" (Kerr et al., 2006: 73) of new media offering "transportation" online (Simon, 2006: 62).

As a technology of "perpetual contact" (Katz and Aakhus, 2002), the cellphone offers a mobile means of keeping in touch with distant others or "relational maintenance" (Wei and Lo, 2006: 68). While "stretched," our friendships are nonetheless continued: "the couple, those lovers" (or when "you're feeling very close to the other person") (female CSP, Chinese-KL) communicate more intimately. A distressing sense of being separate can be surrendered, temporarily denied through using this technology of "distanced relatedness" (Nafus and Tracey, 2002: 207): "you know that the message will go through" (female customer, Chinese-KL). Correlatively, immersion "sunders spatial and geographical ties" (Hemment, 2005: 32) with immediate surroundings.

Handphone communication places us in private digital contact, defining immediately surrounding space and time as more openly shared. Seeking pseudo-privacy we look away from those around us, producing invisible "social partitions" (Ling, 2004: 132). The teenager's domestic phone use constructs a personal space, an "intimate oasis" (Caronia, 2005: 99) of absent play set against which the family home is present and "public."

Space and time take shape in particular cultural terms. With his handphone programmed for "roaming" while "on vacation" in Singapore, a Chinese male enthusiast for such communication could be said to be doubly *at play* when making use of a technology he regarded as "*very* convenient" (emphasis in the original). He is *in absentia* both from home and from his chosen recreational city. More widely, both caller and content can be said to be displaced or positioned in the "cross-call" zone of speaking to another where the narrative of saying is unfolded. An SMS message may be left in that technologically underwritten separate but interactive "third place" (Williams, 2006: 14) and time for collection while the sender "returns" to a location "here and now." "The moment the 'line' is back again, straight away [the addressee] can receive it" (male customer, Chinese-K).

Invitations to play, to instantly extract oneself from one's immediate environment, can be resisted: customers complain about a "call and SMS disturbing them: they want to know when or who is the person" (female CSP, Chinese-KL). Determining its human source is "pivotal" (Katz and Aakhus, 2002: 304) in understanding cellphone contact.

While we escape, extracted from material immediacy by handphone use, the latter does not evade the necessity of conforming to principles of best practice. As if in a game, we engage in a rule-governed pursuit of goals in receiving and sending cellphone content; prescriptions of how to behave may be more or less explicit (in the latter case constituting "tacit knowledge").

Handphone use can aim at simply intrinsic enjoyment in calling or be extrinsic in purpose (e.g., arranging an offline meeting). As a situated social practice (Murtagh, 2002) each mode of employment has its own appropriate address to intended recipients: "To meet up with clients I prefer to call. It's more respect[ful], right. If you SMS, the client's not very happy.... I will *call.*... If you just send an SMS he will say, *whah,* 'how to do business!'" (male customer, Chinese-KL, emphasis in the original).[4] In such ethical reasoning on social competence, "etiquette and politeness rules" (Caronia and Caron, 2004: 54) are expressed. Successful communication through each message mode has its own requirements and difficulties to be avoided. Sometimes phone use can be regarded as a "galling social violation" (Ling, 2004: 128) and must be suspended: "we discipline the child on the usage of the phone" (female customer, Chinese-KL).

Customers can misunderstand the "call divert" function and the rules for its use; others need assisting to connect through the data Internet mode. Some "thought that it's nothing, they just divert the calls and [are] complaining that they didn't receive [them]" (female CSP, Malay-K). "We will help the customer to do the setting until they can connect to the Internet" (female CSP, Chinese-K).

Cellphone use can further infringe on ethical rules, as when long-distance calls were made to far-off places from an interviewee's illicitly accessed phone number "*without my notice*" (female customer, Bidayuh-K, emphasis in the original). Customers become annoyed with offensive communication manifestly disregarding others' rights to privacy and respect. "I find it's quite irritating" (female customer, Chinese-KL).

Anticipating mediated meaning

Immersion is fundamentally fore-structured or interpretative. Our absorption in cellphone use is simultaneously guided by anticipation: reception occurs within a cognitive horizon of fore-concepts. Remembered calls, in other words, allow us to project or expect to hear and see likely narratives from identified sources. Classifying content, we seek sense in sender stories:

if successful, meaning "flows" (Kerr et al., 2006: 71). Phone use is continually future-goal oriented.

Mobile phone users generate or read content, categorizing or identifying it within cultural horizons of understanding as instantiating a type (e.g., as conducting business). Employing research questionnaires ("What is the main topic of your conversations?") seeking single-word answers can often efface these extended narratives of individual calling, truncating stories of creative media engagement. Rather than providing a brief customer autobiography of cellphone use (as is sought in the present inquiry), respondents must agree reductively to one term in a list of alternatives as summarizing their often complex call content: "social," "work," "emergency," etc. (Cohen and Lemish, 2003: 172).

During commentary on handphone use a new media literacy is apparent: people are well versed in reading and writing codes. Knowledge of these patterns permits prediction of content. "Our group of people here [in Malaysia], they are very good in using SMS. They know how to use short forms and whatever" (female customer, Chinese-KL).

Anticipation is implicit within media use. Complaints about connections can occur where the "call divert" (to another phone) function is in operation without the user's knowledge and callers find themselves talking to an unexpected person: "why do you have this service. I want to talk to my friend!" (female CSP, Chinese-KL). Message content from sources whose identity is not already known cannot be anticipated, leaving the recipient vulnerable to the person making contact (Humphreys, 2005: 825). On the other hand, a handphone ringing with a familiar caller identification number prefigures the communication of broadly predictable information. Under such conditions, content can be regarded as carrying a guarantee of being safe to access (not likely to be offensive).[5] "You only answer calls that you know?" (FT-KL). "Yah, that's right!" (female customer, Chinese-KL).

Where he or she identifies familiar narrative the reader anticipates future events. Placing content in categories supports prediction: a horizon of expectations is formed. Anticipation should be achieved. On the other hand, misidentifying content generates mistakes. Interpreting an online offer as free clashes vigorously with subsequently being charged. "Customers, they don't even realize that they're actually subscribing to something and then they're being charged for it" (female CSP, Indian/Kadazan-KL).

Messages using "SMS-ing language" (female CSP, Chinese-KL) can arrive meaningless. Identification of content and its implications is impossible. A wider horizon of understanding may need to be sought from additional multimedia resources. "Normally [recipients] will just reply '?'": but after clarification (sometimes through other communication modes such as logging on to Internet messaging) there will be "no more question marks ... absolutely no question marks" (male customer, Chinese-KL).

With corporate requests to register phones "sometimes [customers] don't really understand what is the content of the SMS" (male CSP, Malay-KL). More fundamentally, generational confusion may occur in identifying digital communication, with older people referring to SMS "texting" as "messaging": "we are calling 'texting' SMS, but for them it's 'messaging'" (male CSP, Malay-KL).

The affective poverty of SMS texting can lead to recipients misconstruing or misplacing emotions therein. "What they *see* is only the text actually.... People may think you're angry because of the SMS you type and you send lah, but actually you're not.... The lack of expression in the SMS lah, that's why" (male customer, Chinese-KL, emphasis in the original).

As customers we buy products towards which in the "practice of citizenship" (Hermes, 2006: 295) we may have a political response (see chapter 9). Handphone purchasers focused on use are also people entertaining social concerns, perhaps with cynical anticipation. "Some people, they try to make more money so they are doing the wrong thing" (female customer, Chinese-KL).

Anticipation may meet uncertainty. Customers can confront indeterminate events (e.g., not knowing whether a connection can be made); the outcome of sport is likewise unpredictable. Satisfaction in mobile phone use rests on service provision, sometimes interrupted by congestion or maintenance (one could devise a political economy of cellphone silence). Uncertainty in communication may be cultural in its source: "Let's say during the festival season, our SMS, our voice call might be congested so customers will be very angry with the service" (female CSP, Chinese-K).

One CSP (female, Iban-K) told us of a customer's experience, outlining a narrative moving from difficulty or concern (disequilibrium) to solution or closure. She cleared up his mistake ("it was sort of a misunderstanding"), interpreting for him an issue emerging from the "configuration of the phone" in seeking to use the voice call mode. Likewise, another's failure to access data because of a "network problem" gained resolution in a CSP (female, Chinese-K) narrative of success. In both stories a final equilibrium was emphasized: "After that he was OK"; "the customer ... appreciated our effort that time."

Because of their wide experience customer service personnel have sub-stantial ability to classify clients seeking solutions and support in cellphone enjoyment (the subject of earlier research by De Run and Thang, 2005). Indeterminacy can provoke irritation:

> there are some customers, they are very nice, kind, *patient*. But there are some customers who are very, you know, impatient, they get angry very fast, and sometimes they say nasty things to you as well so you just have to [let the latter] go in your right ear, go out your left ear. (Female CSP, K, emphasis in the original)[6]

Clearly, people with phones can be variously classified: "How would you categorize customers?" (FT-K). Grouping consumers into different catego-ries generates expectations of them. On the other hand, refusing to distin-guish underwrites a conviction (at least for public consumption) that all will behave in the same way. One of us invited a consultant to nominate a generational, gendered, or "even" a group of customers identified by ethnic-ity as being more knowledgeable of phone use. But she remained silent, reluctant to embark on a sensitive issue:

> "How would you categorize customers? ... I mean whether you think that the customers are all the same or there's a certain group which is more knowl-edgeable ... or can't you differentiate them in terms of age, or gender, or even ... race? Is there a difference?" (FT-K) *Silence.* "So you're not quite sure about that?" (FT-K, laughing)
>
> "Yeh, I'm not sure about that." (female CSP, Malay-K)
>
> "Not sure about that, ah. OK." (FT-K)

Articulating mediated meaning

We articulate meaning by relating text to its context or narrative part to whole (Iser, 1978) within a message. Demonstrating a "cognitive flexibility" (García-Montes et al., 2006: 68) or play in their thinking to and fro (or sentential tacking), media users aim at integrating "story elements" (Gee, 2006: 59) coherently.

Constructing a consistent account of content is important not only to people engaged in cellphone use but to those researching and supporting this communication. Understandably, company employees were unable or unwilling to talk about customer calls/messages/texts in detail: "this I cannot comment on behalf of customers" (female CSP, Chinese-KL). "I don't see anyone mis-communicating. They never tell us. Oh, my girlfriend … Never encountered lah. Hopefully not lah! I don't want to know" (*laughter by all*) (female CSP, Chinese-KL).

Nonetheless, we were told that customers may comprehend codes erroneously, producing contradiction. Media users' assumptions can incorporate a faulty correlation of data leading to them making mistaken judgments in particular cases. When asked to evaluate customer service on a 1–5 numerical scale signaling increasing satisfaction, the "misinterpretation is when they think that 1 is good and 5 is very bad, so they rate us wrongly" (female CSP, Indian/Kadazan-KL). A discrepancy appears between private rating and public reputation of a CSP.

Two customer service providers appeared to us to conflict in their claims about frequency of cellphone use to send business email: "business people," "they use a lot of email" (female CSP, Iban-K): "adult people like business men, working people [are] more to voice call": "email is seldom" (female CSP, Malay-K). Attempting to resolve this apparent contradiction characterizing our narrative of mobile phone experience in Malaysia, the second contributor was asked:

"So are there still a group of, maybe a minority of customers using this email service?" (FT-K)

"Email services [are] normally used by corporate people like … businessmen whereby they really like to get in touch even though they [are] traveling …" (female CSP, Malay-K)

"So usually do they connect to laptops or do they use cellphones most of the time, or PDA [personal digital assistant]?" (FT-K)

"OK, some of our customers, they are using [a] laptop together with the phone and then some of them using PDA." (female CSP, Malay-K)

As investigators, we seek of course to avoid contradiction in our narratives. Here clarification is pursued towards the goal of establishing an integrated account from customer service personnel. Moving back and forth across her memory of answers, FT produces a coherent story of email use. It is relied upon, it appears, by business people but "seldom" merely equipped with basic handphones. Rather than "connect directly from [their] phone" (FT-KL) they employ the latter as modem attached to a laptop in receiving/sending "data."

Appropriating mediated meaning

Alasuutari (1999) writes of an emerging "third generation" or "constructionist view" of audience studies where texts are seen as narratives supporting readers in developing a sense of identity. As well as sending messages, handphone use is "performative" (Kerr et al., 2006: 74), conveying the "self" to others. In the "playful quality" of text messaging (Oksman and Turtiainen, 2004: 326), engaging in a "virtual reality" (329), "face becomes interface" (328). Mobile consumption is "tied to selfhood" (Nafus and Tracey, 2002: 209). We are "mobile selves" (Green and Singleton, 2007) able to construct ourselves in cell space and time.

Use of a cellphone, like sporting activity, can be related to life, appropriated to form self-image (Caronia and Caron, 2004). We develop a collective or individual identity by "dressing" our communication equipment in a particular style or simply by choice of technology. As a consequence we enjoy aesthetic (dis)satisfaction with our purchase. Possessing a "sleek mobile phone" signifies social status among Chinese "yuppies" (Wei, 2006: 1003). People often individualize their portable information technology in a coupling of presentation and personality, to "symbolize your personality," as an "accessory" (female CSP, Chinese-KL).

Establishing an "intertextual matrix" (Kerr et al., 2006: 77) of icons, consumers "capture photos and put them at the display" or "download ringing tones" or "the songs that you like" (FT-K) (e.g., "from my CDs": male customer, Malay-K). Some purchase a "cover only with the beautiful colors" (female customer, Bidayuh-K) to adorn their machines. Complex cellphones further consumer identity: "managers, CEOs, they are the ones who normally use, I would say, a very high tech. telephone" (female CSP, Iban-K). Such handphones organize both data and presentation of the self.[7]

Katz and Sugiyama argue that heavier mobile phone users in America and Japan are "fashion-attentive" (2006: 332) in equipment choice. For many, personalizing phones is clearly a statement of selfhood: "that is the basic thing because they want to differentiate their own personality ... you want to show that this is 'you'" (male CSP, Malay-KL). But downloading (sometimes digitally amending images) can also constitute an additional mode of playful relaxation: "after my work, I cannot think about it, then I'll go, just relax ... browse through the [cellphone company] [website] to see if [it's] got any song or photo to download lah" (male customer, Chinese-KL).

Finally but importantly, several customer service people considered there to be a gender difference in knowledgeable phone use: "*men*, most *men*, they are more knowledgeable compared to the girls, I mean, compared to ladies"; yet "there are some women as well, those who are very, you know, into this phone thing, into this IT kind of world" (female CSP, Iban-K, emphasis in the original). Others agreed with the latter view: "nowadays, more females [are] in IT business or IT savvy" (male CSP, Malay-KL).[8] Consistent with international trends (Madell and Muncer, 2005: 74) most CSP we talked to believed that similar skills are emerging across genders:

> "now even women know about IT, and they use Internet and ... our services for Internet browsing the *same*" as men (female CSP, Malay-K, emphasis in the original). "No difference" between genders, "no difference at all" (female CSP, Chinese-K).

But a Malay-K female CSP did perceive a gendered variation between modes of mobile use: "female, more to SMS: male, more to voice [calls]": "females, they like to SMS rather than call." Indeed Ling writes of young women being the "literary stylists of texting culture" (2004: 148). On the other hand, for a Chinese-KL female CSP: "women use cellphones to talk and then men, I think, basically use cellphones to SMS. 'Cos they don't like to talk so they SMS."

In regard to content, "it's different lah, what they talk and what we talk": "most girls that come in actually request for MMS [multimedia] service *more* than GPRS [for downloading Internet data]" (female CSP, Chinese-KL, emphasis in the original). Women are more likely to send "grooming" texts (Ling, 2004: 155). Male interest is in GPRS accessing of web content.

As a category for distinguishing between contributors, "gender" was made problematic by one customer providing an (indisputably) female name who then talked of men as "we" and "ladies" as "they." Our interviewee thereby entered a discussion with FT as female and left as male.

> "Male customers usually need handphones that ... we can *organize* our things there, in terms of function lah! Yeh, we go for function." "I think for ladies, they go ... for fashion" (female customer, Chinese-K, emphasis in the original).

Locally ludic: multiple modes of cellphone use

Play (ludic activity), we have argued with Kerr et al. (2006: 69),[9] is a "key concept" for interpreting new media use. Everywhere, cellphone use features multiple aspects of being in-play. We enjoy ludic, line-free distraction – albeit anchored to the mundanely instrumental (perhaps tethered to the tedious) when telephoning is determined by duty. Physically instantiating this liminal positioning, some communicate in business from an entertainment space, using time *efficiently*. "I hang out at kind of Starbucks. It's more efficient" (male customer, Chinese-KL).

Handphone use can be "work-related, always work-related" (male customer, Chinese-KL), "work, profession oriented, not for play" (male customer, Chinese-KL). But even such unremitting task-related telephoning involves one's co-presence in another's space and time, functionally constrained rather than freely creative. There we exist on the edge of escape, liminally ludic.

In arguing that multiple aspects of "play" can be used as a model for analyzing even dutiful employment of cellphones, we are drawing upon "new" generation activity to gain insight into media use by older groups: "above forty they are less on entertainment side, they are more on business" (male CSP, Malay-KL). Like other screen-based communication technologies phones support departure from the daily here-and-now. Even when motivated by obligation, using a cellphone remains on the margin of play. Distraction can shift easily from duty to "entertainment" (FT-K): "they want to check the football result" (female CSP, Chinese-K). "[If] we dug deeper, if we start going through their phones, then we'd see all sorts of things inside their phones" (female CSP, KL).

Phoning is purposive. We buy not only on the basis of cost but choose a basic or "smart" model according to our anticipated needs. A person's picking up a handphone may be prompted by many motives ranging from business ambition to recreational anticipation. Across such multiple use our aesthetic experience over the airwaves is fundamentally format-focused. Within the phone modes of data download, email, SMS/MMS texting, and voice call we engage in rule-governed but varying cognitive activity: the latter can be characterized (perhaps a little paradoxically) as being at one and the same time both generally distracted and goal directed.

The mobile phone is a "textual and cultural technology of considerable ramification": we need to establish the "forms, genres, economies, representational systems, and architectures" of its everyday employment (Goggin, 2006a, 2006b). In the wake of its omnipresent use, analytical categories of media and social theory require reconsidering (Cooper, 2002). Exploring people's perceptions of using mobile phones in mediated interaction with others shows these accounts to be diverse. Talking to customer service personnel and clients at walk-in support centers placed this variety on record as occurring in a multi-ethnic Asian nation. It soon became clear that there is increasing use of multifunction cellphones or smart phones incorporating both PDA and facilities to communicate substantially in text.

> There's a lot of changes. Last time customers mostly use for voice call, for incoming call and outgoing call. Now most of the customers, a lot of the teenagers, especially teenagers, they use it for SMS messages, and also for email, and Net surfing for data connection also. (Female CSP, Chinese-K)

"[I will] call, if cannot reach, and then I will leave a message to his handphone and then I will SMS. So hundred percent, he will get it!" (*laughter*) (male business customer, Chinese-KL). Multicultural Malaysia is characterized by multi-modal phone use.

Conclusion: Beyond the Phenomenology of Phone Use

In discussing the circulation of meaning through cellphones we have argued that consumer deployment of an apparently integrated media technology is accompanied by a fundamentally similar experience across varying message modes. The five philosophical "universals" (Campbell, 2007: 359) of phoning can be identified as ludic.

Accessing different communication channels for contacting others does not represent an irreducible diversity in structured experience. Narratives of cellphone use employing these formats can be considered local inflections of a global cognitive process, culturally particular accounts of a core universal undertaking.

Nonetheless, cellphones are daily deployed within national horizons of understanding the technology (Campbell, 2007: 343–8). Considering young phone users in South Korea, Yoon suggests three distinct sources of such images: "those of the state, the market and the mass media" (2006: 754). Mobile marketing advises consumers on purchase and practice in competitively branded landscapes and locations. Research is required on consumer-citizen responses to these "brandscapes." How do they fit the "fine-grained practices" (Graham, 2004: 17) of everyday life?

Cellphones enable groups to achieve a certain semiotic particularity. Research planned to follow this volume will investigate handphone use by travelers – people in the public space and time of tourism and those temporarily "othered" by a subjective journey through mental illness. Universal cognitive and local cultural characteristics of cellphone use need to be connected.

Phenomenology returns a universal subjectivity to audience studies, as hermeneutic process rather than human substance (Descartes's *res cogitans* or thinking thing). We project and position meaningful content on screen. In doing so, we draw on a context of experience, our sometimes contested horizons of fore-structured understanding – wider knowledge supporting interpretation.

As Morley sought to show in his *Nationwide* research, our more or less advantageous access to categories of comprehension (our "placing" or positioning within horizons of understanding) can be accounted for in a political economy of constructing meaning. Economic class and education enable interpretation. Thereby supported by broad awareness, the play of signifiers initiated by media users is centered or "fixed" on the process of achieving understanding of a particular text.

Meaning is actualized by audiences in sought-for comprehension through a projective goal-directed movement between their cultural horizons allowing generic fore-sight and the specific fore-conception of a text as type-embodying example. Knowledge of soap operas guides our making sense of an instance. Here, we have begun to explore a realist psychological account of screen use as cognitive-expressive play between the fore-structure of understanding, as culturally capable readers anticipate content, and their realizing, refining, or rejecting their expectations in the light of an emerging text. Familiar content confirms while faulty call diverting subverts anticipation. We have seen that this narrative theory of comprehension is testable in focus groups or interviews "used as a discursive generator for obtaining an insight into the interpretative repertoires at the disposal of the informants as they make sense of a specific media product" (Schroder et al., 2003: 143). Informants understanding media instantly would nullify the theory.

Interpretation is ludic. An audience's anticipation frames a text within horizons of understanding, re-presenting its stories, setting meaning in play to completion. We assemble narrative: readers move cognitively in a hermeneutic circle between the prefiguring projection of content drawing on tradition – where the mind is "in play" between "protension (expectation) and retention (memory)" (Iser, 1978: 2–3) – and the configuring present of establishing anticipated text. In practice, projection of meaning may emerge as problematic. Focused on the Internet, "usability testing" discloses difficulties in reading menus to establish content. "Websites live and die by their navigation schemes" (Theofanos and Mulligan, 2004: 470). We have seen here how drawing upon a philosophical psychology – phenomenology – can elicit the narrative structuring of media use by audiences – sometimes desperately – seeking meaning.

Notes

1   I worked with a co-researcher in these discussions of cellphone use – Florence Thang Chin Yin – to whom I am immensely grateful.
2   In denoting interview location, Kuching is henceforth referred to as "K" and Kuala Lumpur as "KL": "CSP" are Customer Service Providers.
3   On the first day in Kuching, we talked to five consumer service personnel and on the second, four visiting customers. Each was interviewed individually for ten to fifteen minutes mostly by the Chinese Malaysian female co-researcher. In Kuala Lumpur (at Berjaya Times Square) we spoke likewise to the same number of CSP and their information requesting clients (in a couple of instances for longer than in Kuching).

   We considered the "cellphone experience in messaging, phone calls and also network accessing" (FT-K). Conversation was loosely focused on three questions (altered as appropriate if we were talking to customers rather than CSP):

   (1)   "What is your perception of how customers use cellphones, email and texting?" "Has this use changed?" "How would you categorize customers?" "What expectations do you have of different groups?" "Do customers access websites using cellphones?"
   (2)   "To illustrate your views, can you give us some examples of customers wanting to overcome difficulties or enhance their experience of sending voice or text messages or website access?" "Do some involve misunderstanding of message or technology?"
   (3)   "What solutions or encouragement – if any – did you give to these customers?" We also asked about how people saw cellphone use developing.

   Following university practice of Ethics in Human Research we sought and received permission from the transnational telecommunications company to conduct these interviews and very much appreciate their agreement.
4   A female CSP (Chinese) in Kuala Lumpur supported this view of appropriate business cellphone use: "mostly they don't text, they will just call."
5   "So familiarity is almost a guarantee of safety?" (TW-KL). The female Chinese interviewee to whom this question was directed responded: "Yes, yes, something like that!" (*laughing*) "Yes, yes, yes, yah!" Here we were negotiating across our distinct cultural horizons surrounding cellphone use to establish the most accurate form of understanding.

6   Ethnicity is not attributed here: this meets our undertaking to maintain anonymity.

7   Mobile phone charges for email are "quite expensive," "very high" (male customers, Chinese-KL). We presume these customers are referring to limited plan Internet data access.

8   Identity formation can be political (the Malaysian government is requiring prepaid cellphone users to be registered). Gender equality is furthered in handphone use. Callers may affirm or subvert organizational power (e.g., through supporting corporate profits or protesting in text messages); likewise sport has effects on nation-building. Users are empowered by mobilizing the compressed codes of cheap texting (Gordon, 2002: 19).

In regard to the relationship between gender, generation, and cellphone use, an earlier (1998) study in Hong Kong shows some similarities to our own research in correlations between age, employment in business, and possessing a handphone: "mobile telephone have-nots were distinguished by an older age, females with lower monthly household income, and not engaging in business in terms of occupation" (Leung and Wei, 1999: 217). Later Israeli research (2001) claimed gendered variation: "more mobile phones are registered to men" (Cohen and Lemish, 2003: 170). Domestic fixed line phone use and gender is discussed by Moyal (1992).

9   We argue for ludic experience as a source of theory building in representing media experience. Nonetheless distinctions can be drawn within media use between screen-based (video) game playing and being an audience more widely. The processes of gamer alignment are distinct from those (for instance) of identifying when watching television.

First, acceding to the game's positioning of oneself with a character is a condition of playing but not of program consumption. Second, players positioned with on-screen participants strive to construct and control the game narrative rather than merely anticipating it (at best) accurately, as do television viewers (though reality television phone-in blurs this distinction).

7

Selling on Screen: From Media Hermeneutics to Marketing Communication

The very idea of cultural imperialism has long been abandoned – in its naive or simplistic form. Two decades of audience or reception studies have enabled the recognition that Asian consumers do not passively absorb from screen mediated advertising an aggressively active Western content. Instead, this superficial opposition of stimulus-cause and effect-response has been replaced by theories of glocalization (in cultural studies) or product morphing (in marketing theory). In these more recent accounts, global advertising practice is represented as frequently constructing its television or Internet narrative in terms drawing from the presumed local culture of intended consumers. In Malaysia, McDonald's hamburgers are marketed as Makan (meals). Converging horizons of understanding events are sought, easing audience identification with stories of product purchase.

Culturally appropriate screen mediated marketing (successfully synthesizing the terms of global and local) enables people's interpretative accomplishment of meaning in transnational advertising. They can understand. Comprehension of a screen narrative focused on heuristic use of a marketed product is a clear first step in its acquisition by consumers. Through drawing on media user theory of audience response to audio-visual content, we shall see more than a "relatively vague specification" of how narrative "elements" of advertising and marketing can be linked to readings (McQuarrie and Mick, 1999: 37). Studying consumer "creativities and constraints" (Moores, 1993: 138), we review the five-fold phenomenology of screen reception as the process of narrative telling being *absorbed, anticipated, articulated* and *appropriated* or resulting in audience *alienation* and sometimes *apathy* (consumer *absorption-anticipation, articulation, appropriation/alienation* or *apathy*). In this "epistemology of consumption" (Firat and Venkatesh, 1995: 239) media users simultaneously perceive and project meaning on screen, subsequently producing a coherent narrative, and position themselves accordingly. Patterns of consumption result (Holt, 1997, 1998).

Phenomenology has always been on the horizons of media theory, past, present and probably future. Its hermeneutic research focuses on the "processes by which individuals construct a coherent sense of self-identity (i.e., a life narrative) ... living in a world of pre-existing cultural meanings" (Thompson, 1996: 389). In perceiving we project and position meaning informed by our surrounding horizons of understanding. Interpretations of one's "masculinity" as connoting "man-of-action," for instance, are clearly distinct from considering oneself in terms of embodying "breadwinner masculinity" (Holt and Thompson, 2004: 425–6).

Our cultural horizons or "interpretive frameworks" (Holt, 1995: 3) are often so familiar they are scarcely noticeable. They are thus "precognitive" but nonetheless informing frameworks upon which we draw in making judgments, fundamental to knowledge claims. When constituted by concepts of formats and genres, horizons shape our processing screen narrative. We are active audiences at the center of our assumptions, drawing on them to make predictions.

Significantly, distinguishing hermeneutics from earlier structuralism there is a "gap" (Couldry, 2000: 49) between cultural horizons and constructive agency. A place is left for projection or "inferential comprehension" (Mathieu, 2007). Our perception of texts is not predetermined by our position in a social structure. Rather, viewing from our horizons of understanding we engage in a "dynamic process" (ibid.) of synthesizing meaning. As we have seen, content is actively articulated or linked together (Moores, 1993: 105) by media users – not passively absorbed by their audiences. Constructing narrative occurs slowly, swiftly, with different "timestyles" (Cotte et al., 2004: 333).

Responding to mediated marketing, people project meaning in response to uncertainty or "perceived indeterminacy" (Vosgerau et al., 2006) on screen. When anticipating and articulating narrative, text and pictures are "cognitively processed" (Scott, 1994a: 252) in an "ordered, knowledgeable and inferential" (ibid.: 255) "normative reading" (ibid.: 256). The logic implicit in this process is necessarily local, cultural reasoning often grounded in consumer alterity (difference). More simply, viewers interpret in their own terms. Researchers' own horizons of understanding consumers or "interpretive horizons" (Thompson, 2002: 143) have been dismissed as too narrow, excluding the "world views of social classes other than the middle class, of racial groups other than whites" (Hirschman, 1993: 537). The study of media use needs to address reading as "culturally embedded" (ibid.: 549).

Focus group and interview participant "self-reports" (Schwarz, 2003: 588) serve in this mode of qualitative investigation to "challenge" (Holt and Thompson, 2004: 430) or confirm theoretical interpretations of audience activity. Respondents may (or may not) talk of anticipating content (moments of projecting meaning). People's accounts of their responses can be elliptical, fragmented stories of all but invisible or "implicit" subjective processes (Johar et al., 2006: 139). Nonetheless, claims about "structural frameworks" (Rossiter, 2003: 306) of audience perception and positioning underwriting screen reception, if corroborated by contributor narratives, constitute scientific knowledge of consumer behavior (ibid.: 305).

Our five-fold phenomenology of media user experience is an account of people engaged in "microcultural meaning" (Thompson and Troester, 2002: 550) construction across varying formats (cellphone, Internet, television) of screen use. The theory is implicit within much consumer writing about screen reception – on the "interactivity of the brand" (Lury, 2004). Audience absorption in screen content is considered to constitute "media transportation" (Wang and Calder, 2006: 151). Media user articulation of coherent textual meaning in a hermeneutic circle of relating narrative part to whole has been called "dialectic tacking" (Kates, 2002c: 385).

As among those who drink in response to Coca-Cola television marketing, subsequent appropriation of media advertising materially substantiates prolonged or short-term ways of "being in the world" for groups or individuals. Media-using consumers pursue biographies of buying, exemplifying "regulatory focus theory": "people seek to align their behavior with relevant goals" (Chernev, 2004: 557). Yet affirmation can be ironic, as in "niched" gay readings of popular culture (Kates, 2002c: 391). Alternatively, we shall see Chinese Malaysian consumers regard advertising which shows people phoning distant friends throughout a family reunion dinner as undermining valued close relationships: these responses demonstrate an alienated "contested meaning cluster" (ibid.: 383) of reactions. More widely, such a televised "marketplace mythology" (Thompson, 2004) of human interaction can be resisted from within recipients' cultural horizons of understanding life and media narratives.

Using screen studies concepts of "identification" (alignment) and "distanciation" (alienation) (Wilson, 1993, 2004) introduced in earlier chapters enables our analytical focus on the "blur" of consumer response to be sharper.

Referring to research on consumers absorbing/anticipating narrative we shall see how audience alignment and "empathy responses" (Escalas and Stern, 2003: 566) with product purchase are supported or subverted (positioned or made problematic) by texts experienced as "transparent" and "tacky," respectively. In our gaze of inspection, both narrative marketing and its reception are interrogated. Chapter 7 outlines a converging of media and consumer studies in a shared focus on "hermeneutic processes" (Jansson, 2002: 10). After all, "what is lacking is rich empirical research that actually gives us insights into the practices, processes and consequences – in addition to the possibilities – of the uses of new media technologies" (Tacchi, 2004: 92).

Exploring media user theory from the perspective of reception studies, we saw in chapter 5 that much audience research (such as Buckingham's work with soap opera viewers) is already hermeneutic in its interpreting responses to the screen. Chapter 7 traces out how communication and consumer theory have shared hermeneutics as a philosophical account of understanding. Resisting the construction of audience response in effects studies (chapter 1) as the "always-ready-determined effect" (Morley, 2005: 175) of screen content, we are developing a political psychology of media use for which "macro-structures can only be reproduced through micro-processes" (ibid.). Capitalism's advertising addresses consumers' cognitive activity. Glocal Coca-Cola media marketing, as we shall see, succeeds through students comprehending (and being convinced) that imbibing the drink is identifiably Asian while also enabling cultural access, the illusion of immersion in a global society (La Pastina, 2005: 37).

Advertising is able to simultaneously address particular audiences in parallel mode (e.g., Chinese, Indian, Malay groups). As recipients of marketing, some groups may be deemed "subcultures of consumption" (Schouten and McAlexander, 1995: 43), such as bikers. While each set of consumers interprets within its own horizons of understanding, as we shall determine there is also a shared focus of identification for viewers – often narrative agents or people on screen themselves making sense of circumstances (e.g., engaged in the process of producing a prescriptive narrative of imbibing Coca-Cola).

Shedding light on this process, reader response theory overturned the assumption that a "singular meaning" was "produced by the author," "resided in the text," and was "received by the reader" (Stern, 1993: 557). Instead, the production of meaning is a "*continuum*" (ibid., emphasis in the original), a sequence of activities undertaken by audiences in an "inferencing process" (ibid.: 561). Displaying culturally diverse manifestations, anticipating and articulating understanding are fundamental "structural commonalities" shaping "local appropriations" (Kjeldgaard and Askegaard, 2006: 231–2) of global texts.

Our interpreting screen content with its "goal-evoking marketing promotions" (Lee and Ariely, 2006: 60) is "culturally underpinned" (Thompson and Hirschman, 1995: 140). Viewing is enabled and enclosed, created from and constrained by our occupying continually contested horizons of understanding the world. We have seen that these powerful "media-related frameworks" (Couldry, 2001: 157) or "categorizations" (ibid.: 158) function as the basis of our anticipating and articulating narrative whose prescriptive implications many "appropriate" (Haddon, 2007: 26). In responses to the screen we can be our own worst enemies.

We may refer to screen perceptions as conforming to psychological "laws of functioning" (Bourdieu, 1995: 72). The latter are both invariant (the anticipatory moment of projection in perception) and instantiated in different ways across the reception of varying media forms. These processes of media use need to be "traced" (Couldry, 2001: 171) through successive stages in people's contributions to focus groups and interviews. Here we shall study responses to television advertising and the corporate characterizing (or branding) by these latter narratives of an audience's everyday landscape. We shall engage with the marketing screen's mediating "horizon of experience" (Bassett, 2007: 46). In the "playfulness" (Rojek, 2004: 303) of consuming, brands offer "security and freedom *in one package*" (ibid.: 304, emphasis in the original).

Our construction of media meaning, like tourism, is continually in play, "perpetually in motion" (MacCannell, 2002: 147). Understanding is interpretative, intellectually "infinite play on a field of divergent meanings" (Stern, 1996: 136): it is a process during which readers add that which is not already in the text. Perceiving content from widely differing horizons of understanding, media users seek to resolve indeterminacy of meaning by projecting narrative. In studying through "phenomenological interviews" (Thompson, 2005: 237) the "cultural embeddedness of consumer cognition" (ibid.: 246), the audience's interpretative "panoply of otherness" (Stern, 1996: 144) or vast variation in vision can be disclosed.

Advertising addresses the consumer's past experience and projection of a future: hence reading its narrative content appropriately is both "retrospective and anticipatory" (Krishnamurthy and Sujan, 1999). We remember and speculate. In doing so, audiences need not be persuasively aligned.

"Consumers are trapped within a hegemonic marketplace" (Denzin, 2001: 325) to which their response can be nonetheless one of alienation rather than appropriation.

Sensitivity to the cultural framework of consumption – consumers' categories or horizons of understanding the world – should precede but does not preclude applying quantitative methods of analysis. "Cultural category analysis" needs to be used "prior to quantitatively oriented research instruments" (Applbaum and Jordt, 1996: 204). Here we look at audience and advertising narrative as a "principal medium" (ibid.: 211) conveying cultural understanding (e.g., through repetition defining that which is regarded as "familiar"). For however subsequently subjected to quantification, behavior is "embedded in particularistic sociocultural circumstances" (ibid.: 216).

Mediated Marketing: Consumer Hermeneutics

Consumption of screen content (e.g., gaming on a casino "fruit machine") can literally consist of playing (Casey, 2003: 251). Here, however, we are looking at screen mediated marketing. How appropriate is thinking in terms of the processes of play to understanding our consuming – or interpretative responses to – media advertisements? Is consumer cognition ludic?

Expectations we entertain of a marketing story's development around a product invariably generate our subsequent reading to confirm them. Audiences engage in a discursive drive to secure intelligibility. Thereby structured teleologically by the goal of a coherent meaning for narrative, purchaser response to mediated product promotion can be regarded as "all psychological play, I shall say" (Chinese male research participant). We have considered at length people's cognitive processing of screen content: their perception-projections of storylines, continuing production of meaning and concluding prescriptive appropriation for everyday life from programs. Product acquisition following advertising results in "narratives of identity, consumption stories" (Thompson and Tambyah, 1999: 215). People use consumption to maintain their sense of "selfness" as a narrative through time (Ahuvia, 2005: 180). Drinking Coca-Cola enables our creativity, say some Malaysian student respondents.

Analyzing media reactions in terms of a transnational theory of reading, reception and (re)alignment displays the singular hermeneutic activity sustaining their variety. Cultural difference in responses to a screen can conceal the existence of a cognitive process of understanding which is everywhere identical. Viewers articulating a narrative (making sense of a story) eventuates in accord with – or antipathy towards – their perception of program meaning.

Reminding us of the realist psychology of media user response outlined earlier, the present chapter addresses fundamental questions about the qualitative underwriting of quantitative marketing research. Who counts what? How do consumer reactions occur? Is the investigator or subject best equipped to conceptualize them? Who should attach meaning to the experience investigated? To support our discussion we shall draw upon illustrative exemplars, small but semantically rich Southeast Asian reception studies of culturally complex advertising.

Following Arnold and Fischer (1994), Thompson (1997) and others, we shall further a hermeneutic cognitive or constructivist approach to understand the process of brand morphing and its audience reception. Branding is a "commercial variant" of storytelling (Twitchell, 2004: 484) about corporate entities from Amazon to Starbucks. "Brand morphing" as it takes shape in "glocalization" refers to the ways that brand meanings are developed (or "morphed") by "cultural intermediaries" (Cronin, 2004) to secure an appropriate mode of address to different consumer groups across international markets. We shall gain insight into how consumers' identification with/distancing from product use is promoted by strategic communication in advertising. Close cultural proximity with the world on screen supports "our" purchase of "their" product.

Advertisements position: they "argue" that (implied) audiences should buy. Hermeneutic research into consumer perception of this commercial logic posits (as elsewhere) that responses to texts draw on a background of cultural frames of reference (horizons of understanding) which underwrite media users' interpretative construction (projection) of specific content.

"Cultural narratives" provide a "cultural frame of reference for interpreting the meanings of commercial messages" (Thompson et al., 1994: 438). According to one of Thompson et al.'s female interviewees, "*shopping is a game*" (ibid.: 446, emphasis in the original), with its "sense of total involvement," a "flow experience" characteristic of play (ibid.: 448). She will anticipate that advertisements associate product acquisition with games or game-like experience (as in Coca-Cola marketing we shall shortly discuss).

Recognizing a narrative as marketing enables fore-structured anticipation of events: classifying a storyline supports construction of its likely future direction. Drawing on past experience, media user projection of a developing narrative is immanent or implicit within our perception of screen content. Absorbing Coca-Cola advertising, we anticipate it will involve drinking. This does not exclude counter-factual thinking (Krishnamurthy and Sivaraman, 2002) or considering (articulating) an alternative chain of cause and effect events when we commence reading a story. What might have happened otherwise in this advertisement?

Where they identify with narrative agents' product-based understanding of events on screen, consumers comprehend advertising not only as marketing information but also as a resource for interpreting life (Hirschman and Thompson, 1997; McQuarrie and Mick, 1999). Articulation of meaning enables appropriation of content. The product's purchase is promoted.

Audiences, of course, arrive at alternative interpretations of a text from advertisers. Different categories of consumers can construct multiple meanings depending on the personal histories through which their horizons of understanding have been generated, their frames of interpretative reference formed (Kates and Goh, 2003; Mick and Buhl, 1992; Ritson and Elliott, 1999). Hermeneutic theory of glocalization and its consequences illuminates the practical difficulties inherent in strategically addressing multiple market segments.

In "Hermeneutics and Consumer Research" (1994), Arnold and Fischer establish the "relationship of hermeneutic philosophy to the interpretive and critical theory traditions in consumer research." Here, they address fundamental questions. How is marketed/ing meaning understood on screen? How is it received – or rejected – by consumers?

Accounts of audience response to advertising, as of viewer reactions more widely, need to be structured by a generic psychological narrative in terms of which particular cognitive histories of processing screen content can be located. Understanding, that is, has an "ontological status": we engage in the "continuous act of coming-into-understanding" (Arnold and Fischer, 1994: 55, 56). Relating the consumer's cultural horizons to those of the text, reading advertisements should be shown to be a goal-directed "process" (Scott, 1994b: 461) by drawing upon the reception theory we discussed in earlier chapters. "Every response to an advertisement depends first on the cognitive activity of reading text" (ibid.). Below we consider both global structure and local instance of psychological stories establishing marketing consumption.

Hermeneutics represents meaning as interactively constructed. In their 1994 positioning pieces, Arnold and Fischer, along with Thompson and colleagues (1994), signal some of the approach's core concepts, initiating a reception theory of screen mediated marketing's persuasion of consumers. Writing on advertising, these authors raise a fundamental question in the philosophy of social science. How is a marketing investigator's "pre-understanding" of a research topic (her or his framework of analysis or horizons of understanding the investigated) related to consumer self-understanding? Academic perception of the analyzed subject inextricably involves a fusion of horizons or making the "other" intelligible within the conceptual perspective of the researcher.

Arnold and Fischer take on board the productively spatial (spacious?) metaphors of understanding as both projection (and confirmation) of meaning and as a circular (or dialectical) construction of sense. The former emphasizes reading as temporal, the latter its focusing to and fro on a text. We have seen these models employed in hermeneutic cognitive or reception theory as images of culturally located active thought. "When the interpreter moves or changes position through developing understanding, his or her horizon moves as well" (Arnold and Fischer, 1994: 63–4). The subjective space and time of understanding, wherein the consumer's processing of marketing meaning occurs, is theorized as constructively "ludic."

The spatiotemporality of screen comprehension, in other words, is primarily structured by audience cognitive play aimed at accomplishing the goal of an advertisement's intelligibility. Games are engaged in by players who emphasize attaining an outcome (the goal) which continually occupies a prominent location on participant horizons of thought. Likewise, viewing a screen advertisement is structured by the audience-consumer's future-oriented focus on establishing its emerging narrative – through a projection of meaning in response to marketing.

Thompson's "Interpreting Consumers: A Hermeneutical Framework for Deriving Marketing Insights from the Texts of Consumers' Consumption Stories" (1997) further secured hermeneutic theory within consumer response studies. Drawing on this philosophical psychology, "key patterns of meaning" in the "narrative structuring of cognition and understanding" (Thompson, 1997: 438) can be discerned embedded in focus group participant reactions to screen advertisements. Respondents show both intrinsic and instrumental interest in screen advertising content, enjoying it for what it is (as "fun to watch") and what it may secure (Yoon and Ok, 2007). Listening to accounts of either in research reveals the audience's hermeneutic project of securing narrative intelligibility, the "narratological nature of human understanding" (Thompson, 1997). We have seen earlier that this goal is fundamental to the consumer's identification with character on screen, an alignment at the rational core of marketing's successful persuading to purchase. We can call this alignment *identification in/with a narrative project*.

In this "hermeneutic/narratological model of understanding" (Thompson, 1997: 440), as reading takes place "perceptual information is assimilated to preexisting schematic knowledge" (ibid.: 441). Consumers "pre-understand" or presume being able to construct (or project) and confirm a series of consecutive connections between cause and effect on screen to constitute an advertisement. Audiences articulate parts to form a narrative: a "desire for completeness and closure is a prominent consumer motivation" (ibid.: 444). The point at which it is considered complete depends on perception of the story's generic membership: advertisements need less detail than a product information guide. Reading thereby exercises two functions, a "chronological function" or "narrative movement" and a "holism-creating function" or "narrative framing" (ibid.: 443). Identifying a story as meaningful precedes identification with its prescription.

Identification of/identification with narrative content is enabled by a consumer's "personalized cultural frame of reference." Where marketing is successful, respondents can "relate to" actions on screen, locating them within a "broader cultural system of meanings" (Thompson, 1997), their horizon of understanding. "Cues" (Scott, 1994b) for classifying advertising are recognized by the audience or are culturally close. Already acquainted with their type, people are able to anticipate and actualize stories, supporting alignment with narrative agents. The reader's "recognition of the genre of a given text frames and guides the reading experience" (Scott, 1994b: 464). We expect – project – a Coke advertisement to tell a story celebrating consumption and articulate it accordingly.

Developing content we appropriate (Arnold and Fischer, 1994: 59) advertising, drawing upon its events to form a "coherent narrative of self" (Thompson, 1997: 447). Consumers act as advised (sometimes). We can refer to this response as *identification with a normative proposition*. In the appropriative moment of reading, an audience ascribes to itself a product-focused social identity (Eckhardt and Houston, 2002: 69). We are as we admire. Following a phenomenological path, Fournier (1998) classifies as "process phenomena" (ibid.: 344) the subjective meaning of consumers' "lived experiences" (ibid.: 347) with brands. Some appropriate/appreciate Apple computers.

Addressing the "salient conditions of their lives" (Thompson, 1997), advertising constructs "goods" as means of achieving consumer goals. Through narratives on screen, it invites potential users to align with product purchasers already shown attaining their objectives. Television marketing seeks consumers who will "buy" both its stories and their featured goods.

People purchasing read interpretatively to identify meaning on screen and consequently identify with narrative agents themselves engaged in making sense of product acquisition. Thompson writes of the "apt description of interpretation as a playful endeavour," and goes on to discuss how "hermeneutic interpretation exhibits this player-in-a-game quality" (1997: 452). The cognitive process informing consumer response to mediated marketing is mental activity (a "play of interpretation") (ibid.) aligning viewers with characters themselves making meaning out of the world through purchasing product on screen. In one Southeast Asian research exemplar (chapter 8) our contributors identified with Coca-Cola consumers at play both semantically and in the street.

Listening to participants in focus groups, the ludic universal categories of analysis employed by marketing theorists are enriched by contributors' particular narratives in a "hermeneutic process of assimilation and accommodation." Academic theory and interviewee talk together generate a "more richly textured understanding of the consumption meanings that arise from these constructions of self identity" (Thompson, 1997: 448), allowing "more nuanced conceptualizations of market segments" (ibid.: 439). Consumers exercise a cognitive interest in establishing coherent (advertising) narrative, and as a consequence align themselves with those making sense on screen. Where identification fails because "elements" of a story seem unfamiliar or impossible to identify, audience alienation/distanciation arises. Consumer perception of transparently available narrative content gives way to critically analytical reading of advertising.

Consumer Positioning: Alignment, Alienation, Apathy

Ludic activity is paradoxical. Associated with a "separate and self-contained world," it is "experimental" while also "rule-bound" (Kozinets et al., 2004: 662, 668). Counter-factual, it is controlled. Though immersed in virtual gaming, we must "learn the machines" (Green, 2001: 75).

We have seen that play (Huizinga, 1970) can function to model meaning construction by media user: its disciplined escape captures the creative freedom of audience agency both enabled and enclosed by rules. Cultural experiences of media structured by conventions "set up certain expectations in the reader" (Scott, 1994b: 471). Viewing the screen from the "perspectival diversity" (Kozinets et al., 2004: 661) of these varied (if limiting) horizons of understanding content, we project – expect and establish – distinct narratives. Meaning is always constructed (supported) from – as well as constrained (shaped) by – the cultural perspective of the reader.

Accessing web page, watching TV program, one can refuse to undertake their interpretative processing on pain of incomprehension. Gaze elsewhere: gain no understanding! Otherwise, looking and learning with a narrative goal, media users speculatively strive to articulate and achieve meaningful stories with whose narrative agents they align – or by whom they are angered. What one viewer finds a "self-actualization experience, we can find repulsive," "deceptive persuasion" (Kozinets et al., 2004: 662).

The intense "inundating" immersion of consumers in a media spectacle (from cinema advertising to multi-screen sport in Chicago) has been argued by scholars and spectators to exclude the very possibility that buyers can be critical, entailing ideological impotence. "We're going to overwhelm you with the sports theme" (a visitor assessing intentions behind the "entryway of ESPN Zone, Chicago" in Kozinets et al., 2004: 661). Absorbing media users on screen is said to result in conformist reading of content.

Yet paradoxically, attempts to overwhelm audiences with mediated event management presuppose an ability on the part of these viewers to "cocreate" or "coconstruct" (Kozinets et al., 2004: 658, 660) identifiable narratives of meaningful content. This capacity for rational activity ("ludic dynamics") (ibid.: 658) can continue to be demonstrated in an audience's distanciated dislike of would-be submerging spectacle.

In the *semantic* (meaning-creating) mental play of anticipating and achieving interpretative understanding of stories, we align or position ourselves with narrative agents and other media users equally engaged in the process of seeking intelligibility. This does not entail that one is also politically recruited to – or indeed resists – the latter's *substantive* ideological propositioning. For reading is "critical versus celebratory" – like play itself, ambivalent or "simultaneously seductive and subversive" (Kozinets et al., 2004: 668, 660) in its potential political result for media users. Understanding is compatible with not believing. Securing sense for – and succumbing to – advertising are separate mental processes.

Media generally facilitate without interruption the cognitive play of constructing meaning, easing viewer accounts of events. They enable the process of being an audience to be elided from our thought. Television marketing seeks consumer reception for its advertising on screen as immediately comprehensible despite its status as mediating narrative requiring interpretation. Camera shots, for instance, conform to patterns intended audiences have experienced, to their horizons of expectation (Gadamer, 1975). Where a sequence of sutured edits does not draw attention to itself as unusual, consumers gain apparently transparent and truth-telling access to content (a "window on the world"). Viewed thereby as *veridical*, advertising's immersing stories enable identification with characters. Audiences align with narrative agents, cognitively and expressively as well as ontologically – sharing the latter's view of a world into which they have momentarily plunged. The flow of images is edited to the measure of consumer desire, enabling absorption. Seemingly without constraint, we see what we wish: we are there, in the action.

The veridical sequence is a series of shots apparently disclosing reality as immediately present to the consumer-viewer. Meeting audience expectation, edits are self-effacing. In Gadamer's words, the function of the (veridical) sign is "to point away from itself …. It should not attract attention to itself in a way that would cause one to linger over it, for it is there only to make present something that is not present, and in such a way that the thing that is not present is the only thing that is expressed" (Gadamer, 1975: 134). As we shall learn, narrative sequences of advertising signs can also draw attention to themselves, alienating audiences.

Television consumers identify with veridical program content. They align themselves with characters' concerns, finding themselves in accord with behavior and belief. At other times, they vent harsh criticism. Or are simply agnostic, apathetic. Here we consider at length the processes of viewers identifying with those whom they watch in television advertising, a precondition of media-motivated consumption. Aware that the emphasis on audience involvement may seem to suggest viewers are "dupes of the text," we also discuss their distancing of self in critical resistance to this beckoning to buy. Consumers can construct "countervailing cultural meanings" in responding to advertising's "social prescription" (Thompson and Haytko, 1997: 15–16). In more developed alienated responses to advertising, "culture jamming" (Carducci, 2006) ventures to place brands in jeopardy, deconstructing their images and texts (perhaps by revealing the backstage of the brand, allegedly problematic production practices).

Identity and Internet: Consumers in Cyberspace

As with television, the intrinsic enjoyment of the Internet is of being playfully absorbed, "cognitively immersed" (Zwick and Dholakia, 2006: 23) apart from the materially mundane. In the "translation of self into the digital domain" (Schau and Gilly, 2003: 395), the focus of those accessing cyber-space is on the opportunity to freely celebrate their creativity. Allowing immersion online, digital environments can "free cyber participants from their corporeal selves and the confines of their material worlds" (ibid.: 388).

Using a digital device, consumers establish meaningful narratives about themselves, occupying the space and time of the Web. An online author "'played with the content,' manipulating his original and appropriated elements until 'it seemed just right' and was 'most me'" (Schau and Gilly, 2003: 394). Recognition is of achieved meaning – me! Informants consistently state that "their sites enact selves with which they choose to communicate with other Web participants" (ibid.: 394). Articulated through the cognitive goal-driven play of anticipating and actualizing online content (projected with a purpose), these will be synthesized cyberspace stories ascribing personal identity. "Multiple selves are made comprehensible" (ibid.: 400): assembling such self-focused meaning provides pleasure.

Just as offline, through ascribing meaning to brand images the consumer can present an identity in virtual life. In consumer appropriation of marketing icons, "digital association" with a brand image (e.g., Harley-Davidson motorcycles) on personal websites is a "new form of possession not dependent on ownership or proximity" (Schau and Gilly, 2003: 398). Digital association is "based on signification systems that do not require brand use, only an eventual material referent" (ibid.: 401).

Associating online with a product to construct narratives of the self, the consumer is bound by rules – the brand's pre-existing connotation – but at liberty not to possess the item in real life. In a ludic crossing of categories, constructing personal websites can thereby be declared serious fun, norm-governed release. "Mark admits that his [dating] site is 'comical' but also 'quite serious'" (Schau and Gilly, 2003: 394).

In a "self-presentation project" (Schau and Gilly, 2003: 392), posting a personal website may be liminally ludic, a process on the edge of the playful. Beyond the materially spatiotemporal, on the Web authorial concern is with the other than physically present self, with a "highly contrived digital self" (ibid.: 395). But this autobiographical "game" of meaning construction can be not entirely ludic. On such occasions it serves a further instrumental aim offline, stretching beyond cyberspace, industrializing the Internet. A male computer enthusiast created a site to "show off his programming skills" which would both attract web authoring work and promote his "family's motorcycle restoration business" (ibid.: 392). Here "his digital likeness directly serves his RL (real life) goals" (ibid.: 396).

Media Brandscapes and Their Morphing:
Consumer Appropriation, Alienation, and Advertising

Advertising is the "pathway" through which brands address consumers (Scott, 1994b: 463). Screen mediated marketing which engages in brand morphing "rewrites" advertising content to appropriately address its audience. Morphing is self-conscious and sensitive. For otherwise the marketing message would be unacceptable, unfamiliar, or unrelated to potential consumers. Successful brand micromarketing effaces semiotic distance between product meaning and the cultural conditions of its reception, defining an "exclusive cachet of meaning" for consumption by an interpreting community (Kates, 2002a). Brand morphing can accommodate global item within local values "connecting to the consumer" (Kates and Goh, 2003).[1]

In the research exemplars which follow in the next chapter we discuss the reception of televised brand morphing by Chinese, Indian, and Malay citizen-consumers in Malaysia. We focus analytically first on reactions to the fluid images of Coca-Cola, then more extensively on responses to accounts of cellphone connections in media marketing's narrative images or brandscapes. Rather than discussing "large-scale surveys" we seek to safeguard the "complexity and singularity" of people's perceptions (Murdock, 1997: 181–2).

Integrating hermeneutic theory with the data of purchaser response to product marketing we develop a global thesis of successfully immersing buyers in brandscapes as a four-stage process. Intrinsic or instrumental interest-led consumer absorption in content initiates her or his anticipation (projection) and articulation of narrative in a hermeneutic circle of understanding: the play-like process of constructing meaning concludes at the liminal moment where recipients appropriate content apparently illuminating their life-world.

Audience alignment with (or alienation from) media marketing's narrative agents is complex, contained by cultural horizons of understanding. It takes shape in people's shared articulating and appropriating that which they see as perceptibly authentic. Our Chinese, Indian, and Malay students mostly "bought" the prescriptive maxim that "Coke consumption is creative!" In the appropriative moment of reading, "consumer meanings" "further their identity and lifestyle goals" (Arnould and Thompson, 2005: 870, 871).

Sensitively mediated brand adjustment addresses the "cultural milieu" (e.g., Chinese New Year) in which it is "embedded" (Eckhardt and Houston,

2002: 68). By doing so it is likely to achieve unproblematic consumer align-ment rather than their critical attention to an advertisement's mode of audio-visual narration and its meaning. Brands both enable "customary ways of interacting" to continue and "engender social change" (ibid.: 70).

Purchasers identify with product consumers on screen, reading their practice as culturally comprehensible and close, sharing these people's sense-constructing play. In research participants' statement of their "real-ized positioning," "interpretations of brand communications follow a dis-cernible cultural logic that can be empirically explored and mapped" generating "subtle varieties of meaning" as well as shared readings (Kates, 2002b). We see in chapter 8 how referring to the cognitively ludic, to the play-like processes involved in securing sense, can be used to map particu-lar consumer interpretative strategies and identification in response to Coca-Cola and cellphone mediated marketing on screen.

In the process of product glocalization, familiar life-worlds of consumer philosophy and practice are often absorbed: this "cultural logic of global-ization" generates a hybrid content (Kraidy, 2005). Global marketing meets the local purchaser with the aim of achieving a brand's "cultural fit" (Kates, 2004: 455). For instance, a company with its corporate headquarters in Norway providing cellphone connection in Malaysia advertises use of its services in the latter nation to bring families together at Chinese New Year celebrations. One advertisement (February 2007) showing a reunion dinner where each and all are talking on cellphones bears the tag line, "Longevity Calls." This is a polysemous (or "polysemic") brand slogan carrying multi-ple meanings (Dimofte and Yalch, 2007: 515) supporting local Chinese New Year aspirations – long lives for family members and long calls to friends.

A brand's cultural fit may succeed to the point of it becoming "invisible." Part of the daily familiar life-world in which it is placed, a domestic product can be "considered mundane and blends into the household environment in an inconspicuous manner" (Coupland, 2005: 106). A brand of tea stored in an anonymous container emerges to become tea *simpliciter* – dispos-sessed of its distinctive labeling.[2]

Marketing research investigates varying moments of consumer response to advertising. Thompson and Arsel (2004) consider reactions as proposi-tions asserting a judgment rather than a process of rendering text intelligi-ble. Their discussion is of purchaser identification (alignment) with – or indignation at (alienation from) – the brand's hegemonic message and not the local media user's success in assigning meaning to global advertisement content. In other words, they focus on appropriation.

In the Wilson and Tan (2006) research on media user responses to Coca-Cola's construction of a hegemonic (lifestyle advocating) brandscape in television advertising, the process wherein audiences articulate meaning as well as their appropriation of content is considered. In forming people's identity the latter is itself "processual" (Cherrier and Murray, 2007: 1). Focus groups signaled their absorption without resistance in the Chinatown life-world located on screen in this briefly glocalizing flow of branded liquified enchantment (Langer, 2004: 251). The swiftly moving narrative of basketball play was read by participants as privileging a philosophy of striving to succeed with little (except Coca-Cola). People appropriated the "message," personalizing a public narrative (Caldwell, 2004: 5) of winning. Consumers made local their generation of meaning, constructing global phenomena as familiar presence – as "part of the local landscape" (ibid.: 20). They learned.

Analyzing alienation not alignment, Thompson and Arsel explore the more critically detached "underlying cultural meanings, ideals, and anti-corporate identifications that cafe *flaneurs* (seeking the special) and oppositional localists, respectively, enact in [Starbucks'] hegemonic landscape" (2004: 632). In responses opposed to Starbucks' message of global consumption, oppositional readings emerge constructing the company as less than widely concerned with consumer satisfaction and health – as "Charbucks" or "Frankenbucks."

Elsewhere, consumer identification is both sought and secured. "Viral marketing" encourages potential users of a product to identify with its existing customers (for instance, sending Yahoo! email relays an Internet application to other likely enthusiasts). Similarly, "social marketing" in public information campaigns encourages pursuing an acquisition (e.g., health) on the basis of consumer identification with people already in possession of that "good."

Conclusion

Audiences align with – or become alienated from – narratives they themselves have constructed in cognitive play. Speculating on potential meaning with the goal of coming to comprehend on screen is wholly ludic when not being undertaken with extrinsic purpose. Consumer theory's image of purchaser-players focused on the process of understanding advertisements (in the next chapter) is indeed akin to considering the media user as a *flaneur* or *flaneuse* becoming "immersed in the hyperkinetic, sensory-saturated world of the large metropolis, with little regard for time, schedules, or instrumental outcomes," "suspending the press to squeeze more productivity out of their day" (Thompson and Arsel, 2004: 634).

Notes

1 Glocalization or adaptive product morphing to suit local cultural conditions takes place beyond the television or Internet screen: for example, the spatiotemporal segmenting of the Christmas season in Japan (Kimura and Belk, 2005).
2 Focusing on different brands (from Apple to Nike), Holt (2002) argues that far from them becoming invisible, "postmodern consumer culture" "insists that meanings – any, take your choice – must be channeled through brands to have value": brands have to "insinuate themselves as the most effective palette" for consumers' "sovereign expressions" (ibid.: 82–3) of self. He articulates a changing justification of brand significance.

8

Buying Brandscapes:
A Phenomenology of Perception and Purchase

At the core of society and culture, brands define "where capitalism meets consumerism." Aimed at guaranteeing goods with a shared corporate source, their marketing narratives invoke "intangible ideals" but also "prey upon anxieties and concoct false desires." Brands are "parasites riding the coat-tails of other more powerful cultural forms," proselytizing their own "ideological revisions" (Holt, 2006a; 2006b). In the narratives which form the focus of the research exemplars below, their advertising pirates cultural constructions of security and success.

Brand marketing occurs in an "expanded range of everyday spaces" (Moor, 2003: 40) and times. It colonizes a broad environment from three-dimensional shopping malls to flat screen media with narratives of seemingly inhabitable landscapes which we are calling "brandscapes" (Thompson and Arsel, 2004). Imagining or actually using its products, we inhabit or buy into a brandscape from Coffee Bean to Starbucks. Does reality match representation?

The paradox in branding episodes of life as product-focused "special time" lies in offering opportunity to escape to a space where consumers are "free to play" (Moor, 2003: 55) with goods. Enjoying malls or media, we can immerse ourselves in brandscaped experience. Sex tourist brandscapes offer travelers the opportunity to relive otherwise discarded discourses of patriarchy, to inhabit ludic space on Internet screens or sex tours (Chow-White, 2006).

As we have seen, screen users "engage" (Askwith, 2007: 20) with new content from established horizons of expectation: their mode of reading can be characterized as absorbed anticipation. Through their "transmedia" (ibid.: 42) involvement they operate across delivery platforms to establish a hermeneutic circle of understanding multimedia text. Media consumers "make connections among dispersed media content" (Jenkins, 2006: 3). Television audiences for *Big Brother* branded reality television expect associated website discoveries (*Big Brother Uncut*): the latter are included in their holistic accounts of the show's narrative. Stories receive our "elaboration" (Rehak, 2003: 478) into lives beyond texts. Marketing of brandscapes can encourage such elongated experience with products, whether convergent media texts (like the BBC's sites) or their modes of access (like cellphones).

Brandscapes: Advertising and Acquisition

Enjoying a game, we have seen, involves "psychological immersion" (Mathwick and Rigdon, 2004: 325). Consumers can immerse themselves playfully in coffee-drinking scenarios as well as dramatic media landscapes. The "hegemonic brandscape" associated with Starbucks Coffee outlets and similar global brand names is written into lifestyles where it functions "as a cultural model that consumers act, think, and feel through" (Thompson and Arsel, 2004: 632). Marketing "scapes" may incorporate a "brand-leveraging process" (Keller, 2003: 595) where a brand is shown linked to persons or places (e.g., youth drinking Coca-Cola) in an attempt to define its attributes or character. Cellphones are represented as enhancing relationships, denying distance to integrate families. Reciprocally, people can leverage their own identity in a group through association with a range of products (Escalas and Bettman, 2005) – or even joining a brand cult, such as that formed around Macintosh computers (Belk and Tumbat, 2005).

Shopping malls are places of possibility characterized by multiple brandscapes. They are corridors of contemplated consumption where (as in media use) we cross loosely defined thresholds to envelop ourselves for a short time in a segment of promoted lifestyle.[1] We become absorbed in speculative consideration of potential purchase, articulating subjective narratives of consumption: when marketing succeeds we actually appropriate the goods. Fantasy issues in reality. Our enjoyment of situated branding is thereby characterized by "moments of 'escape' and moments of 'capture'" (Moor, 2003: 58). Our subjectively articulated experience of brandscapes and cellphone content more widely can be considered immersion in a "cellscape."

Malls can be real world or virtual. Arriving at an online retail display "stimulates a fundamental sense of place" (Currah, 2003: 8): (passive) absorption into the website is accompanied by (active) anticipation. Potential purchasers "set off into the site" guided by brand expectation.

They articulate "virtual *landscapes*" of shopping, representing these "*expe-riential spaces*" (ibid.: 8–9, emphases in the original) in stories of their own appropriating consumption. Enjoying branded malls involves "border crossing" (Lindridge et al., 2004). We pass over the threshold of the screen or shop, engaging in a play-like cultivation of content not because our focus is superficial but because it is short-lived. Subsequently, we return to everyday life.

Brands are product-related "platforms" for human activity. Their market-ing management lies in commending profitable programs or narratives of customization by consumers. A brand "stands for a specific way of using the object, a propertied form of life to be realized in consumption" (Arvidsson, 2005: 244). Malaysian Boh teas are promoted to "bring people together." Brands are a cultural resource or story-set where each forms a brand-space creatively reshaped by consumers, made particular within the latter's life-world. In appropriating their products we make the goods our own (Ilmonen, 2004: 34) through practices which can be presented in subjective narratives. Placing a digital product in the home may allow us to transform the domestic sphere into a user-centered technoscape (Lehtonen, 2003: 364).

Responses to brand marketing are characterized like readings of screen media by an initial immersive moment in which we absorb-anticipate narrative: sense structures sight. Similarly, our subsequently appropriating consumer items is both active and passive, a time of contextualized creativity. We may cross categories of traditional gender experience in "gender tourism." Men can enjoy "conventionally feminine" entertainment (Thompson and Holt, 2004: 313, 334).

Consumption is a "process whereby agents engage in appropriation and appreciation" (Warde, 2005: 137) of frequently branded goods and services. Our Chinese female contributor told us that receiving her niece's message on a cellphone "made my day." Emotions have a "cognitive component" (Ilmonen, 2004: 41). Appropriation can be affective, a narrative wherein personal identity is constructed from an emotion-packed understanding of an object. Thereby enthusiastically (or critically) circulating our concep-tion of the brand, we contribute to its economic value. Our five-fold phe-nomenology of screen response as an interpretative process should further explicate such generalizations about perception and purchase as the "higher the number of connotations a brand generates, the greater its psychological force" (Danesi, 2006: 37).

We shall discuss as research exemplars Southeast Asian case studies of television brand advertising ("brandscaping") and consumer response from absorption to appropriation – or alienation. Implicit within this process is the ludic cultural literacy of audiences reading media. My reception study in late June 2004 of one glocal text (a US Coca-Cola advertisement) shows consumer consent or audiences appropriating and aligning with advertising (albeit a "fuzzy capitalist metanarrative": Goldman and Papson, 2006: 328). In making the "brand meaningful to themselves" (Coupland, 2005: 106), they negotiate "brand legitimacy" (Kates, 2004: 456). On the other hand, responses to a local text incorporating global icons (such as the Eiffel Tower) to market a music CD are characterized by consumer contestation, our audience's failure to articulate and appropriate a narrative or their alienation from this television advertising.

Subsequent research in early April 2007 investigated further consumer responses to media advertising, in this case telecommunications brand narratives marketing corporate capacity to connect our cellphones, providing a "portal" (Livingstone, 2007b: 17) to the world. Prior to considering young mobile phone users in South Korea, as we saw earlier Yoon outlines discourses of "the state, the market and the mass media" (2006: 754) contributing to images of technology deploying youth. Setting on one side such issues as state legislation following on from media constructed "moral panics" over perceived abuses of new communication modes, we focus on television narratives marketing cellphone use. In a variety of ways, each aligns its intended viewer-consumers in absorbed anticipation of a narrative which they can articulate and appropriate to guide them in product purchase. Stories cultivate pleasurable audience identification with commodity enjoyment on screen, even while some narratives represent the latter as exaggerated or excessively playful. Groups of successfully aligned enthusiastic consumers can form appreciative "brand communities" (Muniz and Schau, 2005).

Branding by Basketball

Our research exemplars are "polyphonic narratives" (Currah, 2003: 31) constituted collectively by marketing, consumer, and theoretical accounts – presenting and gaining a purchase upon the five-fold process of audience response. The Malaysian television advertisement to which we have referred showed young people playing basketball in a busy Kuala Lumpur city center street while drinking Coca-Cola.

> "The [Coca-Cola] ad. starts off with a question: 'Perlukah ada gelanggang?'
> [The Malay on screen is "Mesti ada gelanggang ke?" or "Must there be a
> court?"] Then it shows a bunch of guys playing street basketball and the ball

bounces in front of a girl. She picks up the ball and scores a basket. Then the question is answered: 'Tidak sangat!' ["Guess not!']" (Female Indian research participant) [The Malay on screen is "Tidak juga!" or "Not really!"]

Viewed from our hermeneutic perspective (interpreting participant and purchaser understanding), the question raised on screen at the opening moment of this narrative can be read as setting out these people's underlying concerned perception of their apparently not very ludic location. "Must there be a court?" Skepticism is buried beneath their investigative behavior in an environment inappropriate to play. But pushing aside doubts, consuming Coca-Cola (if seeing is to believe) enables girls especially to creatively conquer difficulty: "Guess not!"

Intended audiences (appropriately culturally equipped) recognize both basketball game and its challenging circumstances. Caught up in anticipating its outcome with uncertainty, their future-oriented focus on the condition of its success is equally set out on screen in the question: "Must there be a court?" Their intrinsic interest is in constructing a narrative. Assembling the images they share with the camera into a coherent narrative of people at play, viewers achieve a behavioral answer, an enigma-resolving story of screen events from difficulty to restoring equilibrium: "Guess not!"

In our reception study, many respondents projected from highly edited but transparently accessible (veridical) narrative fragments a "storied" account of screen content. Answering the question "Mesti ada gelanggang ke?" that is, aligned our *absorbed* Malaysian Chinese, Indian, and Malay audience with actants in the parallel and simultaneous interpretative process of *anticipating* and *articulating* a coherent outcome to the game – of unusual basketball (for the physically ludic) and textual understanding (among the cognitively ludic). Viewers are passive-active perceivers.

Seeking understanding of a text, we have noted, viewers resemble those on screen engaged in similar construction of intelligible practice, in forming the meaningful "texts" of living. The hermeneutic necessity of coherently comprehending the world, of deploying interpretative strategies infusing everyday life with meaning, is experienced both within and beyond the narratives of television. Audience-consumer identification with those on screen is fundamentally hermeneutic, an implicit or explicit positioning of oneself alongside people always already in the process of understanding the world through action.

Respondents positioned themselves not only epistemologically but ontologically, sharing the players' view of a world in which the audience has become momentarily immersed: watching "makes me feel like I'm one of them" (female Indian). Such intense involvement is to be distinguished from the disconnected distancing which focus group members expressed towards another televised local advertisement for a music CD they regarded as "so made up and unrealistic" (female Indian): "it just went from scene to scene to another scene, and I could not see the transition in the scenes, so it was very messy" (male Chinese).

Expecting and establishing a narrative of Coca-Cola consumption on screen, research participants *appropriated* this prescriptive story: for them it proposed creativity with which the constructively engaged can identify. Audiences align – showing consumer if not civic awareness.

> The message to me was "challenging the norms" where proper courts are not needed to have a good game, and girls can be good at basketball too! [Concluding the advertisement with] "Cuba!" "Try!" is their challenge to consumers to beat the norm.
>
> "Cuba!" "Try!" – the company's "Shout Out" – proves effective with its message in urging youths to experiment with the drink. It encourages youths like us to be more creative, vibrant and exciting – to make us think out-of-box. Playing basketball in the streets and using the waste basket as a rim is a way of creative thinking. (Male Chinese participants)

Consumer identification in such circumstances, then, is a cognitive activity. It involves hermeneutic sharing, a participatory coming to understand content: we align with (our perception of) a narrative agent's transparently accessible project of sense-making. Playing basketball provides its city location with meaning. And the identification process concludes in our adopting that emerging story's more or less explicit normative proposition: "Cuba!" "Try!" So in the eyes of a male Chinese research participant "the whole theme of challenging the norm, it appealed to me very much." Perceived to be enabling, product purchase is a likely result.

The conditions of consumer consensus or audience alignment with narrative actants are three-fold. First, screen advertising needs to be *veridical*. Editing of a visually elaborated story must conform to viewer expectation: it should escape conscious awareness, enabling audiences to easily immerse themselves in events. In the case of the Coca-Cola advertisement, rapid elliptical MTV-style editing meets youthful horizons of expectation with ease. New generations "read" the screen in different ways from their predecessors (Hafez, 2007: 131). During our focus group discussions, one would expect participants to say little on this invisible subject.

Second, narrative content must be *culturally close* to consumers, sufficiently recognizable to support those watching in initiating the process of anticipating and articulating a story from events seen on screen. "I think the Coke ad., the background was, it was a very natural setup, and we can really relate to it because we see it everyday, and 'we are the people,' and they're talking about us" (female Indian). "Basketball is an American game but they use Malaysian context, like the basketball net, they use rattan basket, very traditional basket, but Malaysians can identify that very well" (male Malay).

Thirdly, if establishing a narrative is to align audiences with actants themselves articulating meaning, *signs of projection* need to be present on screen. In our advertisement, physical projection (of the basketball) embodied cognitive anticipation. "We can do it!" Identification with a story's characters and the form of understanding at which they arrive informs consumer comprehension of their own everyday life-world: "Coke is no more ... for the foreigner, the Malaysian can adapt this product, the image of this product very well" (male Chinese).

The Coca-Cola television advertisement succeeds in "glocalizing," "indigenizing," or "morphing" the US product through its imbrication of the drink's consumption with Malaysian cultural practice. Absorbed viewers identify the product in local rather than global terms, giving free passage to their identification with those who playfully build a story of imbibing and victory on screen. Rewriting the Occidental cultural association of Coca-Cola as Oriental supports its easy absorption by an Eastern audience.

Successful transnational advertising is bi-polar in its appeal. On the one hand, it recognizes its intended audience, making global content indigenous with widespread sensitivity to particular cultural pleasures and values. On the other, local consumers are supported in recognizing "our friends" on screen, "adapting" or aligning themselves in global product purchase "very well."

Windows on Wireless Connections

"Brand cultures" (Pettinger, 2004) add value to products in advertising and marketing narratives, relating them to furthering a lifestyle. Such idealized use of the purchasable is seen to occur on screen in a brandscape. These articulated sets of sounds and images can be classified by reference to the social class, ethnicity, gender, and generation of those inhabiting them, as well as associated with secondary phenomena such as the nationhood of people represented.

Branding stories told on screen thereby forge an identity defining dimension to product appropriation (for gendered readings of advertisements and acquisition, see Schroeder and Zwick, 2004). We know who ought to buy. Global youth advertising, for instance, addresses adolescents when "questions of identity are subject to particularly intense negotiation" (Gillespie, 1995: 2). Consumption brings meaning (as well as goods) back home: indeed, in the case of household products, it can be instrumentally fulfilling, a ludic release in shopping circumscribed by dutiful service, the need to subsequently labor. Screen narratives connecting people on cellphones branded their use as both playful and productive.

Brand advertising and packaging are "narrative vehicles" (Kniazeva and Belk, 2007: 51) constructing a mythical status for product achievement through a profundity of association (successful cellphone connections recognize "family is everything"). Stories incorporate principled practice to be appropriated, prescriptive advice to alleviate pain or the otherwise problematic. Purchase a particular cellphone contract, "because distance should bring you closer."

The distinction between branding and other genres (Stern and Russell, 2004: 372) of advertising is that the former employs narratives representing a brandscape (at least implicitly) occupied by a range of related products. Such a construction (not infrequently cinematic in quality) may emphasize space or time – be it geographical or historical in focus. Its scopic vision can give privileged position to an individual's (e.g., pop star's) or a group's (e.g., family's) activity incorporating a theme (e.g., bringing people together). The products themselves need not be visible (corporate capacity to provide successful cellphone connections can be demonstrated only through depicting their consequences).

Our second deployment of hermeneutic consumer theory interprets multicultural consumer responses to telco (telephone company) narrative constructions of brandscapes in Malaysia during Chinese New Year 2007. These advertisements were institutionally authored by the national telecommunications provider (Telco D), a subsidiary (Telco A), two independent companies (Telcos B and C) and collectively expressed a thematic core.[2] They emphasized people's capacity using the cellphone to generate togetherness transcending space and time – sustaining a continual closeness in corporate-customer companionship or extended family. Subtitled images proposed propositional conclusions aligning question-asking potential purchasers with phone users – "because you (we?) can't wait to share" news (Telco C). Camerawork (point of view shots) allowed us (as Telco C audience) to literally share their (narrative agents') world-view (which could be the return look of child, father, or wife).

In most of these advertisements handphone use advances the harmony of linking friends and family. But in one text, the principle that there is value in thus celebrating human relationships is subverted. This advertisement's "consumption narrative" (Stern, 1995: 165) involves a Chinese New Year reunion dinner. The latter's potential for harmony is undermined by prescriptive images of people using the phone there and then – distracting from the immediate friendship of the family.

The cellphone companies' brandscapes or narrative advertising of national coverage can be summarized as follows, notably exemplifying global themes of celebration and continuity:

Telco A enables cellphones to continually connect all regions of the country:
Life never stops in (Telco A) 3G Territory

Telco B cellphone signals are as flourishing and vigorous as *feng shui* energy:[3]
Always with you celebrating this [Chinese New Year] festivity   Telco B

Telco B's cheap long calls engross Chinese New Year reunion diners:
Longevity calls   Free after 5 mins

Telco C's cellphone connections bring distant family members closer:
Because you can't wait to share. Because you want to keep that promise. Because distance should bring you closer. Because family is everything.

Telco D's national history of communication celebrates "eras" of Chinese pioneers:
Era Yap Ah Loy   Era Loke Yiew   Era Tan Cheng Lock   Era Tan Siew Sin[4]
(A patriarchal history of the Chinese Malaysian "family's" national contribution).

Building *visible* brandscapes to represent a company's *invisible* network of cellphone call routes requires creativity. Telco B employs an iconic corporate image – a vigorous if bulky "yellow fellow" – as embodiment of its energetic omnipresent signal, symbolizing its flourishing strength. The yellow fellow with his accompanying theme song "I Will Follow You" has become part of Malaysian popular culture, generating a brand-focused community.

[Telco B]'s Yellow Men have become icons. And, of course, this friend that stands for the brand promises to cover you wherever you go. Before long, he has a *persona* of his own. The Yellow Man grows into an icon that is everyone's friend. Many adults and children alike found ways to relate to him, and found their own scenarios where he would be there for them. The buzz began. (*Star* newspaper, March 17, 2007)

Our reception study of twenty media users and their narratives projected in response to telco brandscapes was conducted at both regional and urban locations in West Malaysia: the town of Titi and city of Kuala Lumpur.[5] Drawing on Heidegger's phenomenology of understanding discussed earlier, the structured process of consumer reaction to these televised advertisements was analyzed as five-fold: interest-led absorption-anticipation, articulation and appropriation of/alienation from meaning, with silence perhaps indicating apathy.

Media users' active absorption in content (interest-led immersion)

The *intrinsic* interest of realizing a story on screen can promote the media user's *absorbed* immersion in content:

"this one you can just imagine yourself" in the space and time of the advertisement: "they didn't show the very detailed thing exactly," "they leave a space for you so that to continue ... you have to think yourself." Even "after you know it, it's still [of] interest for me ... still got some space for us to think about the story." (Female Chinese)

When one reader fails in this hermeneutic task of story construction, another may succeed. The screened advertising from Telco A "is not interesting anymore" (laughing) because "there is not any story inside" (male Chinese): "the story is there, that means that they're connecting each [Malaysian] state, from one to the other, from north to south, east to west" (male Eurasian).

People also have an *instrumental* interest in products advertised.[6] What is the special "benefit they give me ... bonus benefit?" If none is indicated, it is "too normal" (female Chinese).

Anticipating narrative from a horizon
of understanding (projecting)

Consumers engage in fore-structured imagining: when you first see Telco B's coverage advertisement,

> "you won't know what happens next. So that you have to imagine first ... you will think many things, 'Eh, what [are] they going to do?' 'Eh, what happened?'" "You will just watch it out. Eh, actually, what's going [to] happen?" "You will imagine it, what they're going to do." "[I] wait, wait and then to see what happens next" in Telco B's advertising. (Female Chinese)

We look at television content from a horizon of understanding: "we have a mindset before we watch the advert" (male Chinese). Events in standard stories are easily anticipated on the basis of our knowledge (fore-concepts) of formats and genres. Comprehension is eased where the cultures of audience and advertising are close, as where Chinese consumers watch Telco B's *feng shui* narrative: then "people get closer" (female Chinese) in a fusion of horizons or conceptual understanding. But new material inhibits our informed expectation of specific content: "if I view a new ad. I don't expect anything: you must just let it happen" (female Chinese).

Our *anticipating* an advertisement's development on the basis of presuming its association with a brand may meet problems. Consumers can initially classify screen content erroneously, mistaking the advertiser: in subsequent viewing of material clashing with expectation they become aware of their misguided reading. Much Malaysian marketing is alike in drawing upon consumers' awareness of being citizens of a nation. "I'm always confused" (female Chinese).

> "The first frame [of Telco B's coverage advertising], I thought it is a [national oil company] ad." but "actually it was not" (female Chinese). "I thought [Telco D advertising] was [the national oil company's]" "because [the latter] always does this type of ad. where it tells you about [the country's] history, then you relate history and the past to the future, present": "it was like very different from what I thought" (male Chinese).

Under such circumstances, projected – or expected – events on screen do not eventuate. When advertisements do not unfold as anticipated, "if that's not the way," one is a "bit disappointed": "I expect something better than the end" (Chinese females). Expectations need not be explicitly entertained:

they can be implicit or buried in one's understanding of a marketing narrative awaiting disclosure amidst the discourses of a focus group or interview.

Articulating narrative meaning (in a hermeneutic circle of understanding)

In successfully responding to swiftly identified advertising, *we articulate* or assemble a coherent narrative: "from the beginning they already show the telephone company ... This one I guessed out what they are trying to say" (female Chinese). Our stories integrate the abruptly edited: Telco D "'jumps' to ancient times" (female Chinese). Nonetheless viewers can encounter unexpected sights from horizons of interpretative looking at content established after identifying the advertiser:

> "I don't expect to see the UTAR [Universiti Tunku Abdul Rahman] logo in the [Telco D advertising]. I mean, it's kind of odd. What is it doing there?" (male Chinese): likewise "we do not expect the ending for the [Telco B] advertisement would be like that lah ... it stays in your mind" (male Chinese). There are enigmas to be resolved: in Telco B's first marketing narrative "they never use the phone, this one not 'normal'" (female Chinese).

We sometimes have to postpone classification of narratives and hence *articulating* (or expecting and establishing) the events which constitute their specific stories. In respect of Telco B's second narrative (with its high production values), "I don't know [whether] this one is advertisement or this one is movie or what" (Chinese female). The corporate authors of Telco advertisements B, C, and D remained unannounced until the final frames.[7]

> "You have to go until the end of the advertisement, only you know [then] that it's telephone, telco advertising [for Telco B].... You can't expect anything because you don't even know what's the ad. going to be like" (female Chinese). Viewing an elliptical national story of communication, "until the end only you know it's about [Telco D]" (male Chinese).

Appropriating the "message" to inform the consumer's life-world (identification)

Consumer identification with content can be several-layered. It may take shape as sharing the process of articulating a story and its resulting narrative.

Telco B "knows *what* we're thinking about" (female Chinese, emphasis in the original). In constructing (or projecting) Telco C's content, students align with the advertisement's storytelling (of a daughter's phone call from the city, delighting her distant mother in the countryside or *kampung*). They likewise phone home from a distance. Emotions may echo from a text's narrative agents to being repeated amidst an audience: "sometimes I talk with my mum, I also cry" (female Chinese): "[Telco C] touches your heart lah" (male Chinese).

Identifying can travel further. As citizen-consumers with material and moral concerns, media users also *appropriate* a text's normative proposition or positioning ("message") to inform their lives.[8] In recommending purchase, Telco C addressed our ethical need for intimacy:[9]

"Because distance should bring you closer." (Telco C advertisement)

"Because of [Telco C], the family is getting closer." (Male Indian)

"If I buy" "I could really connect me with my mum, me and my dad." (Male Chinese)

Addressing consumer-citizens with material and moral interests

Telco C "cares about ... family values" (male Chinese). Advertising such as the Telco D narrative communicates with media users presumed to occupy the role of consumer-citizens: it shows not only products but the history of communication and how "Malaysia is today" (female Chinese facilitator). Multicultural participants in Telco B's Chinese New Year dinner were regarded by a Malay couple in Titi as signifying an integrated nation. Appropriating the message, the latter indicated when they celebrate their festivals, "we invite our friends ... our family, sit together and eat together and share the story."

Marketing can be expensively movie-like but nonetheless limit its national audience: use of Mandarin entails "only Chinese can understand" and appreciate being the addressees of advertising by Telco B (female Chinese). What are the "meanings of [the] advertisement? ... I'm not understanding.... What is the story?" (female Malay). "I don't understand ... the meaning" (female Malay). Enthusiastic Chinese consumers may translate this content, extending horizons of understanding to embrace other groups.

Malaysian telco advertising consists of substantial narratives establishing brandscapes at times of celebrating national or ethnic identity: the marketing addresses consumer-citizens. In our research on responses to this advertising, some Chinese citizens distanced themselves from the position of telco consumer. They express their "citizen interest primarily through their active role as consumer in the marketplace" (Livingstone et al., 2007: 107). Not citizens with equal rights, they may be disenchanted consumers. Researchers, as Ruddock remarks, need to be aware of the nexus between these roles: for otherwise they can have a "blinkered view" both of political engagement and its occasioning (2007: 31).

Immersion in advertising may be motivated by an instrumental interest in the particular mediated marketing on screen: how can we use the product? But consumers can subsequently extract or distance themselves from an advert because of ethical concerns appropriate to a citizen. Responding to a narrative showing a Chinese reunion dinner where all are telephoning friends elsewhere, a Chinese female remarks: "It seems like the relationship between the family is not very close because of [Telco B]." "[When] the whole family is taking the dinner, you're supposed ... don't answer the phone." "A bit offensive, it breaks the [Chinese] tradition.... You really have to focus on the dinner, not on the phone" (laughter) (male Chinese): it is "out of your culture" (male Eurasian). "You better go out to talk with your friends lah!" (female Chinese).[10]

Viewing Telco D's brandscape history of communication at the heart of a harmonious and egalitarian nation, a Chinese female responded as a distanced recipient of this address to Malaysian consumer-citizens: "Sometimes reality is not the same as what they try to produce"; "in reality it is not like that"; "I have put my own perception and principle into the advertisement, that makes me, actually I don't buy it." "Listening beyond the echoes" (Couldry, 2006a), we hear prescribed public consumer connections challenged within the citizen's experiential life-world.

Conclusion

Branding functions as an assertion of corporate conscience, an ongoing guarantee of good behavior towards consumers. Purchasing a brand reassures, offering the buyer a "predictable and secure" environment (Cronin, 2004: 363). Brands establish valuable "social capital" (Kobayashi et al., 2006) prompting trust. "Trust is central" (Hardey, 2004: 208) online.

Private product acquisition presupposes an ethical concern as citizen with public corporate activity. Yet some would reduce being a citizen to the role of consumer, with the "subjectivity and freedom of the consumer-citizen" being "produced and shaped in the market" (Moisander and Eriksson, 2006: 272). Here we have seen that our immersion in (or "buying") a narrative brandscape presumes that the latter is ethically as well as epistemologically acceptable to customer-citizens. Not only when evoked by political institutions (Couldry et al., 2007: 18) but more widely, trust involves mutual moral recognition.

Notes

1 Media screens and mall spaces both incorporate brandscapes. Keller (2005: 68–70) outlines how (parallel to media use) inhabiting a mall brandscape can be ludic (recreational) or laborious, delightful or dutiful. "Shopping comes to objectify a form of absolute freedom" or a "complicated labour of love" (ibid.). Hence we can argue for a phenomenology of shopping in such places as absorbing-anticipatory, articulating coherent narratives, and appropriation of self-defining goods.

2 Other advertisements in this Chinese New Year series by Malaysia's major telephone companies were not used because we found their narrative too simple or were simply alienated.

3 In this advertisement, a geomantic master is gauging the flow of *feng shui* energy in a house. He finds a place that is very vigorous and he shouts out: "Wow! Here it is! Very wong, very very wong!" ("wong" in Cantonese means "vigorous," "powerful," "flourishing," "prosperous," or "lucky" – and "yellow"). At this point, Telco B's iconic Yellow Fellow appears, a flourishing signal of the company. Jenny Siow Ai Wei (JSAW), who investigated brandscapes with me, contributed this information and other valuable insights in the chapter and notes.

4 Chinese (male) pioneers who developed the capital city and nation in education and industry as well as political leaders of the Malaysian Chinese Association and sporting "heroes."

5 I have referred elsewhere to the further articulation of hypotheses as a result of these interviews as the "Titi turn in theory." "Titi" is both the name of a Malaysian town about one hour's scenic drive south of Kuala Lumpur and Malay for a small bridge (in this case built by the British in colonial times). In March, small group discussions were held in the town cybercafé. Subsequent meetings were with communications students in April at Universiti Tunku Abdul Rahman, Kuala Lumpur. Tan Huey Pyng generously enabled these

responses to brandscapes to be invoked. Finally, in May, one of the Titi contributors met us with two friends in the business center of a Kuala Lumpur
hotel to review the advertisements and an early account of responses. ("So
what about what?") Questions asked in all locations were as follows: (1) Was
the advertisement interesting? (2) What did you expect would happen in the
advertisement? Did it? (3) What was the advertisement's story? (4) What was
the advertisement's "message"? Did you "buy" (accept) it?

6   Telco D's advertisement is said to be not marketing (asking you to "use their
     system") but rather a national history of communication. As such it cannot
     function as an appropriate focus for the reader's instrumental interest. It does
     not "have interest inside but the advertisement is beautiful, it's good enough
     lah." Both Telco C's and Telco B's (second) advertisement lacked instrumental
     address: "Actually I lost my patience to wait for it. Eh? What you going to tell
     me? Faster, faster" (female Chinese).

7   The corporate owner of a brandscape may be immediately discerned: "The
     blue color ... that is [Telco A]" (female Chinese): but Telco B's advertising is
     identified "late" (trans. JSAW) (male Chinese). Given the casual conditions
     under which many watch television, advertisements which postpone disclos-
     ing their corporate source to a diminutive announcement in the final frame
     risk consumers failing to take note. In the Telco C advertisement "the words
     are so small, if you just sit so far [away] then you won't see" (female Chinese).

     Advertising can inappropriately address audiences: "Some aunties are less
     educated, they can't understand what the advertisement is trying to promote"
     (trans. JSAW) (female Chinese, housewife). Other "texts" may not be easily
     regarded as adverts: "They sit and eat together: I didn't know what was hap-
     pening. Finally I saw them holding cellphones, then I just understand" (trans.
     JSAW) (female Chinese, housewife).

8   Media user discussion of these advertisements is important in forming a brand
     community focused on corporate products: "I will always ask my friends '[Has
     Telco B] got the new advertisement?' then I want to see it lah!" (female
     Chinese).

9   A male Malay respondent in Titi provided a more materially focused reading
     of Telco C's message: "In rain you still can talk, communicate" (trans. JSAW).

10   In a reading distinct from the Chinese preference for a single-minded focus on
     the reunion meal, a female Malay interviewee in Titi did not find Telco B's
     conjunction of dining and telephoning objectionable. She agreed to the nor-
     mative proposition "when you are eating together with your family, you still
     can communicate with others" (trans. JSAW).

9

Consumer-Citizens: Crossing Cultures in Cyberspace

In this final chapter, we explore media users' Internet immersion as people who through the process of consuming screen content come to entertain the ethical and political interests of citizens. We long ago rejected a Cause and Effect Theory of television influencing passive viewers. Instead, we have argued for the Media User Model as a five-fold phenomenology of screen perception, integrating earlier theory on a platform of literary and philosophical thinking. Looking at content from their conceptual horizons of understanding, motivated by intrinsic and instrumental interest in its development, active audiences *absorb* and simultaneously *anticipate* narrative. They engage in subsequent goal-directed *articulation* of fragmentary meaning into a coherent content which media users *appropriate* (informing their lives) – or from which they distance themselves in *alienation* (or apathy).

Like one's involvement in the time and space of a game, we have seen that media use is immersive: it is characterized by many aspects of playful experience or is fundamentally ludic despite more liminal dutiful or instrumental uses of the Internet for work. To perceive and play is to project. Sport and spectating are outcome-focused, engaged with while expecting a particular result. People perceive, project, produce narrative on screen and position themselves accordingly.

Consumers sooner or later disclose an identity as citizens. Our media use is "entwined" (Dahlgren, 2006: 276) with citizenship. For Alneng, to be a "modern citizen" is to "exercise the right to consume other cultures" (2002: 123) with the "civil right of tourism" (ibid.: 138) being an instance of the latter. In this last chapter we shall note, on the one hand, consumer-citizens' alienated responses to journalism (Wilson, 2006) and, on the other, accounts of how their trust (or mutual identification) is evoked by tourism web pages (Wilson and Suraya, 2004; Wilson, 2007: 131–54). Here political issues are infused with personal in rejecting or recognizing the "worthwhile-ness"

(Schroder, 2007) of media content. One's sense of citizenship is "dispersed" across responses to such "sites" of reading (Couldry, 2004: 25) narratives of "pushed down" reality and recreational release.

In chapters 7 and 8 we considered from a cultural perspective media marketing and the consumer's response to its brandscapes of prescriptive space and time on television and Internet. Post-viewing narrative readings were contingently occasioned by the presence of researchers: people were asked to talk about their screen perceptions. Writing within hermeneutic horizons of interpreting media user activity, we focused on the conditions and cognitive processes of people constructing intelligible content. Projecting a possible narrative of events on screen, informed viewers watch to test their conjectures and establish their accuracy. While doing so, regarding content with intrinsic interest they immerse themselves in the story's "mediatized space" (Edensor, 2001: 61).

However, people also view media marketing with an instrumental interest in products. Why buy? In this regard consumers are citizens concerned not only with economic but ethical issues (e.g., veracity in advertising). Corporate marketing seeks to communicate a civic message: Trust us! You can believe in our branded goods! Some marketing which connects brand with national identity to emphasize the permanence of a product addresses people as consumer-citizens: our manufacturing in/of your nation. Advertisers invoke their alleged "civic virtues as part of product branding" (Hartley, 2002: 61). Purchasing cannot be separated from politics.

Here we reflect on consumer-citizens' understanding of media content in everyday use, particularly where with differing interests in mind they access the "transnational culture" (Franklin and Crang, 2001: 8) of online news sources or travel sites and make a "public connection" (Couldry, 2004) to ethical-political topics from their private concerns. "Civic agency" (Dahlgren, 2006) issues arise concerning how we or others respond to media images. Digital divides exist between economic, ethnic, gender, and generational groups in their interpretative immersion (Hargittai, 2004) and appropriation of narrative as purchasers and percipients of morality.

Consumers value citizenship if only because it brings an enforceable public dimension to "consumerist rights" (Stevenson, 1995: 113). The active purchaser is always already immersed in the legal obligations as well as the ongoing creativity of citizenship. He or she views society and state from "civic horizons" (Hermes and Dahlgren, 2006: 259). Being a buyer means others sometimes have to say "sorry."

Lewis argues that news ought to focus on "what it is useful for people to know" (2006: 315). It should address consumer-citizens' hybrid horizons of understanding. Looking at the world from that dual perspective, people are politically as well as commercially concerned with issues of morality, power, and status. Likewise, consumer-citizen tourists seek authenticity and truth. Elsewhere horizons of understanding can be uncertain – what frameworks of comprehension shed light on an occurrence? (Scannell, 2004).

In this chapter we discuss media use by individuals taking part in focus groups constituting a "field of civic talk" (Dahlgren, 2006: 280). They are considered as participants transcending consumerism, engaging with the political beyond the personal in a public sphere of debates on matters evoked by journalism and tourism. In Couldry's words (which have a wider focus) "what lies on the other side of the line from things they regard as being of only private concern; what makes up *their* public world?" (2006b: 328, emphasis in the original). What horizons of understanding do they cross in moving from an agenda of private purchasing to public topics regarded as relevant – of interest? How do media sustain (or subvert) our perceptions as consumer-citizens of a private-public connection between aspects of an issue? People reflectively interpret journalism and tourism websites which practice identity politics. Who is seen as commercially or culturally powerful in circulating images prompting recognition or resistance?

Concluding our account of media user theory, we view people as consumer-citizens online albeit recognizing the "unstable, indeed contested, relation" between these roles (Livingstone and Lunt, 2007). We consider their media use from cultural, commercial, and civic perspectives. Need cultural tourists be politically informed? Writing on "young citizens," Olsson tells us how their "individualization" has led to a hybrid "re-moulding" of "civic subjects" into "consumer subjects" (2005: 133). May civic consciousness nonetheless develop within consumer awareness?

Engaging in "deliberative politics" (Wiklund, 2005: 701), participants in groups focusing on the websites of e-journalism or tourism can assess the discursive complicity of their pages in asymmetries of economic and cultural power. We hear East discussing the merits of digital West. They present their distancing identities at the moment the second US Iraq intervention was initiated in response to apparently "unassailable evidence" that the country possessed weapons of mass destruction (Arsenault and Castells, 2006: 284). The symbolic status accrued simply by a message appearing on a media screen is resisted (Couldry, 2001: 172): conflation of authorial and audience interests or "cultural hegemonization" (Chadha and Kavoori,

2000: 416) is questioned. Such public sphere debate concerns "dimensions of citizenship, the feeling of belonging, social integration and the experience of disempowerment" (Sassi, 2005: 690).

Our phenomenology of media perception seeks to underwrite insight into an audience's achieving self-described or "emic experience" (Kane and Tucker, 2004: 217) of screen narrative. Analytical interpretations can be provided of particular reactions. Our focus has been on media use in context, on a screen's significance for someone located within particular horizons of conceptual understanding – within "frameworks of meaning" (Qureshi, 2006: 217) not always easily acknowledged. Reading occurs from ethnic, gendered, generational perspectives on the narrative constructions of media genres.

Journalism and tourist websites engage with the practice of politics in spaces understood as public (Siapera, 2006: 6). So likewise do our consumer-citizens. Through examining a range of responses to the Internet we can discuss the distance between the "rhetoric and the reality of web-assisted democracy" (Ridell, 2005: 31). In discussion groups focusing on reading the media, people "think meaning-making and belonging" from the perspective of "power, power relations and identity construction" (Hermes and Dahlgren, 2006: 261).

Bracketing political identity obscures power (Squires, 2002: 450). Offering an apparently "Asian sort of perspective," CNN.Asia's[1] subtext was regarded in research with Malaysian students (Wilson, 2006) as "actually a very pro-Western sort of ideology" (male Indian) legitimating American action and attitudes as they entered Iraq. Web pages may be posted as "Asian," but their content privileges the West, developing unequal relations between an "identity of dominance and an identity of marginality" (Shome, 2003: 42). Participants discerned a hierarchical opposition structuring these news sites: "it starts off with the Western and then they'll come down to the Asian part" (female Indian). America, foregrounded as the "good guys," is juxtaposed to a marginalized "bad" Asia:

> "Americans are always portrayed as the good guys kind of thing, you know, like 'we are the saviours of the day!'" (female Indian); "even when you click on 'Asia,' it will still go back to 'World'" [and "world news" is American] (female Indian); "Western news has always written bad stories about Asians, only the bad stories, a little of the good stories" (female Malay/Kadazan), suggesting Malaysia to be chaotic and in need of control – "so militant, so terrorist, so religious!" (female Malay).

With titles of news items in "tiny little words up there," CNN.Asia margin-
alizes Asian issues: "ultimately it's still biased towards the Americans"
(female Chinese). In their discourses of "othering" (Parameswaran, 2002),
alienated citizens in these focus groups did not regard its narratives as
supporting possibilities of identification, of gaining eudaemonic self and
social insight. Such public data excluded their deliberative agency (Couldry
et al., 2007: 194–5). Malaysians were not among the news site's implied
addressees: they were not "recognized" or "accorded equal status and worth"
(Siapera, 2006: 8).

A second genre of web authorship builds Internet sites for travelers.
These cyberspace constructions of cultural identity are discussed here by
audiences as consumer-citizens. Media users reflect on the ethics and justice
displayed in representing people on tourist sites they recognize to be both
civic and commercial. Why is a Southeast Asian nation characterized as
both pleasurable haven and potential hell? In doing so, people regard these
cultural web pages for travelers as contributing to a political public sphere.
Tourist icons are "hybrid forms, fusions of historical, local and visitor
imagery" (Adams, 2004: 129) with "politics and power dynamics" embedded in their genesis (ibid.: 116). "Touristic consumerism" (Tomlinson, 2005:
90) here calls upon the civic within us, evoking the citizen's awareness of
nationhood.

Phenomenologies of Web Access:
Our Absorbed Anticipation of Narrative

Drawing audiences from television, in a mainstreaming of new media
(Lievrouw, 2004: 10) the Internet has become embedded in the everyday
lives of many (Wellman, 2004: 125). Yet economic, ethical, gender, generational, technological, and other digital divisions (Gunkel, 2003: Hargittai,
2004) or distance still exist between those who do, and those who do not, go
online. The economically successful can be defined by their capacity to
access a "digital hearth," enjoying virtual games away from the "mess and
routine" of daily domesticity (Flynn, 2003: 557).

Escaping the materially mundane, surfer-tourists play in cyberspace,
striving to secure a meaning "construed and bent" (Feenberg and
Bakardjieva, 2004: 39) in virtual ways.[2] Despite the impedimenta of pop-up
pages, spam, and virus, they enjoy a livable environment on the web

(Herring, 2004: 32), new "geographies of screen space" (Flynn, 2003: 559). Surfer immersion in seamless cyberspace is challenged only at the point of the Internet user's necessary navigation, her or his conscious clicking between menu items or hypertext links (MacGregor, 2003: 13).

We project particular meaning at Internet sites. Web access may involve cultivating personal relationships of a character intrinsic to the Internet (e.g., in a chat room). Or on the margins of such mediated play, people instrumentally strive in cyberspace towards progressing business offline. On the Internet one can discern convergence not only of technologies (film, radio, television) but between intrinsic and extrinsic goals in escape and endeavor (Mehra et al., 2004: 781). Displaying online/offline "crossover" (ibid.: 781, 790) in the purpose of cyber-activity, web access exhibits ambivalence between play and work.

Depending on participant purpose, online forums stage "fun" or functional exchanges (Feenberg and Bakardjieva, 2004: 39). Use of the web can swiftly alternate between considering it to be wondrous toy or "work tool," focus for serendipitous surfing or seeking information relating to business and study (Selwyn et al., 2005), mediated virtual escape or material empowerment, cyberspace distraction or civil society development. Conjoining profitable labor with ludic pleasure, games production in cyberspace can be demanding as well as "fun" (Postigo, 2003: 601).

Audience cyberplay with its intrinsic focus on Internet mediated content as an "object of fascination" and the "practical necessity" (Herring, 2004: 33) of dutiful work on websites towards achieving an extrinsic goal offline share a core of ludic caring. For both are focused, albeit from differing virtual and material perspectives, on anticipating and achieving meaning on the Internet. The instrumentally driven – however – are less than wholly immersed in cyberspace.

Internet user studies are of responses to web narrative by those knowing its generic mediating forms (e.g., tourist blogs) structuring page or site related by hypertext menu: "connectivity matters as much as content" (Schneider and Foot, 2004: 116, 117). Reception is creative of audience identity, for chat rooms and other community times and places in cyberspace feature a "staging of the self" (Axelsson et al., 2003: 480). Destabilizing "categories of knowing, relating, and being" (Taylor and Kolkob, 2003: 497), that self can be a fictional morph of the real life person. As in play (e.g., football) and television (e.g., the talk show) so on the Internet, perceptions of identity are interpersonally constructed, emerging from the social nature of online interaction (Lamerichs and Te Molder, 2003: 452) often to inform the offline. In this ludic slippage between our "selves," we are consumer-citizens, empowering those who profit from our playful engagement.

Tourist Gaze, Ludic Look:
A Phenomenology of Far-away Play

Gazing, seeking sense in what they see, tourists everywhere play perceptually. Travel online as well as offline is (in)formed by anticipating and assessing meaning across pages – whether hard or soft copy. Constructing multiple narratives is at the core of the "hypothetical tourist consciousness" (Tomlinson, 2005: 84). We pursue understanding of both material and virtual site in the stories we develop. Our interest in content is intrinsic: our focus is specific and special. Accessing the Internet instantiates processes of interpretation which, while universally shared, draw on different cultural contexts. Media users perceive content in diverse ways.

Advertising addresses the "process of consumption before consumption" (Crouch, 2005: 77). Tourism's marketing images are safe, tamed texts familiar to intended audiences who are customarily Caucasian (Alneng, 2002: 123). Knowledge-seeking viewers identify with narrative agents. Processing – anticipating and actualizing – projections of potential advertising storylines, consumers can validate a prescriptive meaning for these texts by purchase, or resist through rejection of attempted persuasion. Where we fail in the hermeneutic circle of informed and integrated story-building, reflexive (distanciated) reading of tourist narrative is a likely result. We wonder why the site lacks sense.

Drawing upon accounts of the "tourist gaze" (Urry, 1995), in this research exemplar we explore the structure of this traveling gaze or perception in play across web pages – media users projecting possible narratives, speculating upon and synthesizing stories. Writing from the perspective of hermeneutic Internet theory, we share the "(cyber)spatial turn in tourism studies" (Saarinen, 2004: 163) through discussing consumer-citizen responses to the tourism information and marketing screens of government and industry: for these organizations cannot afford to be invisible in cyberspace (Milne et al., 2005: 106). Tourism sites engage in commercial, community/cultural, and political/public sphere modes of address, presenting "distinct identities" in "corporate face" and "community face" (Campbell, 2005: 665). Travel advertising and travel warnings can collide.

The Internet offers "prior texts for prospective tourists" (Adams, 2004: 115). "Checking out" destinations online, travelers assume an e-presence in cyberspace. But the "look" evoked in surfing tourism sites bears a metonymic relationship to the traveler's gaze more widely. Albeit focused on the virtual, this perceptual process exemplifies touristic construction of meaning everywhere. Real world or virtual, "tourist destinations are symbolically characterized spaces" (Saarinen, 2004: 166). Making sense of them – ludic looking – takes time.

Occurring both teleologically (purposefully) and to and fro (perceptually), the cyber-traveler's look-in-play assembles web page content. We make meaning in media use. Whether online or offline, we gaze from informed horizons of understanding where even the exotic is recognized as exemplifying the typically unknown. Awareness of such (sometimes contested) conceptual frameworks defines the cultural conditions of our making sense.

Drawing on this "mental grid" through which audiences form and "filter their experiences" (Adams, 2004: 116) our ludic gaze develops a familiarizing narrative from special experience. Informed anticipation of a story is confirmed – in making coherent sense of a complex Internet marketing guide to holiday opportunity or on an informative if meandering tour of a historical site. Narratives of web and world are achieved. Being online and benign tourism engage in a parallel process of perceptual play.

If travel broadens the mind, intending tourists customarily entertain wide possibilities of enjoying experiences "missing and missed in everyday life" (Franklin, 2004: 277). They cultivate choice of route and remarkable site. Preparing online, travelers anticipate assistance from appropriate web pages provided by commercial and national tour agents and authorities. Their Internet use is cognitively focused and goal directed. Tourists cover long distances both virtual and material, checking on perceived possibility and consuming marketed destinations. Aligning themselves with the latter's cultural associations, they define social identities (Murray, 2003: 15) and acquiesce in political power.

In the following pages, Chinese, Indian, and Malay young people travel online with multiple Malaysian identities. They subsequently consider in focus groups their responses to local and overseas (Australian) private sector, as well as government sponsored, tourism and travel websites. Invited to become research participants by virtue of their being able to articulate readings signaling multicultural awareness, these youthful contributors underwrite the development of hybrid (or in Malay, "rojak") reception theory. Such client responses are set alongside professional perceptions of corporate home pages provided by the office manager in a large Malaysian travel company (www.reliancetravel.com).[3]

On Australian and Malaysian government tourism sites which our contributors visit, sociocultural aspects of religious practice (from the hostile to the "heavenly") are represented as relevant to citizen-consumer travelers. To explore this issue further, the online editions of two Malaysian newspapers (*New Straits Times* and *Harakah*), with their view of Islam as a fundamental aspect of that nation, were included for discussion by a focus group.

In the *Asian Journal of Communication*, Lim argues that shopping is play involving "recreation," "fantasies and fun" (2002: 79): it engages consumers in a "diversion from their daily routines" (ibid.: 81). Travel sites offer would-be tourists an immersive opportunity to "daydream about holidays" (ibid.: 90), the intrinsic interest of imaginative speculation. Here, cyberspace is considered "heterotopian" (Liff and Steward, 2003: 319), "not a medium but a place to be or to dwell" (Slater, 2002: 534).

Play brackets the banal place, moving it to memory. In games we anticipate going beyond tedium: the ludic is characterized by "exterritoriality" (Diken and Laustsen, 2004: 102) or "extraterritorial" (Graml, 2004: 146). Equally, the "tourist's project" is to "escape the social: to go beyond limits, cross borders, go native" (Diken and Laustsen, 2004: 109). Party tourism, in particular, can be constructed as "transgression/enjoyment" or "forced enjoyment" (ibid.: 99). Both phrases capture the conceptual opposition or tension within the ludic between "serious" and "fun": in party tourism the "serious" is constituted by a continually invoked conformity to rule-breaking.

Tourism's transgression/enjoyment, with its intrinsic focus on sustaining stories of serious fun, involves structured play for the sake of play in a "state of exception" (Agamben, 1998: 105) to duty. Ludic time and space is "other," characterized by rule-governed alterity (Diken and Laustsen, 2004: 101). Likewise "tourist" connotes a sense of "impermanence, difference, foreignness, otherness, temporariness" (McCabe: 2005: 99). The ludic is special, closer to the sacred than the secular, which as a characteristic of screen content confers a status which may need to be resisted (Couldry, 2001). Equally, there is "something quasi-religious to tourism" (Diken and Laustsen, 2004: 105). Tourism/play can change participant identity and subsequent practice – unlike a carnival's temporary inverting of hierarchy altering nothing.

In this research exemplar, also, focus group exchanges suggest that tourist travel online as well as offline is fundamentally diverting fun seriously (in)formed by the playful purpose of understanding site and self, or ludic. Like surfers, computer "users are presented with a scintillating surface on which to float, skim, and play" (Turkle, 2003: 21). Referring to Urry's (1995) work on the "tourist gaze," we advance an argument for the screen-absorbed traveling gaze as ludic looking online at the tourism information, marketing and purchasing screens of government and industry. Implicit in this perceptual process is a play-like singular structure underwriting "highly differentiated" (MacCannell, 2001: 24) "multiplicities of tourist gazes" (Urry, interviewed by Franklin, 2001: 123) at real and virtual worlds. Alongside a masculine focus on beach and bodies there is the feminized "family gaze" (Haldrup and Larsen, 2003) of cameras "making family memory-stories" (ibid.: 43): online looking is likewise variously gendered.

Recognizing an "increasing interest in conceptualizing questions of desire" (Featherstone, 1991: 13), tourist consumption is considered as active ludic pleasure rather than loss of autonomy to profit-accumulating ventures. For a critical hermeneutics, cultural theory focuses on the "passages of mediation" (Fornas, 2002: 104) where audiences cognitively respond to (or mediate[a]) texts themselves interpreting (mediating[b]) the world. We address a number of associated questions about client readings of Internet travel sites. Can the perspectives of commercial providers and consumers be reconciled in a coherent theoretically informed account of tourism web page access? How does screen-mediated marketing address audiences, communicating beyond the "playfulness of white masculinity" (Frohlick, 2005) to a cultural diversity of consumer and citizen interests? How is trust (the Internet user's perception of brand identification with client interest) established in cyberspace – through construction of a welcoming community on the tourist website?

The "Tourist Gaze" as Ludic Looking

Tour agents, hoteliers, and others engaged in selling tourism offer a holiday experience, leisure activity whose identity presupposes its opposite, namely "regulated and organized work" (Urry, 1995: 132). Both the ludic and tourism involve a separate space and time from the mundane: the "journey and stay are to, and in, sites which are outside the normal places of residence and work" (ibid.) A holiday consists in being "removed from the quotidian," placed far away from "imbrication in the everyday (Edensor, 2001: 59–60). We enjoy a ludic "*looseness* of ties" (Bauman, 2003: 207, emphasis in the original).

For Urry, the tourist experience is to be understood in terms of consuming opportunities to look (the "tourist gaze"), a distracting gaze "upon aspects of landscape or townscape which are distinctive, which signify an experience which contrasts with everyday experience," "which separate them off from everyday and routine experiences" (Urry, 1995: 132). Like ludic looking at screens, the tourist gaze crosses a threshold to serious fun, anticipated experience of the special which can be evaluated aesthetically or even as "functionally equivalent to the objects of religious pilgrimage in traditional society" (ibid.: 144–5).

> Places are chosen to be gazed upon because there is an anticipation, especially through day-dreaming and fantasy, of intense pleasures, either on a different scale or involving different senses from those customarily encountered. (Ibid.: 132)

The tourist's gaze is characterized in Urry's epistemology of escape by mobility (shifting to and fro) enabling visual absorption in the other than everyday, whether he or she is "literally mobile or only experiences simulated mobility through the incredible fluidity of multiple signs and electronic images" (ibid.: 148). Reaching destinations "chosen to be gazed upon," the leisure traveler's hermeneutic experience is quintessentially ludic, of distracting cognitive play. He or she enjoys a constructive focus on exploring intrinsic difference, insolated/isolated from dispossession by the instrumentally mundane. Here, we investigate the structure of the touristic ludic gaze online.

Online Travel Sites:
Generic Address, Goal-Focused Consumption

Consumers' interpretations of business and holiday travel agency, and associated sites, constitute complex formations of understanding. People's subjective reactions to cyberspace content, often reading online across cultures, are fore-structured by public concepts and rationally formed. Those interested in marketed mobility understand web pages as instances of a generic type (the "travel site"). They form assumptions guiding their expectations of content or project a particular meaning in hypotheses tested by subsequent reading.

Using travel websites, potential purchasers articulate aspects of a play-like formation of meaning, multiple moments of goal-directed epistemological activity in establishing content. Screen reception theory which constructs the interpretative processes involved as ludic is tested here in focus groups against contributors' awareness of their own Internet access to travel sites. For universalizing "Western theoretical practices at the expense of local articulations" (Cheung, 2003: 7) is to be avoided.

Focus groups are forms of philosophical analysis. "You begin to see how concepts are related in the participant's world" (Morrison et al., 2002: 53). The abstractions of screen reception hermeneutics are found to be embodied in contributors' responses, albeit discursively enriched. For instance, we have noted that the European philosopher Hans Gadamer claims (1976) that readers seek coherent accounts of content, relating story segment to a contextualizing narrative structure, thereby completing a full hermeneutic circle of understanding texts. Such theory conceptually reverberates in one of our male Chinese student's evaluations of web pages. "For me, I go for websites which give more and complete information" (male Chinese, trans.).[4] Urry argues that much tourism is involved in a "kind of hermeneutic circle" (1990: 140), placing travel images in context. Ethnographic research regards it as important to "ground" global statement in local self-reflexive perceptions (Green, 2003: 136).

Using cyberspatial cognitive play as an interpretative model to investigate audience reception of the Internet "captures the event character of understanding" (Risser, 1997: 140). Moreover, it foregrounds the fundamental aspect of going online, the player or web user's "decentring" departure from a focus on material to virtual phenomena. Internet users negotiate the intersections of cyberplay and offline space (Taylor, 2003: 23).

Motivated by an intrinsic interest in the discursive media specificities of screen content, the player-tourist "gives him or herself over to the game, participates in the playing of the game" (Risser, 1997: 140), the "serious fun" (Huizinga, 1970) of surfing cyberspace. But on other occasions, web pages are used instrumentally to search for travel solutions. While still a game-like construction of meaning, this is planning on the edge of play, at the limits of the ludic, work.

The Tourist's "Ludic Look" as Process:
A Hybrid Hermeneutics of Consumption

Qualitative research confronts empirical and logical difficulty inductively generating widely applicable theory from individuals' first-hand experience. Limited data can never justify extrapolation to universal conclusions. Instead, as we have seen, the methodology underwriting this investigation involves assumptions in philosophical psychology about the ludic nature of Internet reading being scrutinized for potential error (Popperian "falsification" (1963)) by setting them alongside accounts contained in research participant narratives. Is touristic reception theory compatible with user response to web pages? Do travelers read Internet sites as moral citizens as well as in the role of materialistic consumers? These are increasingly pertinent questions in an era of environmentally conscious tourism.

Focus group discussions in Malaysia[5] distinguished between web pages with different generic functions (e.g., advertising/promotional or advisory/prescriptive, in the latter case sometimes discouraging tourism). Travel sites can construct radically opposed accounts of a nation (as a female Chinese student observed in her role of citizen, Malaysia is "really two different worlds" on the Australian government travel advisory and Malaysian government tourism sites).

Visitors to sites could be surfing extensively online (with an intrinsic interest in creatively mediated content for its own sake, such as enjoying images supporting ludic "e-escapism" or "cybertourism": Mascheroni, 2007: 531). Alternatively, they may be searching intensively online (displaying an instrumentally motivated interest in finding information (e.g., costs or routes) on the Internet related to their own or another's extrinsic "real world" travel). Such searching can be considered dutiful work, an epistemic seeking sharply separated from escapist surfing. But both modes of accessing the Internet engage in cognitive processing, the creative activity of constructing a comprehensible cyberspace and identity for travelers. Searching for travel information can therefore be considered liminally ludic, as working on the "experiential threshold" (Fornas, 2002: 90) of fully realized cognitive play.

Whichever form of going online is involved, interaction with a site is grounded in an immersive touristic looking (Tsao and Chang, 2002: 4) as the construction of meaning, albeit a gaze-like immersion sometimes made marginal (glance-like) by a focus on securing extrinsic purpose.

Website contents, like online games, are "texts created (from a provided product) by playing" (Humphreys, 2003: 79).

The Ludic Tourist Look Online: Structured Understanding

Hermeneutic philosophers foreground for study the processes of understanding, of arriving at a text's interpretation. In cognitive play, they assert, significance is created for "meaningful human activity" (Hans, 1980: 312) whether seen on screen or read elsewhere. Watching television, using the Internet, instantiate hermeneutic processes of comprehension resulting in cultural varieties of understanding content. Accessing different forms of life from afar, a semantic fusion of distinctive conceptual horizons is made possible, the particular "power and creativity" (Ang, 2003: 12) of hybridization (Bun, 2002: 4).

Dwelling on four moments or aspects of "play," we explore the multiple ways in which tourists constitute themselves as viewers, their cognitive, pleasure-realizing, and political behavior in response to the screen's mediated meaning. Even where audiences casually engage in watching television or Internet use, they playfully form some understanding, albeit a relatively empty perception of content. Temporary tourists, limited in being ludic, they go online.

A Phenomenology of Touristic Meaning Formation: Discerning Moments of Traveling Consciousness

Moment 1: absorbing perception

Tourist looking as a pleasurable "immersive operation"
Games are "a brief escape from reality" (Taylor, 2003: 36). Likewise, accessing the Internet is to absent oneself from the materially mundane, to engage in the serious fun of cyberspatial play. The worldwide web is a "space of immersive operation" (Lonsway, 2002: 62), the separating space of the ludic online. Internet "connectivity can provide a pass, a port and a presence for entering into a new way of life" where "the peculiar spatial quality of cyberspace as a cultural domain for dispersion, decentring and discontinuity comes into its own" (Luke, 2002: 524, 522).

The Internet allows distracting access to the distant: "all the way to Dubai, you are able to get it on the Net." Pictures – "usually they will use [images of] ladies" (female Chinese travel agent) – can particularly entice those online to ludic immersion. "Some of the people like to look at pictures because of the distraction"; "for me, I think I like to look at pictures first" (male Malay). Some web pages are hermeneutically dense with text, over-crowded with description and information. These repel rather than offer a route to relaxation. Sites should be more "user friendly": some are "not that attractive, for example like the Flight Centre, they put too many words, too many descriptions"; "when we want to travel, of course we want to look more at [attractive?] pictures" (female Chinese).

The tourist's ludic gaze: when play becomes work

Conceptualizing Internet users as ludic in their immediate focus on the hypermediated space of the web overcomes binary oppositions between "virtual experience" and "our larger spatial context," real life (Lonsway, 2002: 61). In rejecting this reductive framework, play is seen as an activity occurring in life-worlds both offline and online. From a ludic perspective, seated in front of a computer screen, we are understood as absorbed by/ in cyberspace not as Cartesian "disembodied minds" released from corporeal existence, but rather as continually refocusing, keyboard using, "corporeal players."

As a place for cognitive play, Internet space is "scapic," read as facilitating "cultural sustenance or human desire" (Lonsway, 2002: 63). For people engage in a "complex sign play" (Featherstone, 1991: 24), with the web seen to support or subvert the accomplishment of readers' goals. A meaningful virtual space and time is a "social accomplishment" (Wakeford, 2003b: 395), articulated by audiences online in cognitive play.

Websites can address a ludic browser who is focusing playfully (with intrinsic interest) on the Internet's remediated content, perhaps after accessing a menu of hypertext connections. Such "menu-based interactivity" (Manovich, 2001: 38) offers those surfing online a list of alternative narratives (parallel possibilities or syntagmatic structures of knowledge) supporting immersion in virtual content.[6]

But travel websites can also meet the more instrumentally motivated, liminally ludic visitor seeking access to particular practical information (e.g., with a site-specific search engine) to satisfy a real world purpose. "Once on the Net, they seek to leverage cyberspace to serve various offline agendas" (Luke, 2002: 519). He or she may be engaged in work, suppressing the playful moment of Internet access, physically placed, perhaps, on the edge of others' ludic online access in a cybercafé (Laegran and Stewart, 2003: 372).[7]

Self-contained enjoyment of cyberspace (celebrating the intrinsic interest of the Internet) is to be contrasted with online access mediated through an instrumental concern with its real world use. For tourist consumer and those manufacturing the experience there is a "shifting boundary of holiday and everyday" (Franklin and Crang, 2001: 7). Likewise, a web page can be read from distinct horizons of understanding. Distinguishing between people's intrinsic and extrinsic interest in websites, comparing the latter's status as ludic spaces with their online support for work, Slater writes of how "immersive experiences, in which identity and sociality are treated with deep seriousness, give way to, for example, more instrumental uses of the Internet, clearly integrated into everyday life" (2002: 539). To study the Internet

> "as culture means regarding it as a social space in its own right, rather than as a complex object used within other, contextualizing spaces," as "a postmodern space of transformation" (e.g., the remediation of content and character in chat rooms) rather than as a "tool, and hence part of a modernist orientation to the new media as something used instrumentally within wider social projects." (Ibid.: 534)

The distinction between an intrinsic and instrumental navigational use of a website is that of a less or more selective accessing of home page and hypertext (an extensive or intensive focus on content); it is between browsing seductive simulacra, pleasurable pictures, or looking for specific travel-related information (e.g., hotels). Content is clearly appreciated differently in either case. Our contributors indicated an intrinsic interest in web content with their recognition that, in an explorative navigation of images and information, Malaysians "like to read much ... when they browse through the websites" (male Malay). A ludic enjoyment of distraction prevails.

On the other hand, an instrumental use of the Internet is declared in such judgments as, "if I want to go to travel ... to make life easier, I surf through the website" (e.g., for hotel accommodation) (male Malay). Corporate sites must allow such a customer to "go straight to the point," "which part they want." In the budget airline Air Asia's (air.asia.com) online ticketing site, "they instantly give you the flight schedules" (male Malay). Web page adequacy is a function of epistemological need, of people not deciding "they need more information than this" (female, Malay, trans.).

For travelers, of course, the instrumental offline motive behind a fact-gathering focus on the Internet can also be ludic, realizing the materially focused tourist gaze in a holiday.

Moment 2: anticipation – projection

The travel site as generic possibility of cognitive play

Travel-related websites were classified by focus group contributors as instances of functional types (or genres), addressing different audiences. Pages online support varying forms of cognitive play, with users assuming (or projecting) likely content. The latter is "checked out" with details further ascertained in the process of reading through the "projective space of online life" (Slater, 2002: 539). Tourism boards and travel agencies engage in generic narrowcasting to consumers, addressing cultural or budget issues, respectively:

> Each type, all the tourism boards and travel agencies, always they have different purposes to publish their website. And as for tourism boards, they will provide more towards cultural insights or information, and as for the agencies they just provide budgets, the locations. (Female Chinese)

Generic address to travelers can invoke the "previously unseen, purchased, or browsed" (Elmer, 2003: 245). Identifying customers' needs can be politically contentious. Encouraging some types of travelers to come from overseas may be at odds with locally preferred perceptions of national character. Constructing authenticity is a "powerful currency in imagining national identity" (McRae, 2003: 238). Here, arguments can be heard for the protection of a country's culture through the regulation of advertising (Frith, 2003: 37). The Australian Visit [the State of] Victoria site welcomes gays and lesbians ("this type of creature ... this type of people": male Malay). But explicit recognition of sexual minorities as citizens in its mode of address to consumers is unlikely on an Asian government tourism web page.[8] The Victorian travel website welcomes the world,

> "lesbian and gay ... everyone can come," "it's a place where, maybe, this lesbian and gay, they can find a life-partner," "more open lah!" "They don't hide, they say what they want to say inside the page," "they give the real thing." Here, "maybe they want to protect the image of Malaysia as a Muslim country, so they don't list [?] this kind of thing." (Male Malay)

Accessing the Malaysian government website (www.tourism.gov.my), distinct visual enjoyment is available for audiences of both genders gazing at the women wearing national costumes: "if males surf through the Net I think they will say, 'wow, they're pretty!,' but as for us, I think, 'yah, that's the way we like the costumes [?]'" (female Chinese). Such pleasure distracts a little from patriarchal "gender-power relations in tourism" (Aitchison, 2001: 134).

Internet travel sites establish a horizon of narrative expectations for a user regarding the latter's real world tourism: "by this information, consumers can decide their expectations for some country, to travel" (male, Malay). Our travel offline tests assumptions generated online.

Moment 3: articulation – production

Cyberspace as circular: the tourist gaze as holistic looking
Pursuing an encompassing hermeneutic circle of understanding, the tourist look achieves a holistic comprehension of narrative content online. Gazing to and fro, readers flexibly focus on Internet page and part, following hyperlinks: "those websites are ok in terms of providing complete information" (male, Chinese, trans.). Seeking facts to fully satisfy her or his information needs in being online, the tourist's attention plays across a text to relate items to their wider context, composing and comprehending a totality (or closure) of "arrangeable" (female Indian) useful knowledge. A travel site (Reliance) is "systematic," but it downloads "one part by one part" (female Indian), slowing this syntagmatic (monolinear) process of integration.

Unstructured "crowded" or "messy" information ("not properly or well arranged": male Chinese, trans.) renders the reader's ludic assembling of coherent web page narratives more problematic, potentially undermining a site's usefulness. A hermeneutically "heavy" Internet location resists the cognitive play of user comprehension: it is possible to become bored rather than browsing or lose one's focus, emerging a "bit dizzy" (female Chinese).

The tourist's ludic look as encountering indeterminacy
Cyber-surfing, like sport, is often uncertain in result. Discussing the Internet from the perspective of her intended customers, the travel agency manager considered travel sites "very friendly, user friendly," "you just get in and they tell you, 'next, next, next'." Here, the reader's anticipation is actualized: the narrative of hypertext use is easy to complete, to form a coherent account of content. (Otherwise, users say "it's incomplete.")

On the other hand, our travel agent pointed out, travelers can find a "website has too many choices," an indeterminacy offering excessive possibility of cognitive (and material) play leaving them confused, challenging their holistic formation of decision-guiding information. Here, a real world travel agency (such as her own) can assist in securing plans.

But website surfer-visitors, like players, can enjoy speculating on uncertainty. The site for Reliance Travel "brings some kind of emotion to the users": clicking on its hyperlinks, different web pages "come out one after another, making the users curious about what will come out next, so it attracts the customers" (female Malay, trans.). A site "stimulates curiosity" (female Chinese), cognitive play, but in different ways, depending on source and sought-for audience.

The look of the website: aesthetic judgment online
Accessing travel sites online, like play on a sports field, can be the focus of aesthetic judgment. Style is emulated and enjoyed. "Design choice is very important in terms of image" to instantly attract the customer's "ten second" focus (female Malay). The Reliance site's "cooling colour is very suitable for travel agencies" (female Indian), a "very good combination of colours" (male Malay). Visit Victoria Australia website has "natural colours" (female Indian). In this aesthetics of ludic engagement, bright colors can promote attention from Internet surfers, be used for color coding or corporate identification. Web pages contain "more colour to attract their customers, sometimes they use bright colours" (male Malay).

Characterized by complexity of color, Malaysian sites foreground images: Western counterparts online emphasize information. The former are "all focused on pictures," "we want something that we can see," whereas Westerners want "information based" "reading material" (female Chinese).

Tourist marketing increasingly relies on designers of new media for which the claim has been made that (through high quality or navigable images) they bring the user closer to an ideal state in which there is (apparently) no intervening mediation of reality at all (Bolter, 2002: 79). But images on a website may also function as icons, prompting user interest, guiding playful interaction, offering hypertext connections (e.g., a picture of a cruise ship).

A website's use of color can produce alternative responses from different ethnic groups. Potentially viewed as lucky by the Chinese, the emphatic "reddish" coding at Flight Centre (red, white) suggests "something regarding fear," the "coloured emotion" (female Indian). Flight Centre, "because of the colour you are not attracted" (female Indian). Flight Centre's red colour is "not very attractive" (Malay female).

Images online may be both pleasurably entertaining and productive of enigma. Looking at the multi-ethnic women on the Malaysian government website, the Chinese travel agent responded, "We ladies, we enjoy looking at beautiful women too": the women "make you look twice" as a speculative response to the enigma, "Why is she in there?"

Moment 4: appropriation – positioning

Tourist play, product positioning, and the cultivation of trust
Culture is electronically endemic to cyberspace, written into personal and professional home pages (Kim and Papacharissi, 2003: 113). As consumer-citizens, Malaysians easily recognized their nation's tourist sites. The cultural proximity between percipients and web page (e.g., www.tourism.gov.my) allowed swift identification of the latter as their own. Assumptions as to content are consistently fulfilled, encouraging these visitors to feel at home on sites with which "we are more comfortable" (female Malay focus group moderator).

Even pages featuring women wearing ethnic costume conspicuously addressing potential tourists "in some ways" looked like Malaysia; "culture plays an important role in tourism" (female Chinese). Such images establish a Malaysian corporate presence in the international tourism industry for "easy identification" by business and consumers alike, "ah, they know it's Malaysia" (female Chinese). Establishing her local identity or "version of self" (Wakeford, 2003b: 389), a Chinese student pointed out that these online representations of nationhood are novel "for outside only" foreigners.

Yet in employing these visual signifiers of feminine ethnicity, the Malaysian government tourism website displays narrative images suggesting welcoming communities of a distinctive national character, implying alignment of would-be hosts with visitors' interests as consumers. Hosts, of course, can themselves imagine being guests at different times and places (Sherlock, 2001: 272). If "I'm not a Malaysian and I see the website, I feel welcomed by the picture, you know, the women, they smile, the way they wear [clothes], quite different from the other countries ... we've got many different racial [groups]." Women, rather than men, invite the tourist, for the former are "more easy to approach, approachable" (female Chinese).

Such elliptical reference to empathetic communities online is also important locally. It allows Internet marketing of tourism in the Malaysian context to constructively embody the "personal human touch" between customer and travel agent. In the absence of such signifiers online, if tourists attempt to make travel arrangements via these web pages, there would be no suggestion of commitment to the personal support they anticipate. This could discourage them from continuing (Suraya, 2003). We are consumer-citizens expecting an ethical response.

Hence web pages need to underwrite consumers' "cybertrust" or "confident expectation" (Dutton and Shepherd, 2006), to "give assurance to the customer" (female Indian) and support their confidence in the tourism products on commercial offer. "We are not made confident enough just by clicking through the Internet" (female Indian). In the absence of an experienced friend's advice, hyperlinks to digital video could allow those interested in purchasing a "package" to share (immersively) online previous customers' holiday pleasures. Likewise, through clients' feedback on locations visited, that's "how they can build a society there ... a community, I think, a tourism community" online (female Chinese). "Some of [the websites] are really lacking about the assurances for customers" (female Indian). "If you need to do online booking, it is very much depending on one's confidence level" (female Malay, trans.).

In displaying communities of citizens, tourism board web pages often focus on cultural aspects of a nation's identity. Websites associated with tourism represent Malaysia in conflicting ways, not always reassuring. "From an Australian point of view it's different from [the] Malaysian point of view" (female Malay). In discourses about the country, the narrative horizons of the Australian government's Department of Foreign Affairs and Trade, on the one hand, and the Malaysian government's Tourism Board, on the other, are opposed. "An Australian, for example, who wants to come to Malaysia," and consequently visited both Australian government and Malaysian tourism sites, "would be utterly confused" (female Chinese) by web page narratives supporting conflicting projections of likely experience in the country. At the heart of these disparate accounts of Malaysia on websites is religious belief. The Australian Travel Advisory site's negative warnings about Islamic terrorism can be set against the Malaysian Tourism Board's positive images of welcoming Muslim women.

> "The Australian website stresses so much on extreme caution, how the traveler should really take care ... everywhere that they go"; whereas on the Malaysian tourism website, "Malaysia is like a heaven," "a lot of words and phrases that were used suggest that Malaysia is a very safe place, everything is

cheap and wonderful, stuff like that"; the Australian and Malaysian sites, "those two are really two different worlds." (Female Chinese)

Readers, then, perceive these travel websites from informed horizons of understanding which allow citizens both recognition of their subject matter (e.g., as Australia or Malaysia) and the realization that constituent pages may construct nations in opposing ways (e.g., as dangerous or safe). The online definition of a country's character can be shared by customers who identify with the perspective taken, or challenged by those who wish to critically distance themselves. In this way, users underwrite their identity, constructing a sense of self through Internet access (Turkle, 1997: 145).

Counter-factual identification, practiced here as imagined alignment with a website's addressee (while distinguishing oneself from such a person) is also a possible response to matters considered online. Positioning herself as a foreign tourist with a consumer's instrumental interest in travel conditions, a Malaysian Chinese student acknowledged that the Australian government site's "advice that they were offering about Malaysia," "some of it, well probably it's not very flattering about Malaysia, but it's true." "If I were a tourist in another country, it's something that I would want to know about, you know, the health situation or the economic crisis."

The tourist gaze at a "playful space" of political consequence
Accessing websites, like engaging in games, maintains and enhances the powerful status and political perspectives of citizens who own their means of production. Football can support familiar bigotry, frequently visited home pages make firm profits. Hence, ludic space and time are continually the focus of political interests: they do not offer an "eclipse of controls" (Featherstone, 1991: 24), a "playful space beyond determination" (ibid.: 84).

On tourist agency home pages, as in less traveled corners of cyberspace, "modes of digital interaction may simply provide a more effective means of co-opting the user" into a website's ideology (Bolter, 2002: 86). In the absence of criticism, political messages (whether explicit or implicit) are consumed, confirmed, and circulated. Representations of a nation as dangerous or delightful, on news or tourism site, are upheld.

Perceptions of enabling tourist web technology
With the advent of the Internet "there has been a liberation of the people in their quest for information" (Halim, 2001: 121). New technology supports finding fresh ways of informing the consumer. Changing screen media

(as from television to the Internet) means changing the message mode. "We have to change our style ... adjusting to the technology." "The message of the advertisement, make it like a story, you know" (female Indian) online, with the narrative structure of its content recognized in consumer understanding.

More often emphasizing fun than serious-mindedness, the Internet chat room is "predominantly recreational" (Crystal, 2001: 169). Such online spaces for "voicing out" could be linked to travel sites, forming communities of just-returned and would-be tourists located at portals in cyberspace. This would be for "generations to come" (female Chinese travel agent), a marketing tool of uneven reliability. On existing web pages, travelers are addressed as consumers of products rather than citizens who would contribute, perhaps, to a chat room public sphere discussion on environmentalism and tourism (Wang, 2002: 74).

Conclusion

"We just understand about the Harry Potter!" (Malay female). Hermeneutics resists accounts of audiences merely absorbing media content. Instead, drawing on a meaning-constitutive background of presuppositions, often crossing unfamiliar cultural horizons, the viewer's interpretative accomplishment of understanding media narrative is given close analysis. Research methodologies make implicit epistemological assumptions about the construction of knowledge by both investigator and investigated – the forming of their respective "subjectivities." Internet hermeneutics posits people's coming to understand a web page as a process which is continually, temporally, in play.

While drawing on past retention (the memory of previous sites), Internet use is simultaneously projected towards the future (protention, or anticipation of developments). Equipped with generic knowledge of web texts as instances of types, viewers anticipate their meaning (e.g., as entertainment, news or media focused). Research employing the close empirical scrutiny enabled by focus groups maps an audience's hermeneutic processing of content through such cognitive activities of media consumption, forming an emic or participant perspective. Listening to contributors' discourse, tacit themes (e.g., pluralism in news reports as a preferred value) may be discerned within their narrative responses, a focus for integrating individuals' reactions.

In discussing the present paradigmatic exemplar, we have thematized and considered analytically the knowledge-constituting structure of the tourist gaze – or ludic looking – online. The traveler's cognitive play on the Internet, we have seen, has both intrinsic and instrumental (extrinsic) motivation. The tourist gaze becomes liminally ludic when play-like in producing meaning, identity, and political power yet seeking information for everyday needs.

From time to time online one needs to engage in persistent play to access useful information beyond the home page. The ludic becomes strenuous, one has to "really search" for good deals, be "hard working," it's "not that easy." Nevertheless, access produces eudaemonic effect, ludic well-being. There is fair play on the Internet, "everybody has got what they paid for": using credit card information, "you go to E-bay, you put it in," "nobody questions that any more" (female Chinese travel agent).

Travel pages on the Internet offer people accessing them possibilities of ludic escape, both virtual and material. For those online motivated by an intrinsic interest in distracting content, site features encouraging absorption are important (e.g., menus hyperlinked to images of interesting destinations). Among tour agents or travelers with an instrumental purpose in using websites for real world achievement (work), easy access to specific Internet content (e.g., using a search engine) is important. This cognitive engagement in constituting meaning is dutiful. Such work abstracts from distracting tourism.

In conclusion, responding to both e-journalism and e-tourism, our consumer-citizens wish to resist their nation's branding as a source of terror. In contesting media power they challenge the way social reality is "defined or named" (Couldry, 2003: 39). Democratically engaged, they distance themselves from an identity they perceive as media constructed. In Malaysian national advertising the corporate voice speaks of a harmonious nation. Who "carries the responsibility" to ensure accuracy of media representation (Livingstone et al., 2007: 106) elsewhere?

Notes

1 The CNN.Asia website has now been redesigned and located at www.edition. cnn.com/ASIA/ (accessed May 11, 2003).
2 The possibility they offer of escape from the everyday must surely promote the popularity of Internet Virtual Environments (Axelsson et al., 2003).

3   Patricia Kho, Manager of the Reliance Travel Agency in Kuching, Sarawak, gen-
    erously provided her professional perception of the role played by websites in
    the travel industry.
4   In extracts from the focus groups, translations from Malay to English (signified
    by "trans.") are by Raja Mazhatul Yasmin Suraya. Transcriptions of contribu-
    tors' Malaysian English were produced by the author.
5   A set of six online travel sites was selected to initiate this media reception
    research on Internet use at the Faculty of Economics and Business, University of
    Malaysia, Sarawak (June 30, 2003). Seeking consumer-citizen responses to vari-
    ous forms of online marketing presence, the investigators asked student par-
    ticipants to access three categories of Malaysian and Australian home pages,
    prior to discussing their experience in focus groups. Aware of the need to
    accommodate ethnic variation in readership (or in Malay terms, establish a
    "rojak" media reception theory), the sites selected were judged by the research-
    ers to constitute prominent private and public sector provision of travel infor-
    mation, marketing and purchasing possibility across Asian and Caucasian
    cultures:

    1   *Websites for travel agencies with shops*
        www.reliancetravel.com
        www.flightcentre.com.au
    2   *Websites for virtual travel agencies*
        www.asiatravelmart.com
        www.travel.com.au
    3   *Websites for tourism boards*
        www.tourism.gov.my
        www.visitvictoria.com

Subsequently (July 15, 2003), at Universiti Putra Malaysia (UPM) in suburban
Kuala Lumpur, the online discourses accessed during this research were extended
to include four further websites providing information to Caucasian travelers
arriving in a Malaysia represented as being "truly Asia": the Australian Department
of Foreign Affairs and Trade (Travel Advisory on Malaysia) site which was compared with the Malaysian government's web pages for tourists: and two sites
established by Malaysian hard copy newspapers, *Harakah* and the *New Straits
Times*, with contrasting Islamic views of current events in the country:

    4   *Government websites*
        www.dfat.gov.au/zw-cgi/view/Advice/Malaysia
        www.tourism.gov.my
    5   *Websites for newspapers*
        www.harakahdaily.net/
        www.emedia.com.my

Participants in focus groups at the University of Malaysia Sarawak were volunteer students from the Faculty of Economics and Business recruited by a notice announcing the research. There were four groups, each with between three to four members from different ethnic backgrounds and hence likely diversity of response, producing a total of fourteen contributors: three female and one male Chinese, two Indian females, five female and three male Malays. After reading the travel sites for one hour, participants met the two academic researchers (a female Malay and male Caucasian) to consider their responses in tape-recorded discussions. Each of these lasted between forty-five minutes and one hour, producing the contributions analyzed in detail above.

The following day, both researchers visited the manager of the Kuching office operated by one of Malaysia's national tourism agencies, who participated in a recorded interview. In her daily experience, online travel sites are clearly associated for the most part with work rather than play. Her response to them could be described as liminally ludic. While her comprehension of their content was specifically goal-oriented in its formation of meaning, she perceived them from the perspective of professional duty as supporting others' escape from mundane life rather than her own. These work-informing reactions are especially valuable here as potential refutation of touristic reception theory in which responses to the screen are considered to be fundamentally ludic.

Finally, at the Faculty of Modern Languages and Communication, Universiti Putra Malaysia, a focus group was conducted by the author in which the four government and newspaper websites (above) were considered at length by three female students (two Chinese, one Malay) of mass communication (broadcasting, journalism, and public relations where "we learn to face the public") (female Malay). Here, across diversity of response, how national and religious identity are represented on travel sites emerged as an important topic.

All the focus group conversations were lightly structured around three questions, which initiated but did not constrict the direction taken by each stage of the discussion. These were:

1   Reading and Information – do you find the sites make "easy reading," supporting users in navigating through them using web page menus and hypertext connections to locate comprehensible and comprehensive information?
2   Recognition and Identification – do the sites encourage potential tourists to visit Malaysia or Australia with accounts of these countries which you can recognize as accurate or with distorted stereotyped representations?
3   Recommendations for Sites – do you want to make any recommendations about altering site content: how do you see future use of the Internet for advertising to, and advising, travelers?

Associate Professor Dr. Ezhar Tamam kindly invited students to attend the focus group at Universiti Putra Malaysia.

6   Influenced by the way screens look online, new television foregrounds fram-
     ing and content menus. A convergent aesthetic has replaced the "transparent"
     simplicities of naturalism with a hypermediated image whose "mediating
     machinery" (Fornas, 2002: 93) is disclosed. "TV content is now increasingly
     stylized to suggest an interface rather than a surface" (Vered, 2002: 41).

7   Luke writes of a historical tendency to move from an intrinsic enjoyment of the
     Internet (play) to its exclusive instrumental use (work). "The initial interface of
     disembodied subjectivity, distributed community and cybernetic play cele-
     brated in the early days of the net is rapidly being eclipsed by newer interface
     values tied to reimagining cyberspace as hyperreal estate, virtual markets and
     online e-commerce" (2002: 523). Yet subsequently he suggests the ludic use of
     the Internet without further extrinsic purpose is increasing. "This effusion of
     humans and machines in a progressive pact of transcendent unity … is leading
     more toward MP3 downloads, $8 online stock trades on Ameritrade, 24 × 7
     swap meets on eBay, and cyberporn on demand" (ibid.: 524).

8   According to Power's (prejudicial) account of Asian values, for the latter the
     (heterosexual) family is foundation and fulcrum of society, marginalizing sexual
     minorities. "For 'collectivist' cultures, the ingroup is usually fairly tight and is
     often limited to family" (2003: 4).

Conclusion

Media User Theory: Going Beyond Accumulation of Audiences

There are "unanswered questions in audience research" (Morley, 2006). Investigations have "got stuck at the level of *accumulation*" of "numbers of studies" (Barker, 2006: 126, 128, emphasis in the original). My aim in *Understanding Media Users* has been a brief narrative of the subject from which I hope has emerged a theoretical grounding which "transcends" or acts as a foundation for empirical accumulation of studies.

My conclusion (from a phenomenological perspective initiated by Heidegger's *Being and Time*) is that media "understanding" is a five-stage process of absorption/anticipation, articulation, and appropriation of or alienation from screen content. Silence may signal apathy. We can arrive at this model through abstract analysis (abduction) of audience claims to comprehend rather than generalization (induction) – and it may be tested in potentially falsifying focus groups or interviews. Not surprisingly after thirty years of media research, there is accord between this philosophical psychology and Barker's own "almost unarguable truths about audiences" (2006: 124). As groundwork for post-positivist studies of perception, the former underwrites the latter.

In media user studies, the "patterns and processes" (Barker, 2006: 124) of audience response are an important focus: an emphasis on "film form that takes into account the mental processes of audiences" is "commendable" (ibid.: 134). Watching the screen we *ipso facto* "build expectations," "guiding selections" providing the "resources for conceiving self and the world" (ibid.: 124). The audience is not always active: it can become absorbed in content, the "deliberate letting go in the face of desired experiences, which require(s) passivity" (ibid.: 125). There is "no way of separating out the cognitive and the [*sic*] emotional responses" (ibid.: 126).

Barker's epistemological ambitions for audience studies are hermeneutic. He calls for work on how interpretative communities are constituted or crossed (in Gadamer's terms how people share "horizons of understanding," generate "horizons of expectation," or engage in a "fusion of horizons"). In her essay introducing his work, Press (2006: 96) indicates that he considers "how to explain the relations between the 'reading positions' of different interpretive communities." We can theorize this relationship as one of occupying different horizons of understanding from which varying projections of meaning occur (to be subsequently tested by audiences checking on narrative events). Positioning on a horizon of claimed conceptual insight may be contested.

Martin Barker argues like Martin Heidegger that there should be a fore-grounding of "typicality" and an emphasis on viewing as "motivated" (by intrinsic or instrumental interest?). He dwells on the concept of audience "projection" (their "understanding of what is happening which may have to be checked and revised as the film proceeds") (2006: 134).

Morley also wishes to interrogate accumulation or generalization in research. The "process of extrapolation from ethnographic examples is one that always needs to be handled with particular care" (2006: 106). Remembering his earlier call to distinguish analysis of perception on the one hand from political scrutiny of a program's power on the other, he writes that we "need to disentangle the elements of comprehension and evaluation" (ibid.: 110). Phenomenology as a philosophical psychology could be said to "put the process back" into perception. It offers us an account of the audience's time-structured decoding activity or the herme-neutic "dimensions" of their discourse about the "processes of audience meaning-making" (Schroder, 2000: 237). Signs support their percipients' focus on both present and future.

In this philosophical psychology, informed absorption in content and anticipation of meaning are simultaneous: they are passive-active aspects of the same media engagement. On the other hand, articulation and appro-priation of meaning are necessarily successive moments in media use. Audience articulation of a narrative checks on the accuracy of their antici-pation: likewise appropriation presupposes a coherent meaning has emerged from constructing a text. Absorption is motivated (cf. Schroder, 2000: 244) by intrinsic interest in a text or weakened by instrumental interest in the use which it may serve ("relevance"). Both are an opposite response from the kind of alienated reading of content which regards it as constructed.

From Decoding Programs to Projecting Narratives

The encoding/decoding model (Hall, 1981) of television programs and viewer response was originally developed to understand the "interpretative gap" between production and reception during mass communication

(Livingstone, 2007c: 167). Roscoe et al. identify the audience's perceptual "decoding" of textual signs as at the heart of the "making sense process" (1995: 90). But while production and understanding are thereby connected by Hall's model, the structured process of reception itself is not considered. It is a "missing link" (Hoijer, 1992: 584). Yet as discursive psychologists such as Harré and Billig have argued, we can hear that activity occurring during focus groups and interviews: the "inner life is constituted by the outer activity of communication" (Billig, 1997: 217). The process of understanding (projection) can be found patterning what people have to say about programs.

We need to look at "specific reception patterns" (Ang, 1990: 244), locating them within wider frameworks. Reception by its very nature relates cultural moments of interpretation: the remembered past enables prediction. For the very moment in which our fore-structured understanding of a text commences designates our deductive projection or fore-concept of future meaning. Earlier in this exploration of media use, our Chinese aunt identified her cellphone numbers as those of friend or foe, making or menacing her day. Where responses to texts are thought through theoretically by researchers as educated expectation, we can relate culture to reading as the platform of informed anticipation by the active audience – and the place of powerful struggle. Phenomenology allows us to place constructing (projecting and positioning) meaning on screen within contested horizons of understanding – conceptualizing reception as a "deeply politicized, cultural [process]" (Ang, 1990: 244).

References

Abercrombie, N. (1996) *Television and Society*. Cambridge: Polity Press.

Adams, K. (2004) "The Genesis of Touristic Imagery Politics and Poetics in the Creation of a Remote Indonesian Island Destination," *Tourist Studies* 4(2) 115–135.

Agamben, G. (1998) *Homo Sacer: Sovereign Power and Bare Life*. Stanford, CA: Stanford University Press.

Ahuvia, A. C. (2005) "Beyond the Extended Self: Loved Objects and Consumers' Identity Narratives," *Journal of Consumer Research* 32 (June) 171–184.

Aitchison, C. (2001) "Theorizing Other Discourses of Tourism, Gender and Culture: Can the Subaltern Speak (in Tourism)?" *Tourist Studies* 1(2) 133–147.

Alasuutari, P. (1999) "Introduction: Three Phases of Reception Studies" in P. Alasuutari (ed.) *Rethinking the Media Audience*. London: Sage, pp. 1–21.

Allen, R. C. (1985) *Speaking of Soap Operas*. Chapel Hill: University of North Carolina Press.

Alneng, V. (2002) "The Modern Does Not Cater for Natives: Travel Ethnography and the Conventions of Form," *Tourist Studies* 2(2) 119–142.

Amerika, M. (2004) "Anticipating the Present: An Artist's Intuition," *New Media and Society* 6(1) 71–76.

Ang, I. (1990) "Culture and Communication: Towards an Ethnographic Critique of Media Consumption in the Transnational Media System," *European Journal of Communication* 5 239–260.

Ang, I. (1996) *Living Room Wars: Rethinking Media Audiences for a Postmodern World*. London: Routledge.

Ang, I. (2003) "Representing Social Life in a Conflictive Global World: From Diaspora to Hybridity," Working Paper Series, *David C. Lam Institute for East-West Studies*, Hong Kong.

Applbaum, K. and I. Jordt (1996) "Notes Towards an Application of McCracken's 'Cultural Categories' for Cross-Cultural Consumer Research," *Journal of Consumer Research* 23 (December) 204–218.

Arnold, S. J. and E. Fischer (1994) "Hermeneutics and Consumer Research," *Journal of Consumer Research* 21 (June) 55–71.

Arnould, E. J. and C. J. Thompson (2005) "Consumer Culture Theory (CCT): Twenty Years of Research," *Journal of Consumer Research* 31(4) 868–882.

Aronson, J. (1994) "A Pragmatic View of Thematic Analysis," *The Qualitative Report* 2(1). www.nova.edu/ssss/QR/BackIssues/QR2–1/aronson.html. Accessed March 23, 2004.

Arsenault, A. and M. Castells (2006) "Conquering the Minds, Conquering Iraq: The Social Production of Misinformation in the Unites States – A Case Study," *Information, Communication and Society* 9(3) 284–307.

Arvidsson, A. (2005) "Brands: A Critical Perspective," *Journal of Consumer Culture* 5(2) 235–258.

Askwith, I. D. (2007) "*Television 2.0: Reconceptualizing TV as an Engagement Medium*." MSc thesis, Massachusetts Institute of Technology.

Axelsson, A. S., A. Abelin, and R. Schroeder (2003) "Anyone Speak Spanish? Language Encounters in Multi-User Virtual Environments and the Influence of Technology," *New Media and Society* 5(4) 475–498.

Baker, R. and S. Ball (eds.) (1969) *Violence and the Media*. Washington, DC: US Government Printing Office.

Bandura, A. (2002) "Social Cognitive Theory of Mass Communication" in J. Bryant and D. Zillmann (eds.) *Media Effects: Advances in Theory and Research*. Mahwah, NJ: Lawrence Erlbaum, pp. 121–154.

Barker, M. (2001) "The Newson Report: A Case Study in 'Common Sense'" in M. Barker and J. Petley (eds.) *Ill Effects: The Media/Violence Debate*. London: Routledge, pp. 27–46.

Barker, M. (2003) "Assessing the 'Quality' in Qualitative Research: The Case of Text-Audience Relations," *European Journal of Communication* 18(3) 315–335.

Barker, M. (2004) "News, Reviews, Clues, Interviews and Other Ancillary Materials: A Critique and Research Proposal," *Scope: An Online Journal of Film Studies*. February. www.nottingham.ac.uk/film/scopearchive/articles/news-reviews.htm. Accessed November 2005.

Barker, M. (2005) "Research Note: *The Lord of the Rings* and 'Identification': A Critical Encounter," *European Journal of Communication* 20(3) 353–378.

Barker, M. (2006) "I Have Seen the Future and It Is Not Here Yet; or, On Being Ambitious for Audience Research," *Communication Review* 9 123–141.

Barker, M. and K. Brooks (1998) *Knowing Audiences: Judge Dredd, Its Friends, Fans and Foes*. Luton: University of Luton Press.

Barker, M. and J. Petley (2001) "Introduction: From Bad Research to Good – a Guide for the Perplexed" in M. Barker and J. Petley (eds.) *Ill Effects The Media/ Violence Debate*. London: Routledge, pp. 1–26.

Barthes, R. (1974) *S/Z*. Trans. R. Miller. New York: Hill and Wang.

Barthes, R. (1977) "From Work to Text" in R. Barthes, *Image-Music-Text*. Fontana: London, pp. 155–164.

Bassett, C. (2007) "Of Distance and Closeness: The Work of Roger Silverstone," *New Media and Society* 9(1) 42–48.

Bauman, Z. (2003) "The Tourist Syndrome" (interview with Adrian Franklin), *Tourist Studies* 3(2) 205–217.

Belk, R. W. and G. Tumbat (2005) "The Cult of Macintosh," *Consumption, Markets and Culture* 8(3) 205–217.

Bennett, W. L. (2003) "Communicating Global Activism: Strengths and Vulnerabilities of Networked Politics," *Information, Communication and Society* 6(2) 143–168.

Billig, M. (1997) "From Codes to Utterances: Cultural Studies, Discourse and Psychology" in M. Ferguson and P. Golding (eds.) *Cultural Studies in Question*. London: Sage, pp. 205–226.

Bird, E. (2003) *The Audience in Everyday Life: Living in a Media World*. London: Routledge.

Bobo, J. (1988) "*The Color Purple*: Black Women as Cultural Readers" in E. D. Pribram (ed.) *Female Spectators: Looking at Film and Television*. London: Verso, pp. 90–109.

Boczkowski, P. J. (2004) "Books to Think With," *New Media and Society* 6(1) 144–150.

Boellstorff, T. (2006) "A Ludicrous Discipline? Ethnography and Games Studies," *Games and Culture* 1(1) 29–35.

Bolter, J. D. (2002) "Formal Analysis and Cultural Critique in Digital Media Theory," *Convergence* 8(4) 77–88.

Bordwell, D. (1989) *Making Meaning: Inference and Rhetoric in the Interpretation of Cinema*. Cambridge, MA: Harvard University Press.

Bourdieu, P. (1995) "Some Properties of Fields" in *Sociology in Question*. London: Sage. Quoted in Rocamora, A. (2002) "Fields of Fashion: Critical Insights into Bourdieu's Sociology of Culture," *Journal of Consumer Culture* 2(3) 341–362.

Bovenizer, E. (2000) "Presentation 02/06/00: Chapter 5: *A Hermeneutical Circle from Theory to Cultural Literacy*." www.sw2.euv-frankfurt-o.de/Doktoranden/hermeneutics.html. Accessed March 5, 2004.

Brehony, K. J. (1996) "Texts, Meaning and Interpretation: Hermeneutics and Historical Research." Paper presented to the Joint Conference of the *Canadian History of Education Association* and the *History of Education Society* (USA) at OISE, University of Toronto, Canada.

Brewster, B. (1975) "Editorial," *Screen* 16(1) 5–6.

Brewster, B. and C. MacCabe (1974) "Editorial," *Screen* 15(1) 4–10.

Brewster, B., E. Cowie, J. Halliday, K. Hanet, S. Heath, C. MacCabe, P. Willemen, and P. Wollen (1976) "Reply to 'Why We Have Resigned from the Board of *Screen*,'" *Screen* 17(2) 106–116.

Brey, P. (1997) "Philosophy of Technology Meets Social Constructivism," *Techne: Journal of the Society for Philosophy and Technology* 2(3–4).

Brunette, P. (2000) "Post-Structuralism and Deconstruction" in J. Hill and P. C. Gibson (eds.) *Film Studies: Critical Approaches.* Oxford: Oxford University Press, pp. 89–93.

Brunsdon, C. and D. Morley (1978) *Everyday Television: Nationwide.* London: British Film Institute.

Bryant, J. and S. Thompson (2002) *Fundamentals of Media Effects.* New York: McGraw-Hill.

Buckingham, D. (1987) *Public Secrets: EastEnders and Its Audience.* London: British Film Institute.

Buckingham, D. (ed.) (1993) *Reading Audiences: Young People and the Media.* Manchester: Manchester University Press.

Buckingham, D. (2000) *The Making of Citizens: Young People, News and Politics.* London: Routledge.

Buckingham, D. (2006) "Studying Computer Games" in D. Carr, D. Buckingham, A. Burn and G. Schott (eds.) *Computer Games: Text, Narrative and Play.* Cambridge: Polity Press, pp. 1–13.

Bun, C. K. (2002) "Both Sides, Now: A Sociologist Meditates on Culture Contact, Hybridization, and Cosmopolitanism," Working Paper Series, *David C. Lam Institute for East-West Studies,* Hong Kong.

Caillois, R. (1961) *Man, Play and Games.* New York: Free Press.

Caldwell, M. L. (2004) "Domesticating the French Fry: McDonald's and Consumerism in Moscow," *Journal of Consumer Culture* 4(1) 5–26.

Campbell, J. E. (2005) "Outing Planet Out: Surveillance, Gay Marketing and Internet Affinity Portals," *New Media and Society* 7(5) 663–683.

Campbell, S. W. (2007) "A Cross-Cultural Comparison of Perceptions and Uses of Mobile Telephony," *New Media and Society* 9(2) 343–363.

Carducci, V. (2006) "Culture Jamming: A Sociological Perspective," *Journal of Consumer Culture* 6(1) 116–138.

Caronia, L. (2005) "Mobile Culture: An Ethnography of Cellular Phone Uses in Teenagers' Everyday Life," *Convergence* 11(3) 96–103.

Caronia, L. and A. H. Caron (2004) "Constructing a Specific Culture: Young People's Use of the Mobile Phone as a Social Performance," *Convergence* 10(2) 28–61.

Casebier, A. (1991) *Film and Phenomenology.* Cambridge: Cambridge University Press.

Casey, E. (2003) "Gambling and Consumption: Working-Class Women and UK National Lottery Play," *Journal of Consumer Culture* 3(2) 245–263.

Chadha, K. and A. Kavoori (2000) "Media Imperialism Revisited: Some Findings from the Asian Case," *Media, Culture and Society* 22 415–432.

Chan, A. and J. Garrick (2003) "The Moral 'Technologies' of Knowledge Management," *Information, Communication and Society* 6(3) 291–306.

Chan, J. K. and L. Leung (2005) "Lifestyles, Reliance on Traditional News Media and Online News Adoption," *New Media and Society* 7(3) 357–382.

Chandler, D. (1998) "Notes on 'The Gaze'." www.aber.ac.uk/media/Documents/gaze/gaze.html. Accessed February 29, 2004.

Chernev, A. (2004) "Goal Orientation and Consumer Preference for the Status Quo," *Journal of Consumer Research* 31 (December) 557–565.

Cherrier, H. and J. B. Murray (2007) "Reflexive Dispossession and the Self: Constructing a Processual Theory of Identity," *Consumption, Markets and Culture* 10(1) 1–29.

Cheung, M. P. Y. (2003) "Representation, Mediation, and Intervention: A Translation Anthologist's Preliminary Reflections on Three Key Issues in Cross-Cultural Understanding," Working Paper Series, *David C. Lam Institute for East-West Studies*, Hong Kong.

Chitty, N. (2005) "International Communication Continuing into the 21st Century as an Academic 'Commons'," *Gazette: The International Journal for Communication Studies* 67(6) 555–559.

Chow-White, P. A. (2006) "Race, Gender and Sex on the Net," *Media, Culture and Society* 28(6) 883–905.

Coffey, A., B. Holbrook, and P. Atkinson (1996) "Qualitative Data Analysis: Technologies and Representations," *Sociological Research Online* 1(1). www.socresonline.org.uk/socresonline/1/1/4.html. Accessed March 23, 2004.

Cohen, A. A. and D. Lemish (2003) "Real Time and Recall Measures of Mobile Phone Use: Some Methodological Concerns and Empirical Applications," *New Media and Society* 5(2) 167–183.

Connor, S. (n.d.) "Cp or, A Few Don'ts (And Dos) By A Cultural Phenomenologist." www.bbk.ac.uk/eh/eng/skc/cp/whyphen.htm. Accessed March 5, 2004.

Consalvo, M. (2003) "*Zelda 64* and Video Game Fans: A Walkthrough of Games, Intertextuality, and Narrative," *Television and New Media* 4(3) 321–334.

Cooper, G. (2002) "The Mutable Mobile: Social Theory in the Wireless World" in B. Brown, N. Green, and R. Harper (eds.) *Wireless World: Social and Interactional Aspects of the Mobile Age*. London: Springer, pp. 19–31.

Cotte, J., S. Ratneshwar, and D. G. Mick (2004) "The Times of Their Lives: Phenomenological and Metaphorical Characteristics of Consumer Timestyles," *Journal of Consumer Research* 31 (September) 333–345.

Couldry, N. (2000) *Inside Culture: Re-Imagining the Method of Cultural Studies*. London: Sage.

Couldry, N. (2001) "The Hidden Injuries of Media Power," *Journal of Consumer Culture* 1(2) 155–177.

Couldry, N. (2003) "Beyond the Hall of Mirrors? Some Theoretical Reflections on the Global Contestation of Media Power" in N. Couldry and J. Curran (eds.) *Contesting Media Power: Alternative Media in a Networked World*. London: Rowman and Littlefield, pp. 39–54.

Couldry, N. (2004) "The Productive 'Consumer' and the Dispersed 'Citizen'," *International Journal of Cultural Studies* 7(1) 21–32.

Couldry, N. (2005) "The Extended Audience: Scanning the Horizon" in M. Gillespie (ed.) *Media Audiences*. Maidenhead: Open University Press, pp. 183–222.

Couldry, N. (2006a) *Listening Beyond the Echoes: Media, Ethics, and Agency in an Uncertain World*. London: Paradigm Publishers.

Couldry, N. (2006b) "Culture and Citizenship: The Missing Link?" *European Journal of Cultural Studies* 9(3) 321–339.

Couldry, N., S. Livingstone, and T. Markham (2007) *Media Consumption and Public Engagement: Beyond the Presumption of Attention*. London: Palgrave Macmillan.

Coupland, J. C. (2005) "Invisible Brands: An Ethnography of Households and the Brands in their Kitchen Pantries," *Journal of Consumer Research* 32 (June) 106–118.

Cronin, A. M. (2004) "Regimes of Mediation: Advertising Practitioners as Cultural Intermediaries?" *Consumption, Markets and Culture* 7(4) 349–369.

Crouch, D. (2005) "Introduction: Critical Reflections on the Working of Communication in Tourism Cultures," *Tourism, Culture and Communication* 5(2) 75–81.

Crystal, D. (2001) *Language and the Internet*. Cambridge: Cambridge University Press.

Culler, J. (1975) *Structuralist Poetics*. London: Routledge and Kegan Paul.

Culler, J. (1983) *Barthes*. London: Fontana.

Currah, A. (2003) "The Virtual Geographies of Retail Display," *Journal of Consumer Culture* 3(1) 5–37.

Curran, J. (1996) "The New Revisionism in Mass Communication Research: A Reappraisal" in J. Curran, D. Morley, and V. Walkerdine (eds.) *Cultural Studies and Communications*. London: Arnold, pp. 256–278.

Dahlgren, P. (1988) "What's the Meaning of This? Viewers' Plural Sense-Making of TV News," *Media, Culture and Society* 10 285–301.

Dahlgren, P. (2006) "Doing Citizenship: The Cultural Origins of Civic Agency in the Public Sphere," *European Journal of Cultural Studies* 9(3) 267–286.

Danesi, M. (2006) *Brands*. London: Routledge.

Dass, J. and W. Lord (1995) "Where Has the Audience Gone? The Experts Answer." www.bu.edu/com/html/panelarticle.html. Accessed March 22, 2004.

Davis, W. (2007) "Television's Liveness: A Lesson from the 1920s," *Westminster Papers in Communications and Culture* 4(2) 36–51.

De Mul, J. (2003) "Digitally Mediated (Dis)Embodiment: Plessner's Concept of Excentric Positionality Explained for Cyborgs," *Information, Communication and Society* 6(2) 247–266.

Denzin, N. K. (2001) "The Seventh Moment: Qualitative Inquiry and the Practices of a More Radical Consumer Research," *Journal of Consumer Research* 28 (September) 324–330.

Derrida, J. (1970) "Structure, Sign and Play in the Discourse of the Human Sciences" in R. Macksey and E. Donato (eds.) *The Structuralist Controversy*. Baltimore: Johns Hopkins University Press, pp. 247–272.

De Run, E. C. and F. C. Y. Thang (2005) "Telecommunications Customer Service Personnel's Perceptions of Customers: A Quantitative Approach," paper presented to the *Asia Pacific Marketing Conference: Integrating Theory with Practice*, University of Malaysia Sarawak, Malaysia.

Devereux, E. (2003) *Understanding the Media*. London: Sage.

Diken, B. and C. B. Laustsen (2004) "Sea, Sun, Sex and the Discontents of Pleasure," *Tourist Studies* 4(2) 99–114.

Dimofte, C. V. and R. F. Yalch (2007) "Consumer Response to Polysemous Brand Slogans," *Journal of Consumer Research* 33 (March) 515–522.

Di Tommaso, T. (2004) "The Aesthetics of Television," *Crossings: eJournal of Art and Technology*. www.crossings.tcd.ie/issues/3.1/DiTommaso/. Accessed March 2, 2004.

Dorsey, E. R., H. L. Steeves, and L. E. Porras (2004) "Advertising Ecotourism on the Internet: Commodifying Environment and Culture," *New Media and Society* 6(6) 753–779.

Drotner, K. (2005) "Media on the Move: Personalized Media and the Transformation of Publicness" in S. Livingstone (ed.) *Audiences and Publics: When Cultural Engagement Matters for the Public Sphere*. Bristol: Intellect Press, pp. 187–211.

Dutton, W. H. and A. Shepherd (2006) "Trust in the Internet as an Experience Technology," *Information, Communication and Society* 9(4) 433–451.

Eagleton, T. (1983) *Literary Theory: An Introduction*. Oxford: Blackwell.

Eckhardt, G. M. and M. J. Houston (2002) "Cultural Paradoxes Reflected in Brand Meaning: McDonald's in Shanghai China," *Journal of International Marketing* 10(2) 68–82.

Eco, U. (1981) *The Role of the Reader*. London: Hutchinson.

Edensor, T. (2001) "Performing Tourism, Staging Tourism: (Re)producing Tourist Space and Practice," *Tourist Studies* 1(1) 59–81.

Edwards, D. (1997) *Discourse and Cognition*. London: Sage.

Eischen, K. (2003) "Opening the 'Black Box' of Software. The Micro-Foundations of Informational Technologies, Practices and Environments," *Information, Communication and Society* 6(1) 57–81.

Elmer, G. (2003) "A Diagram of Panoptic Surveillance," *New Media and Society* 5(2) 231–247.

Escalas, J. E. and J. R. Bettman (2005) "Self-Construal, Reference Groups, and Brand Meaning," *Journal of Consumer Research* 32 (December) 378–389.

Escalas, J. E. and B. B. Stern (2003) "Sympathy and Empathy: Emotional Responses to Advertising Dramas," *Journal of Consumer Research* 29 (March) 566–578.

Farnsworth, J. and T. Austrin (2005) "Assembling Portable Talk and Mobile Worlds: Sound Technologies and Mobile Social Networks," *Convergence* 11(2) 14–22.

Featherstone, M. (1991) *Consumer Culture and Postmodernism*. London: Sage.

Feenberg, A. and M. Bakardjieva (2004) "Virtual Community: No 'Killer Implication'," *New Media and Society* 6(1) 37–43.

Ferguson, M. (1992) "The Mythology About Globalization," *European Journal of Communication* 7 69–93.

Firat, A. F. F. and A. Venkatesh (1995) "Liberatory Postmodernism and the Reenchantment of Consumption," *Journal of Consumer Research* 22 (December) 239–267.

Fish, S. E. (1972) *Self-Consuming Artifacts*. Berkeley: University of California Press.

Fish, S. E. (1980) "Interpreting the *Variorum*" in J. P. Tompkins (ed.) *Reader-Response Criticism From Formalism to Post-Structuralism*. Baltimore: Johns Hopkins University Press, pp. 164–184.

Fiske, J. (1987) *Television Culture*. London: Methuen.

Flynn, B. (2003) "Geography of the Digital Hearth," *Information, Communication and Society* 6(4) 551–576.

Fornas, J. (2002) "Passage Across Thresholds into the Borderlands of Mediation," *Convergence* 8(4) 89–106.

Fournier, S. (1998) "Consumers and Their Brands: Developing Relationship Theory in Consumer Research," *Journal of Consumer Research* 24 (March) 343–373.

Franklin, A. (2001) "*The Tourist Gaze* and Beyond: An Interview with John Urry," *Tourist Studies* 1(2) 115–131.

Franklin, A. (2004) "Tourism as an Ordering: Towards a New Ontology of Tourism," *Tourist Studies* 4(3) 277–301.

Franklin, A. and Crang, M. (2001) "The Trouble with Tourism and Travel Theory?" *Tourist Studies* 1(1) 5–22.

Freeman, M. (2007) "Performing the Event of Understanding in Hermeneutic Conversations With Narrative Texts," *Qualitative Inquiry* 13(7) 925–944.

Friesen, M. (2002) "Play, Rhetoric and Method in Gadamer's Hermeneutics and Derrida's Deconstruction," *Proceedings of the Canadian Society for Hermeneutics and Postmodern Thought*. www.ualberta.ca/ di/csh/CSHmeetingProgram2002. htm. Accessed March 5, 2004.

Frith, K. T. (2003) "Advertising and the Homogenization of Cultures: Perspectives from ASEAN," *Asian Journal of Communication* 13(1) 37–54.

Frohlick, S. (2005) "'That Playfulness of White Masculinity': Mediating Masculinities and Adventure at Mountain Film Festivals," *Tourist Studies* 5(2) 175–193.

Gadamer, H. G. (1975) *Truth and Method*. London: Sheed and Ward.

Gadamer, H. G. (1976) *Philosophical Hermeneutics*. Trans. D. E. Linge. Berkeley: University of California Press.

Gane, N. (2003) "Computerized Capitalism: The Media Theory of Jean-François Lyotard," *Information, Communication and Society* 6(3) 430–450.

Gant, D. and S. Kiesler (2002) "Blurring the Boundaries: Cellphones, Mobility, and the Line between Work and Personal Life" in B. Brown, N. Green, and

R. Harper (eds.) *Wireless World: Social and Interactional Aspects of the Mobile Age*. London: Springer, pp. 121–131.

García-Montes, J. M, D. Caballero-Muñoz, and M. Pérez-Àlvarez (2006) "Changes in the Self Resulting from the Use of Mobile Phones," *Media Culture and Society* 28(1) 67–82.

Gauntlett, D. and A. Hill (1999) *TV Living: Television, Culture and Everyday Life*. London: British Film Institute and Routledge.

Gee, J. P. (2006) "Why Games Studies Now? Video Games: A New Art Form," *Games and Culture* 1(1) 58–61.

Georgiou, M. (2006) *Diaspora, Identity and the Media*. Cresskill, NJ: Hampton Press.

Gergen, K. J. (2002) "The Challenge of Absent Presence" in J. E. Katz and M. Aakhus (eds.) *Perpetual Contact: Mobile Communication, Private Talk, Public Performance*. Cambridge: Cambridge University Press, pp. 227–241.

Gibson, W. (1980) "Authors, Speakers, Readers and Mock Readers" in J. P. Tompkins (ed.) *Reader-Response Criticism From Formalism to Post-Structuralism*. Baltimore: Johns Hopkins University Press, pp. 1–6.

Gillespie, M. (1995) *Television, Ethnicity and Cultural Change*. London: Routledge.

Gillespie, M. (2006) "Audiences: Living with Media" in M. Gillespie (ed.) *Media Audiences*. Maidenhead: Open University Press.

Goggin, G. (2006a) *Cellphone Culture: Mobile Technology in Everyday Life*. London: Routledge.

Goggin, G. (2006b) "Mobile Media and Ethnography," paper presented to the *International Association for Media and Communication Research* Conference, American University in Cairo, Egypt.

Goldman, R. (1982) "Hegemony and Managed Critique in Prime-Time Television: A Critical Reading of 'Mork and Mindy,'" *Theory and Society* 11 (May) 363–388.

Goldman, R. and S. Papson (2006) "Capital's Brandscapes," *Journal of Consumer Culture* 6(3) 327–353.

Gordon, J. (2002) "The Mobile Phone: An Artefact of Popular Culture and a Tool of the Public Sphere," *Convergence* 8(3) 15–26.

Graham, S. (2004) "Beyond the 'Dazzling Light': From Dreams of Transcendence to the 'Remediation' of Urban Life," *New Media and Society* 6(1) 16–25.

Graml, G. (2004) "(Re)mapping the Nation: Sound of Music Tourism and National Identity in Austria, ca. 2000 CE," *Tourist Studies* 4(2) 137–159.

Green, E. and C. Singleton (2007) "Mobile Selves: Gender, Ethnicity and Mobile Phones in the Everyday Lives of Young Pakistani-British Women and Men," *Information, Communication and Society* 10(4) 506–526.

Green, L. (2003) "Attempting to Ground Ethnographic Theory and Practice," *Australian Journal of Communication*, 30(2) 133–145.

Green, N. (2001) "How Everyday Life Became Virtual Mundane Work at the Juncture of Production and Consumption," *Journal of Consumer Culture* 1(1) 73–92.

Grondin, J. (2002) "Gadamer and Bultmann" in J. Pokorny and J. Roskovec (eds.) *Philosophical Hermeneutics and Biblical Exegesis*. Wissenschaftliche Untersuchungen zum Neuen Testament. Tubingen: Mohr Siebeck.

Gunkel, D. (2003) "Second Thoughts: Toward a Critique of the Digital Divide," *New Media and Society* 5(4) 499–522.

Gurwitsch, A. (1966) *Studies in Phenomenology and Psychology*. Evanston, IL: Northwestern University Press.

Habuchi, I. (2005) "Accelerating Reflexivity" in M. Ito, D. Okabe, and M. Matsuda (eds.) *Personal, Portable, Pedestrian: Mobile Phones in Japanese Life*. Cambridge, MA: MIT Press, pp. 165–182.

Haddon, L. (2007) "Roger Silverstone's Legacies: Domestication," *New Media and Society* 9(1) 25–32.

Hafez, K. (2007) *The Myth of Media Globalization*. Cambridge: Polity Press.

Haldrup, M. and Larsen, J. (2003) "The Family Gaze," *Tourist Studies* 3(1) 23–45.

Halim, Z. A. (2001) "Freedom of Information in Malaysia: A Long and Arduous Journey" in V. Iyer (ed.) *Freedom of Information: An Asian Survey*. Singapore: AMIC & NTU, pp. 97–124.

Hall, S. (1981) "Encoding/Decoding" in S. Hall, D. Hobson, A. Lowe, and P. Willis (eds.) *Culture, Media, Language*. London: Hutchinson, pp. 106–121.

Hammersley, M. and Atkinson, P. (1983) *Ethnography: Principles and Practice*. London: Tavistock Books.

Hans, J. S. (1980) "Hermeneutics, Play, Deconstruction," *Philosophy Today* 24 299–317.

Hans, J. S. (1981) *The Play of the World*. Amherst: University of Massachusetts Press.

Hardey, M. (2004) "Mediated Relationships," *Information, Communication and Society* 7(2) 207–222.

Hargittai, E. (2004) "Internet Access and Use in Context," *New Media and Society* 6(1) 137–143.

Harré, R. (1972) *The Philosophies of Science*. Oxford: Oxford University Press.

Harré, R. (1984) *Personal Being*. Cambridge, MA: Harvard University Press.

Harré, R. (1998) *The Singular Self: An Introduction to the Psychology of Personhood*. London: Sage.

Harré, R. and P. F. Secord (1972) *Explanation of Social Behaviour*. Oxford: Blackwell.

Harris, E. (1970) *Hypothesis and Perception*. London: Allen and Unwin.

Hartley, J. (2002) "The Constructed Viewer" in T. Miller (ed.) *Television Studies*. London: British Film Institute, pp. 60–63.

Hartley, J. (2004) "Television, Nation, and Indigenous Media," *Television and New Media* 5(1) 7–25.

Hassanpour, A. (n.d.) "Voice-over." www.museum.tv/archives/etv/V/htmlV/voice-over voice-over.htm. Accessed March 5, 2004.

Heath, S. (1973) "Introduction: Questions of Emphasis," *Screen* 14(1/2) 9–12.

Heelan, P. A. (1997) "After Post-Modernism: The Scope of Hermeneutics in Natural Science." www.focusing.org/apm_papers/heelan.html. Accessed March 3, 2004.

Heidegger, M. (1962) *Being and Time*. Trans. J. Macquarrie and E. Robinson. New York: Harper and Row.

Hemment, D. (2005) "The Mobile Effect," *Convergence* 11(2) 32–40.

Hermes, J. (2006) "Citizenship in the Age of the Internet," *European Journal of Communication* 21(3) 295–309.

Hermes, J. and P. Dahlgren (2006) "Cultural Studies and Citizenship," *European Journal of Cultural Studies* 9(3) 259–265.

Herring, S. C. (2004) "Slouching Toward the Ordinary: Current Trends in Computer-Mediated Communication," *New Media and Society* 6(1) 26–36.

Hill, A. (1997) *Shocking Entertainment: Viewer Response to Violent Movies*. Luton: University of Luton Press. Quoted by Barker, M. and J. Petley (2001) "Introduction: From Bad Research to Good – a Guide for the Perplexed" in M. Barker and J. Petley (eds.) *Ill Effects: The Media/Violence Debate*. London: Routledge, pp. 1–26.

Hill, A. (2005) *Reality TV: Audiences and Popular Factual Television*. London: Routledge.

Hima, G. (2001) "The Message of the Medium: McLuhan's Media Theory and the Present Media Situation." www.inst.at/trans/10Nr/hima10.htm. Accessed March 20, 2004.

Hirschman, E. C. (1988) "The Ideology of Consumption: A Structural-Syntactical Analysis of *Dallas* and *Dynasty*," *Journal of Consumer Research* 15 (December) 344–359.

Hirschman, E. C. (1993) "Ideology in Consumer Research, 1980 and 1990: A Marxist and Feminist Critique," *Journal of Consumer Research* 19 (March) 537–555.

Hirschman, E. C. and C. J. Thompson (1997) "Why Media Matter: Toward a Richer Understanding of Consumers' Relationship with Advertising and Mass Media," *Journal of Advertising* 26 (Spring) 43–60.

Hoijer, B. (1992) "Socio-Cognitive Structures and Television Reception," *Media, Culture and Society* 14 583–603.

Holbrook, M. and M. W. Grayson (1986) "The Semiology of Cinematic Consumption: Symbolic Consumer Behavior in 'Out of Africa'," *Journal of Consumer Research* 13 (December) 374–381.

Holland, N. (1980) "Unity Identity Text Self" in J. P. Tompkins (ed.) *Reader-Response Criticism From Formalism to Post-Structuralism*. Baltimore: Johns Hopkins University Press, pp. 118–133.

Holt, D. B. (1995) "How Consumers Consume: A Typology of Consumption Practices," *Journal of Consumer Research* 22 (June) 1–16.

Holt, D. B. (1997) "Poststructuralist Lifestyle Analysis: Conceptualizing the Social Patterning of Consumption in Postmodernity," *Journal of Consumer Research* 23 (March) 326–350.

Holt, D. B. (1998) "Does Cultural Capital Structure American Consumption?" *Journal of Consumer Research* 25 (June) 1–25.

Holt, D. B. (2002) "Why Do Brands Cause Trouble? A Dialectical Theory of Consumer Culture and Branding," *Journal of Consumer Research* 29 (June) 70–90.

Holt, D. B. (2006a) "Toward a Sociology of Branding," *Journal of Consumer Culture* 6(3) 299–302.

Holt, D. B. (2006b) "Jack Daniel's America: Iconic Brands as Ideological Parasites and Proselytizers," *Journal of Consumer Culture* 6(3) 355–377.

Holt, D. B. and C. J. Thompson (2004) "Man-of-Action Heroes: The Pursuit of Heroic Masculinity in Everyday Consumption," *Journal of Consumer Research* 31 (September) 425–440.

Holub, R. C. (1984) *Reception Theory*. London: Methuen.

Huizinga, J. (1970) *Homo Ludens: A Study of the Play Element in Culture*. London: Temple Smith. Published previously, London: Routledge and Kegan Paul (1949) and Boston: Beacon Press (1955).

Humphreys, L. (2005) "Cellphones in Public: Social Interactions in a Wireless Era," *New Media and Society* 7(6) 810–833.

Humphreys, S. (2003) "Online Multi-User Games: Playing for Real," *Australian Journal of Communication* 30(1) 79–92.

Husserl, E. (1973) *Experience and Judgement*. London: Routledge and Kegan Paul.

Ilmonen, K. (2004) "The Use of and Commitment to Goods," *Journal of Consumer Culture* 4(1) 27–50.

Iser, W. (1974) *The Implied Reader*. Baltimore: Johns Hopkins University Press.

Iser, W. (1978) *The Act of Reading*. Baltimore: Johns Hopkins University Press.

Iser, W. (1980) "The Reading Process: A Phenomenological Approach" in J. P. Tompkins (ed.) *Reader-Response Criticism From Formalism to Post-Structuralism*. Baltimore: Johns Hopkins University Press, pp. 50–69.

Iser, W. (2006) *How to Do Theory*. Oxford: Blackwell.

Ito, M. (2005) "Introduction" in M. Ito, D. Okabe, and M. Matsuda (eds.) *Personal, Portable, Pedestrian: Mobile Phones in Japanese Life*. Cambridge, MA: MIT Press, pp. 1–16.

Ito, M. (2007) "Introduction" in K. Varnelis (ed.) *Networked Publics*. Cambridge, MA: MIT Press.

Jansson, A. (2002) "The Mediatization of Consumption: Towards an Analytical Framework of Image Culture," *Journal of Consumer Culture* 2(1) 5–31.

Jauss, H. R. (1982a) *Aesthetic Experience and Literary Hermeneutics*. Minneapolis: University of Minnesota Press.

Jauss, H. R. (1982b) *Towards an Aesthetic of Reception*. Brighton: Harvester Press.

Jenkins, H. (1992) *Textual Poachers: Television Fans and Participatory Culture.* New York: Routledge.

Jenkins, H. (2006) *Convergence Culture.* New York: New York University Press.

Jensen, K. B. (2005) "Interactivity in the Wild: An Empirical Study of 'Interactivity' as Understood in Organizational Practices," *Nordicom Review* 26(1) 3–30.

Jensen, K. B. and K. E. Rosengren (1990) "Five Traditions in Search of the Audience," *European Journal of Communication* 5 207–238.

Johar, G. V., D. Maheswaran, and L. A. Peracchio (2006) "*MAP*ping the Frontiers: Theoretical Advances in Consumer Research on Memory, Affect, and Persuasion," *Journal of Consumer Research* 33 (June) 139–149.

Joyce, M. (2004) "'We Thought We Could Sit Forever in Fun': New Media and Literary Studies," *New Media and Society* 6(1) 77–81.

Kahn, R. and D. Kellner (2004) "New Media and Internet Activism: From the 'Battle of Seattle' to Blogging," *New Media and Society* 6(1) 87–95.

Kamir, O. (2005) "Why 'Law-and-Film' and What Does it Actually Mean? A Perspective," *Continuum: Journal of Media and Cultural Studies* 19(2) 255–278.

Kane, M. J. and H. Tucker (2004) "Adventure Tourism: The Freedom to Play with Reality," *Tourist Studies* 4(3) 217–234.

Kates, S. M. (2002a) "The Morphing Brand: An Account of Collective Consumer-Brand Relationships" (working paper).

Kates, S. M. (2002b) "The Morphing Brand: Implications for Advertising" (working paper).

Kates, S. M. (2002c) "The Protean Quality of Subcultural Consumption: An Ethnographic Account of Gay Consumers," *Journal of Consumer Research* 29 (December) 383–399.

Kates, S. M. (2004) "The Dynamics of Brand Legitimacy: An Interpretive Study in the Gay Men's Community," *Journal of Consumer Research* 31 (September) 455–464.

Kates, S. M. and C. Goh (2003) "Brand Morphing: Implications for Advertising Theory and Practice," *Journal of Advertising* 32 (Spring) 59–68.

Katz, J. E. and M. A. Aakhus (2002) "Conclusion: Making Meaning of Mobiles – a Theory of *Apparatgeist*" in J. E. Katz and M. A. Aakhus (eds.) *Perpetual Contact: Mobile Communication, Private Talk, Public Performance.* Cambridge: Cambridge University Press, pp. 301–318.

Katz, J. E. and S. Sugiyama (2006) "Mobile Phones as Fashion Statements: Evidence from Student Surveys in the US and Japan," *New Media and Society* 8(2) 321–337.

Keller, K. L. (2003) "Brand Synthesis: The Multidimensionality of Brand Knowledge," *Journal of Consumer Research* 29 (March) 595–600.

Keller, M. (2005) "Needs, Desires and the Experience of Scarcity: Representations of Recreational Shopping in Post-Soviet Estonia," *Journal of Consumer Culture* 5(1) 65–85.

Kerr, A., J. Kucklich, and P. Brereton (2006) "New Media – New Pleasures?" *International Journal of Cultural Studies* 9(1) 63–82.

Kim, H. and Papacharissi, Z. (2003) "Cross-cultural Differences in On-line Presentation: A Content Analysis of Personal Korean and US Home Pages," *Asian Journal of Communication* 13(1) 100–119.

Kimura, J. and R. W. Belk (2005) "Christmas in Japan: Globalization Versus Localization," *Consumption, Markets and Culture* 8(3) 325–338.

King, N. (2000) "Hermeneutics, Reception Aesthetics, and Film Interpretation" in J. Hill and P. C. Gibson (eds.) *Film Studies: Critical Approaches*. Oxford: Oxford University Press, pp. 210–221.

Kitzinger, J. (2000) "Media Templates: Patterns of Association and the (Re) Construction of Meaning over Time," *Media, Culture and Society* 22 61–84.

Kjeldgaard, D. and S. Askegaard (2006) "The Glocalization of Youth Culture: The Global Youth Segment as Structures of Common Difference," *Journal of Consumer Research* 33 (September) 231–247.

Kluver, R. and I. Banerjee (2005) "Political Culture, Regulation, and Democratization: The Internet in Nine Asian Nations," *Information, Communication and Society* 8(1) 30–46.

Kniazeva, M. and R. W. Belk (2007) "Packaging as a Vehicle for Mythologizing the Brand," *Consumption, Markets and Culture* 10(1) 51–69.

Kobayashi, T., K. Ikeda, and K. Miyata (2006) "Social Capital: Online Collective Use of the Internet and Reciprocity as Lubricants of Democracy," *Information, Communication and Society* 9 (5) 582–611.

Koegler, H.-R. (n.d.) "A Critical Hermeneutics of Subjectivity: Cultural Studies as Critical Social Theory." www.unf.edu/ hkoegler/Postmodernism/KoeglerDocs/ OtherDocs/Koegler.pdf. Accessed March 25, 2004.

Kozinets, R. V., J. F. Sherry Jnr., D. Storm, A. Duhachek, K. Nuttavuthisit, and B. Deberry-Spence (2004) "Ludic Agency and Retail Spectacle," *Journal of Consumer Research* 31 (December) 658–672.

Kraidy, M. (2005) *Hybridity or the Cultural Logic of Globalization*. Philadelphia: Temple University Press.

Krishna, R. S. (2003) "Review of M. Poster *What's the Matter with the Internet?* (Minneapolis: University of Minnesota Press, 2001)," *Information, Communication and Society* 6(1) 127–132.

Krishnamurthy, P. and A. Sivaraman (2002) "Counterfactual Thinking and Advertising Responses," *Journal of Consumer Research* 28 (March) 650–658.

Krishnamurthy, P. and M. Sujan (1999) "Retrospection versus Anticipation: The Role of the Ad under Retrospective and Anticipatory Self-Referencing," *Journal of Consumer Research* 26 (June) 55–69.

Krzywinska, T. (2006) "The Pleasures and Dangers of the Game: Up Close and Personal," *Games and Culture* 1(1) 119–122.

Kuhn, A. (1994) *Women's Pictures: Feminism and Cinema*, 2nd edn. London: Verso.

Kuhn, T. (1962) *The Structure of Scientific Revolutions.* Chicago: University of Chicago Press.

Laegran, A. S. and J. Stewart (2003) "Nerdy, Trendy or Healthy? Configuring the Internet Cafe," *New Media and Society* 5(3) 357–377.

Lamerichs, J. and H. F. M. Te Molder (2003) "Computer-Mediated Communication: From a Cognitive to a Discursive Model," *New Media and Society* 5(4) 451–473.

Langer, B. (2004) "The Business of Branded Enchantment: Ambivalence and Disjuncture in the Global Children's Culture Industry," *Journal of Consumer Culture* 4(2) 251–277.

La Pastina, A. (2005) "Up the Amazon Without a Paddle: Developing Nations and Globalization," *Global Media and Communication* 1(1) 36–41.

Lee, H. (2005) "Implosion, Virtuality, and Interaction in an Internet Discussion Group," *Information, Communication and Society* 8(1) 47–63.

Lee, L. and D. Ariely (2006) "Shopping Goals, Goal Concreteness, and Conditional Promotions," *Journal of Consumer Research* 33 (June) 60–70.

Lehtonen, T.-K. (2003) "The Domestication of New Technologies as a Set of Trials," *Journal of Consumer Culture* 3(3) 363–385.

Lenert, A. (2004) "A Social Shaping Perspective on the Development of the World Wide Web: The Case of iCraveTV," *New Media and Society* 6(2) 235–258.

Leung, L. and R. Wei (1999) "Who are the Mobile Phone Have-Nots?" *New Media and Society* 1(2) 209–226.

Lewis, J. (1991) *The Ideological Octopus: An Exploration of Television and Its Audience.* London: Routledge.

Lewis, J. (2006) "News and the Empowerment of Citizens," *European Journal of Cultural Studies* 9(3) 303–319.

Lie, R. (2003) *Spaces of Intercultural Communication: An Interdisciplinary Introduction to Communication, Culture, and Globalizing/Localizing Identities.* Cresskill, NJ: Hampton Press.

Liebes, T. and E. Katz (1993) *The Export of Meaning: Cross-Cultural Readings of Dallas.* Cambridge: Polity Press.

Lievrouw, L. A. (2004) "What's Changed about New Media? Introduction to the Fifth Anniversary Issue of *New Media and Society,*" *New Media and Society* 6(1) 9–15.

Liff, A. and F. Steward (2003) "Shaping E-Acccess in the Cybercafe: Networks, Boundaries and Heterotopian Innovation," *New Media and Society* 5(3) 313–334.

Lim, S. S. (2002) "The Experiential Dimensions of Internet Shopping: An Ethnographic Analysis of Online Store Websites," *Asian Journal of Communication* 12(2) 79–99.

Lindridge, A. M., M. K. Hogg, and M. Shah (2004) "Imagined Multiple Worlds: How South Asian Women in Britain Use Family and Friends to Navigate the 'Border Crossings' Between Household and Societal Contexts," *Consumption, Markets and Culture* 7(3) 211–238.

Ling, R. (2004) *The Mobile Connection: The Cellphone's Impact on Society*. San Francisco: Morgan Kaufmann.

Littau, K. (2006) *Theories of Reading: Books, Bodies and Bibliomania*. Cambridge: Polity Press.

Livingstone, S. (2004) "The Challenge of Changing Audiences: Or, What is the Audience Researcher to Do in the Age of the Internet?" *European Journal of Communication* 19(1) 75–86.

Livingstone, S. (2007a) "Engaging with Media – a Matter of Literacy?" Keynote presentation to the Conference, *Transforming Audiences: Identity/Creativity/ Everyday Life*. University of Westminster, September.

Livingstone, S. (2007b) "On the Material and the Symbolic: Silverstone's Double Articulation of Research Traditions in New Media Studies," *New Media and Society* 9(1) 16–24.

Livingstone, S. (2007c) "The Challenge of Engaging Youth Online: Contrasting Producers' and Teenagers' Interpretations of Websites," *European Journal of Communication* 22(2) 165–184.

Livingstone, S. and P. Lunt (2007) "Representing Citizens and Consumers in Media and Communications Regulation," *The Politics of Consumption/The Consumption of Politics: The Annals of the American Academy of Political and Social Science* 611 51–65.

Livingstone, S., P. Lunt, and L. Miller (2007) "Citizens, Consumers and the Citizen-Consumer: Articulating the Citizen Interest in Media and Communications Regulation," *Discourse and Communication* 1(1) 85–111.

Lo, S.-H. (2002) "Diaspora Regime into Nation: Mediating Hybrid Nationhood in Taiwan," *The Public* 9(1) 65–84.

Lonsway, B. (2002) "Testing the Space of the Virtual," *Convergence* 8(3) 61–77.

Love, J. G. (1994) "The Hermeneutics of Transcript Analysis," *The Qualitative Report* 2(1). www.nova.edu/ssss/QR/BackIssues/QR2–1/love.html. Accessed March 20, 2004.

Lowery, S. A. and M. L. DeFleur (1995) *Milestones in Mass Communication Research: Media Effects*. White Plains, NY: Longman.

Luke, T. W. (2002) "Power and Political Culture" in L. A. Lievrouw and S. Livingstone (eds.) *Handbook of New Media: Social Shaping and Consequences of ICTs*. London: Sage, pp. 518–532.

Lunenfeld, P. (2004) "Media Design: New and Improved Without the New," *New Media and Society* 6(1) 65–70.

Lury, C. (2004) *Brands: The Logos of the Global Economy*. London: Routledge.

Lury, K. (2005) *Interpreting Television*. London: Hodder Arnold.

Lye, J. (1996) "Reader-Response: Various Positions." www.brocku.ca/english/ courses/4F70rr.html. Accessed March 21, 2004.

MacCabe, C. (1974) "Realism and the Cinema: Notes on Some Brechtian Theses," *Screen* 15(2) 7–27.

MacCabe, C. (1976) "Theory and Film: Principles of Realism and Pleasure," *Screen* 17(3) 7–27.

MacCabe, C. (1981) "Realism and the Cinema: Notes on Some Brechtian Theses" in T. Bennett et al. (eds.) *Popular Television and Film*. London: British Film Institute.

MacCabe, C. (1985) *Theoretical Essays: Film, Linguistics, Literature*. Manchester: Manchester University Press.

McCabe, S. (2005) "'Who is a Tourist?' A Critical Review," *Tourist Studies* 5(1) 85–106.

MacCannell, D. (2001) "Tourist Agency," *Tourist Studies* 1(1) 23–37.

MacCannell, D. (2002) "The Ego Factor in Tourism," *Journal of Consumer Research* 29 (June) 146–151.

McDonnell, K. and K. Robins (1980) "Marxist Cultural Theory: The Althusserian Smokescreen" in S. Clarke, V. J. Seidler, K. McDonnell, K. Robins, and T. Lovell, *One-Dimensional Marxism: Althusser and the Politics of Culture*. London: Allison and Busby, pp. 157–231.

MacGregor, P. (2003) "Mind the Gap: Problems of Multimedia Journalism," *Convergence* 9(3) 8–17.

Machill, M., S. Kohler, and M. Waldheuser (2007) "The Use of Narrative Structures in Television News: An Experiment in Innovative Forms of Journalistic Presentation," *European Journal of Communication* 22(2) 185–205.

Mackenzie, C. (2006) "Imagination, Identity and Self-transformation." Paper presented to the *Practical Identity and Narrative Agency Conference*, Macquarie University, Sydney, Australia.

McMillin, D. C. (2007) *International Media Studies*. Oxford: Blackwell.

McQuarrie, E. F. and D. G. Mick (1999) "Visual Rhetoric in Advertising: Text-Interpretive, Experimental and Reader-Responses Analyses," *Journal of Consumer Research* 26 (June) 37–54.

McRae, L. (2003) "Rethinking Tourism: Edward Said and a Politics of Meeting and Movement," *Tourist Studies* 3(3) 235–251.

Madell, D. and S. Muncer (2005) "Are Internet and Mobile Phone Communication Complementary Activities Amongst Young People? A Study from a 'Rational Actor' Perspective," *Information, Communication and Society* 8(1) 64–80.

Malaviya, P., D. R. John, and B. Sternthal (2001) "Human Participants-Respondents and Researchers," *Journal of Consumer Psychology* 10 (1 and 2) 115–121.

Manovich, L. (2001) *The Language of New Media*. Cambridge, MA: MIT Press.

Mansell, R. (2004) "Political Economy, Power and New Media," *New Media and Society* 6(1) 9–105.

Markova, I. (2000) "Armedee or How to Get Rid of It: Social Representations from a Dialogical Perspective," *Culture and Psychology* 6(4) 419–460.

Marshall, P. D. (2004) *New Media Cultures*. London: Arnold.

Mascheroni, G. (2007) "Global Nomads" Network and Mobile Sociality: Exploring New Media Uses on the Move," *Information, Communication and Society* 10(4) 527–546.

Mathieu, D. (2007) "Cultural Presuppositions in News Comprehension," paper presented at the International Association for Media and Communication Research Conference, UNESCO, Paris.

Mathwick, C. and E. Rigdon (2004) "Play, Flow, and the Online Search Experience," *Journal of Consumer Research* 31 (September) 324–333.

May, H. and G. Hearn (2005) "The Mobile Phone as Media," *International Journal of Cultural Studies* 8(2) 195–211.

Mayra, F. (2006) "A Moment in the Life of a Generation," *Games and Culture* 1(1) 103–106.

Mehra, B., C. Merkel, and A. P. Bishop (2004) "The Internet for Empowerment of Minority and Marginalized Users," *New Media and Society* 6(6) 781–802.

Merquior, J. G. (1986) *From Prague to Paris*. London: Verso.

Michelle, C. (2007) "Modes of Reception: A Consolidated Analytical Framework," *Communication Review* 10 181–222.

Mick, D. G. (1986) "Consumer Research and Semiotics: Exploring the Morphology of Signs, Symbols, and Significance," *Journal of Consumer Research* 13 (September) 196–213.

Mick, D. G. and C. Buhl (1992) "A Meaning-Based Model of Advertising Experiences," *Journal of Consumer Research* 19 (December) 317–338.

Miller, H. (1995) "The Social Psychology of Objects," paper presented to the *Understanding the Social World* Conference, University of Huddersfield, UK.

Miller, T. (2006) "Gaming for Beginners," *Games and Culture* 1(1) 5–12.

Milne, S., D. Mason, U. Speidel, and T. West-Newman (2005) "Tourism and Community Informatics: The Case of Kiwitrails," *Tourism, Culture and Communication* 5(2) 105–114.

Moisander, J. and P. Eriksson (2006) "Corporate Narratives of Information Society: Making Up the Mobile Consumer Subject," *Consumption, Markets and Culture* 9(4) 257–275.

Moor, E. (2003) "Branded Spaces: The Scope of 'New Marketing'," *Journal of Consumer Culture* 3(1) 39–60.

Moores, S. (1993) *Interpreting Audiences*. London: Sage.

Moores, S. (2000) *Media and Everyday Life in Modern Society*. Edinburgh: Edinburgh University Press.

Moores, S. (2005) *Media/Theory*. London: Routledge.

Moores, S. (2006) "Media Uses and Everyday Environmental Experiences: A Positive Critique of Phenomenological Geography," *Particip@tions* 3(2).

Morley, D. (1980) *The Nationwide Audience: Structure and Decoding*. London: British Film Institute.

Morley, D. (1992) *Television, Audiences and Cultural Studies*. London: Routledge.

Morley, D. (2005) "Theoretical Orthodoxies: Textualism, Constructivism and the 'New Ethnography' in Cultural Studies" in P. Leistyna (ed.) *Cultural Studies: From Theory to Action*. Oxford: Blackwell, pp. 171–187.

Morley, D. (2006) "Unanswered Questions in Audience Research," *Communication Review* 9 101–121.

Morrison, D. E. (2003) "Good and Bad Practice in Focus Group Research" in V. Nightingale and K. Ross (eds.) *Critical Readings: Media and Audiences*. Maidenhead: Open University Press, pp. 111–130.

Morrison, M. A., E. Haley, K. B. Sheehan, and R. E. Taylor (2002) *Using Qualitative Research in Advertising*. London: Sage.

Mosco, V. (2004) *The Digital Sublime*. Cambridge, MA: MIT Press.

Moyal, A. (1992) "The Gendered Use of the Telephone: An Australian Case Study," *Media, Culture and Society* 14 51–72.

Muniz, A. M and H. J. Schau (2005) "Religiosity in the Abandoned Apple Newton Brand Community," *Journal of Consumer Research* 31 (March) 737–747.

Murdock, G. (1997) "Thin Descriptions: Questions of Method in Cultural Analysis" in J. McGuigan (ed.) *Cultural Methodologies*. London: Sage, pp. 178–192.

Murphy, E. (1997) "Constructivism: From Philosophy to Practice." www.stemnet. nf.ca/~elmurphy/emurphy/cle.html. Accessed March 23, 2004.

Murphy, P. D. and M. M. Kraidy (2003) "International Communication, Ethnography, and the Challenge of Globalization," *Communication Theory* 13(3) 304–323.

Murray, S. (2003) "Media Convergence's Third Wave: Content Streaming," *Convergence* 9(1) 8–18.

Murtagh, G. M. (2002) "Seeing the 'Rules': Preliminary Observations of Action, Interaction and Mobile Phone Use" in B. Brown, N. Green, and R. Harper (eds.) *Wireless World: Social and Interactional Aspects of the Mobile Age*. London: Springer, pp. 81–91.

Myers, D. (2006) "Signs, Symbols, Games, and Play," *Games and Culture* 1(1) 47–51.

Nafus, D. and K. Tracey (2002) "Mobile Phone Consumption and Concepts of Personhood" in J. E. Katz and M. Aakhus (eds.) *Perpetual Contact: Mobile Communication, Private Talk, Public Performance*. Cambridge: Cambridge University Press, pp. 206–221.

Nettleton, S., R. Burrows, L. O'Malley, and I. Watt (2004) "Health E-Types? An Analysis of the Everyday Use of the Internet for Health," *Information, Communication and Society* 7(4) 531–553.

Nightingale, V. (1996) *Studying Audiences: The Shock of the Real*. London: Routledge.

Nissenbaum, H. (2004) "Hackers and the Contested Ontology of Cyberspace," *New Media and Society* 6(2) 195–217.

Nutt, D. and D. Railton (2003) "The Sims: Real Life as Genre," *Information, Communication and Society* 6(4) 577–592.

Nyre, L. (2007) "What Happens When I Turn on the TV Set?" *Westminster Papers in Communications and Culture* 4(2) 24–35.

Oatey, A. (1999) "The Strengths and Limitations of Interviews as a Research Technique for Studying Television Viewers." www.aber.ac.uk/media/Students/aeo9702.html. Accessed June 2, 2005.

Okabe, D., K. Anderson, M. Ito, and S. Mainwaring (2005) "Location-Based Moblogging as Method: New Views into the Use and Practice of Persona, Social, and Mobile Technologies," paper presented to the *Seeing, Understanding, Learning in the Mobile Age International Conference*, Budapest, Hungary.

Oksman, V. and J. Turtiainen (2004) "Mobile Communication as a Social Stage," *New Media and Society* 6(3) 319–339.

Olson, H. (n.d.) "Quantitative 'Versus' Qualitative Research: The Wrong Question." www.ualberta.ca/dept/slis/cais/olson.htm. Accessed March 20, 2004.

Olsson, T. (2005) "Young Citizens, ICTs and Learning," *Nordicom Review* 26(1) 131–139.

Ortner, S. B. (2005) "Subjectivity and Cultural Critique," *Anthropological Theory* 5(1) 31–52.

Parameswaran, R. (2002) "Reading Fictions of Romance: Gender, Sexuality, and Nationalism in Postcolonial India," *Journal of Communication* 52(4) 832–851.

Pauwels, L. (2005) "Websites as Visual and Multimodal Cultural Expressions: Opportunities and Issues of Online Hybrid Media Research," *Media, Culture and Society* 27(4) 604–613.

Pearce, C. (2006) "Productive Play: Game Culture From the Bottom Up," *Games and Culture* 1(1) 17–24.

Perry, D. K. (2002) *Theory and Research in Mass Communication: Contexts and Consequences*. Mahwah, NJ: Lawrence Erlbaum.

Pettinger, L. (2004) "Brand Culture and Branded Workers: Service Work and Aesthetic Labour in Fashion Retail," *Consumption, Markets and Culture* 7(2) 165–184.

Phillips, D. J. (2004) "Privacy Policy and PETS: The Influence of Policy Regimes on the Development and Social Implications of Privacy Enhancing Technologies," *New Media and Society* 6(6) 691–706.

Philo, G. (2005) "The Mass Production of Ignorance: News Content and Audience Understanding" in C. Paterson and A. Sreberny (eds.) *International News in the Twenty-First Century*. London: John Libbey Publishing.

Plantinga, C. (n.d.) "Movie Pleasures and the Spectator's Experience: Toward a Cognitive Approach," *Film and Philosophy* II. www.hanover.edu/philos/film/vol_02/planting.htm. Accessed March 28, 2004.

Popper, K. (1963) *Conjectures and Refutations*. London: Routledge and Kegan Paul.

Poster, M. (2003) "Perfect Transmissions: Evil Bert Laden," *Television and New Media* 4(3) 283–295.

Postigo, H. (2003) "From Pong to Planet Quake: Post-Industrial Transitions from Leisure to Work," *Information, Communication and Society* 6(4) 593–607.

Potter, J. (2003) "Review Essay: Studying the Standardized Survey as Interaction," *Qualitative Research* 3(2) 269–278.

Poulet, G. (1970) "Criticism and the Experience of Interiority" in R. Macksey and E. Donato (eds.) *The Structuralist Controversy.* Baltimore: Johns Hopkins University Press, pp. 56–88.

Power, M. R. (2003) "Designing Communication for Diversity in a Horizontal Individualist Culture," *Australian Journal of Communication* 30(2) 1–14.

Press, A. (2006) "Audience Research in the Post-Audience Age: An Introduction to Barker and Morley," *Communication Review* 9 93–100.

Prince, G. (1980) "Introduction to the Study of the Narratee" in J. P. Tompkins (ed.) *Reader-Response Criticism From Formalism to Post-Structuralism.* Baltimore: Johns Hopkins University Press, pp. 7–25.

Qiu, J. L. and E. C. Thompson (2007) "Editorial: Mobile Communication and Asian Modernities," *New Media and Society* 9(6) 95–901.

Qureshi, K. (2006) "Trans-boundary Spaces: Scottish Pakistanis and Trans-local/National Identities," *International Journal of Cultural Studies* 9(2) 207–226.

Radway, J. (1984, 1991) *Reading the Romance: Women, Patriarchy, and Popular Literature.* Chapel Hill: University of North Carolina Press.

Raessens, J. (2006) "Playful Identities, or the Ludification of Culture," *Games and Culture* 1(1) 52–57.

Rainie, L. and P. Bell (2004) "The Numbers that Count," *New Media and Society* 6(1) 44–54.

Rehak, B. (2003) "Mapping the Bit Girl: Lara Croft and New Media Fandom," *Information, Communication and Society* 6(4) 477–496.

Rentschler, E. and A. Kaes (n.d.) "Reading a Film Sequence: Preliminary Notes." www.web.uvic.ca/geru/439/seq.html. Accessed March 21, 2004.

Ridell, S. (2005) "Mediating the Web as a Public Space: A Local Experiment in the Creation of Online Civic Genres," *Nordicom Review* 26(1) 31–48.

Riffaterre, M. (1966) "Describing Poetic Structures: Two Approaches to Baudelaire's 'Les Chats'" in J. Ehrmann (ed.) *Structuralism.* Yale French Studies. New Haven, CT: Yale University Press, pp. 188–230.

Risser, J. (1997) *Hermeneutics and the Voice of the Other: Re-reading Gadamer's Philosophical Hermeneutics.* Albany: State University of New York Press.

Ritson, M. and R. Elliott (1999) "The Social Uses of Advertising: An Ethnographic Study of Adolescent Advertising Audiences," *Journal of Consumer Research* 26 (December) 260–277.

Robins, K. (1979) "Althusserian Marxism and Media Studies: The Case of *Screen,*" *Media, Culture and Society* 1 355–370.

Rojek, C. (2004) "The Consumerist Syndrome in Contemporary Society: An Interview with Zygmunt Bauman," *Journal of Consumer Culture* 4(3) 291–312.

Roscoe, J., H. Marshall, and K. Gleeson (1995) "The Television Audience: A Reconsideration of the Taken-for-Granted Terms 'Active,' 'Social' and 'Critical,'" *European Journal of Communication* 10(1) 87–108.

Ross, K. and V. Nightingale (2003) *Media and Audiences: New Perspectives.* Maidenhead: Open University Press.

Ross, K. L. (2002) "Foundationalism and Hermeneutics." www.friesian.com/hermenut.htm. Accessed March 3, 2004.

Rossiter, J. R. (2003) "How to Construct a Test of Scientific Knowledge in Consumer Behavior," *Journal of Consumer Research* 30 (September) 305–310.

Ruddock, A. (2007) *Investigating Audiences.* London: Sage.

Ryder, M. (1995) "Production and Consumption of Meaning: The Interplay Between Subject and Object in Open Hypertext Representation," paper presented to the *Semiotics as a Bridge between the Humanities and the Sciences Conference*, University of Toronto, Canada.

Saarinen, J. (2004) "Destinations in Change: The Transformation Process of Tourist Destinations," *Tourist Studies* 4(2) 161–179.

Salter, L. (2005) "Colonization Tendencies in the Development of the World Wide Web," *New Media and Society* 7(3) 291–309.

Sassi, S. (2005) "Cultural Differentiation or Social Segregation? Four Approaches to the Digital Divide," *New Media and Society* 7(5) 684–700.

Scannell, P. (1996) *Radio, Television and Modern Life.* Oxford: Blackwell.

Scannell, P. (2004) "What Reality Has Misfortune?" *Media, Culture and Society* 26(4) 573–584.

Scannell, P. (2007) Interview with Tarik Sabry. *Westminster Papers in Communications and Culture* 4(2) 3–23.

Schau, H. J. and M. C. Gilly (2003) "We Are What We Post? Self-Presentation in Personal Web Space," *Journal of Consumer Research* 30 (December) 385–404.

Schneider, S. M. and K. A. Foot (2004) "The Web as an Object of Study," *New Media and Society* 6(1) 114–122.

Schouten, J. W. and J. H. McAlexander (1995) "Subcultures of Consumption: An Ethnography of the New Bikers," *Journal of Consumer Research* 22 (June) 43–61.

Schroder, K. (1987) "Convergence of Antagonistic Traditions? The Case of Audience Research," *European Journal of Communication* 2 7–31.

Schroder, K. (1999) "Beyond the Pioneer Days! Where is Reception Research Going?" Inaugural lecture as Professor of Communication, Roskilde University.

Schroder, K. (2000) "Making Sense of Audience Discourses: Towards a Multi-dimensional Model of Mass Media Reception," *European Journal of Cultural Studies* 3(2) 233–258.

Schroder, K. (2007) "Newspaper Readers in the Media Landscape of the Digital Age." Paper presented to the Transforming Audiences Conference, University of Westminster, September 6–7.

Schroder, K., K. Drotner, S. Kline, and C. Murray (2003) *Researching Audiences.* London: Arnold.

Schroeder, J. E. and D. Zwick (2004) "Mirrors of Masculinity: Representation and Identity in Advertising Images," *Consumption, Markets and Culture* 7(1) 21–52.

Schwarz, N. (2003) "Self-Reports in Consumer Research: The Challenge of Comparing Cohorts and Cultures," *Journal of Consumer Research* 29 (March) 588–594.

Scott, L. M. (1994a) "Images in Advertising: The Need for a Theory of Visual Rhetoric," *Journal of Consumer Research* 21 (September) 252–273.

Scott, L. M. (1994b) "The Bridge from Text to Mind: Adapting Reader-Response Theory to Consumer Research," *Journal of Consumer Research* 21 (December) 461–480.

Seiter, E. (1999) *Television and New Media Audiences.* Oxford: Oxford University Press.

Selwyn, N. (2004) "Home Truths: Exploring the Domestic Consumption of Computers (Review Article)," *Information, Communication and Society* 7(4) 575–587.

Selwyn, N., S. Gorard, and J. Furlong (2005) "Whose Internet is it Anyway? Exploring Adults' (Non) Use of the Internet in Everyday Life," *European Journal of Communication* 20(1) 5–26.

Seung, T. K. (1982) *Structuralism and Hermeneutics.* New York: Columbia University Press.

Sherlock, K. (2001) "Revisiting the Concept of Hosts and Guests," *Tourist Studies* 1(3) 271–295.

Shi, Y. (2005) "Identity Construction of the Chinese Diaspora: Ethnic Media Use, Community Formation, and the Possibility of Social Activism," *Continuum: Journal of Media and Cultural Studies* 19(1) 55–72.

Shome, R. (2003) "Space Matters: The Power and Practice of Space," *Communication Theory* 13(1) 39–56.

Siapera, E. (2006) "Multiculturalism Online: The Internet and the Dilemmas of Multicultural Politics," *European Journal of Cultural Studies* 9(1) 5–24.

Silver, D. (2004) "Internet/Cyberculture/ Digital Culture/New Media/ Fill-in-the-Blank Studies," *New Media and Society* 6(1) 55–64.

Silverstone, R. (1999) *Why Study the Media?* London: Sage.

Simon, B. (2006) "Beyond Cyberspatial Flaneurie: On the Analytic Potential of Living with Digital Games," *Games and Culture* 1(1) 62–67.

Slater, D. (2002) "Social Relationships and Identity Online and Offline" in L. A. Lievrouw and S. Livingstone (eds.) *Handbook of New Media: Social Shaping and Consequences of ICTs.* London: Sage, pp. 533–546.

Smith-Shomade, B. E. (2004) "Narrowcasting in the New World Information Order," *Television and New Media* 5(1) 69–81.

Smolka, A. L. B. (2000) "Cultural Diversity and Theoretical Differences: Perspectives and Difficulties in (Cross-cultural) Psychology," *Culture and Psychology* 6(4) 477–494. Review of J. W. Berry, P. R. Dasen, and T. S. Saraswathi (1996) *Handbook of Cross-Cultural Psychology, Vol. 2: Basic Processes and Human Development* (2nd edn.) Boston: Allyn and Bacon.

Smythe, W. (1992) "Conceptions of Interpretation in Cognitive Theories of Representation," *Theory and Psychology* 2(3) 339–362.

Sobchack, V. (1992) *The Address of the Eye: A Phenomenology of Film Experience.* Princeton, NJ: Princeton University Press.

Spiggle, S. (1994) "Analysis and Interpretation of Qualitative Data in Consumer Research," *Journal of Consumer Research* 21 (December) 491–503.

Squires, C. R. (2002) "Rethinking the Black Public Sphere: An Alternative Vocabulary for Multiple Public Spheres," *Communication Theory* 12(4) 446–468.

Stecker, R. (2003) *Interpretation and Construction.* Oxford: Blackwell.

Steinkuehler, C. A. (2006) "Why Game (Culture) Studies Now?" *Games and Culture* 1(1) 97–102.

Stern, B. B. (1993) "Feminist Literary Criticism and the Deconstruction of Ads: A Postmodern View of Advertising and Consumer Responses," *Journal of Consumer Research* 19 (March) 556–566.

Stern, B. B. (1995) "Consumer Myths: Frye's Taxonomy and the Structural Analysis of Consumption Text," *Journal of Consumer Research* 22 (September) 165–185.

Stern, B. B. (1996) "Deconstructive Strategy and Consumer Research: Concepts and Illustrative Exemplar," *Journal of Consumer Research* 23 (September) 136–147.

Stern, B. B. and C. A. Russell (2004) "Consumer Responses to Product Placement in Television Sitcoms: Genre, Sex, and Consumption," *Consumption, Markets and Culture* 7(4) 371–394.

Stevenson, N. (1995) *Understanding Media Cultures.* London: Sage.

Straubhaar, J. D. (2007) *World Television: From Global to Local.* London: Sage.

Sturken, M. (2008) "Memory, Consumerism and Media: Reflections on the Emergence of the Field," *Memory Studies* 1(1) 73–78.

Suraya, R. M. Y. (2003) "Internet Diffusion and E-Business Opportunities Amongst Malaysian Travel Agencies," paper presented at Monash University Asia Institute seminar.

Sutton-Smith, B. (1997) *The Ambiguity of Play.* Cambridge, MA: Harvard University Press.

Sweeney, K. (n.d.) "Constructivism in Cognitive Film Theory." www.hanover.edu/philos/film/vol_02/sweeney.htm. Accessed March 20, 2004.

Tacchi, J. (2004) "Researching Creative Applications of New Information and Communication Technologies," *International Journal of Cultural Studies* 7(1) 91–103.

Taylor, P. A. (2005) "From Hackers to Hacktivists: Speed Bumps on the Global Superhighway?" *New Media and Society* 7(5) 625–646.

Taylor, T. L. (2003) "Multiple Pleasures: Women and Online Gaming" *Convergence* 9(1) 21–46.

Taylor, T. L. and B. E. Kolkob (2003) "Boundary Spaces: Majestic and the Uncertain Status of Knowledge, Community and Self in a Digital Age," *Information, Communication and Society* 6(4) 497–522.

Theofanos, M. F. and C. Mulligan (2004) "Empowering Patients through Access to Information: The United States Department of Health and Human Services' E-Health Enterprise," *Information, Communication and Society* 7(4) 466–490.

Thompson, C. J. (1996) "Caring Consumers: Gendered Consumption Meanings and the Juggling Lifestyle," *Journal of Consumer Research* 22 (March) 388–407.

Thompson, C. J. (1997) "Interpreting Consumers: A Hermeneutical Framework for Deriving Marketing Insights from the Texts of Consumers' Consumption Stories," *Journal of Marketing Research* 34(4) 438–455.

Thompson, C. J. (2002) "A Re-Inquiry on Re-Inquiries: A Postmodern Proposal for a Critical-Reflexive Approach," *Journal of Consumer Research* 29 (June) 142–145.

Thompson, C. J. (2004) "Marketplace Mythology and Discourses of Power," *Journal of Consumer Research* 31 (June) 162–180.

Thompson, C. J. (2005) "Consumer Risk Perceptions in a Community of Reflexive Doubt," *Journal of Consumer Research* 32 (September) 235–248.

Thompson, C. J. and Z. Arsel (2004) "The Starbucks Brandscape and Consumers' (Anticorporate) Experiences of Glocalization," *Journal of Consumer Research* 31 (December) 631–642.

Thompson, C. J. and D. L. Haytko (1997) "Speaking of Fashion: Consumers' Uses of Fashion Discourses and the Appropriation of Countervailing Cultural Meanings," *Journal of Consumer Research* 24 (June) 15–42.

Thompson, C. J. and E. C. Hirschman (1995) "Understanding the Socialized Body: A Poststructuralist Analysis of Consumers' Self-Conceptions, Body Images, and Self-Care Practices," *Journal of Consumer Research* 22 (September) 139–153.

Thompson, C. J. and D. B. Holt (2004) "How Do Men Grab the Phallus? Gender Tourism in Everyday Consumption," *Journal of Consumer Culture* 4(3) 313–338.

Thompson, C. J., H. R. Pollio, and W. B. Locander (1994) "The Spoken and the Unspoken: A Hermeneutic Approach to Understanding the Cultural Viewpoints that Underlie Consumers' Expressed Meanings," *Journal of Consumer Research* 21 (December) 432–453.

Thompson, C. J. and S. K. Tambyah (1999) "Trying to be Cosmopolitan," *Journal of Consumer Research* 26 (December) 214–241.

Thompson, C. J. and M. Troester (2002) "Consumer Value Systems in the Age of Postmodern Fragmentation: The Case of the Natural Health Microculture," *Journal of Consumer Research* 28 (March) 550–571.

Tomlinson, A. (2005) "Picturing the Winter Olympics: The Opening Ceremonies of Nagano (Japan) 1998 and Salt Lake City (USA) 2002," *Tourism, Culture and Communication* 5(2) 83–92.

Tompkins, J. P. (ed.) (1980) *Reader-Response Criticism From Formalism to Post-Structuralism.* Baltimore: Johns Hopkins University Press.

Tsao, J. C. and C. Chang (2002) "Communication Strategy in Taiwanese and US Corporate Web Pages: A Cross-Cultural Comparison," *Asian Journal of Communication* 12(2) 1–29.

Tulloch, J. (2000) *Watching Television Audiences: Cultural Theories and Methods.* London: Arnold.

Turkle, S. (1997) "Constructions and Reconstructions of Self in Virtual Reality: Playing in the MUDS" in S. Kiesler (ed.) *Culture of the Internet.* Mahwah, NJ: Lawrence Erlbaum, pp. 143–155.

Turkle, S. (2003) "From Powerful Ideas to Powerpoint," *Convergence* 9(2) 19–25.

Twitchell, J. B. (2004) "An English Teacher Looks at Branding," *Journal of Consumer Research* 31 (September) 484–489.

Urry, J. (1990) *The Tourist Gaze: Leisure and Travel in Contemporary Societies.* London: Sage.

Urry, J. (1995) *Consuming Places.* London: Routledge.

Valkenburg, P. M., A. P. Schouten, and J. Peter (2005) "Adolescents' Identity Experiments on the Internet," *New Media and Society* 7(3) 383–402.

Valsiner, J. (2000) "Scaling the Skyscraper of the Contemporary Social Sciences," *Culture and Psychology* 6(4) 495–501. Review of D. Holland, W. Lachicotte, D. Skinner, and C. Cain (1998) *Identity and Agency in Cultural Worlds.* Cambridge, MA: Harvard University Press.

Van Dijck, J. (2005) "From Shoebox to Performative Agent: The Computer as Personal Memory Machine," *New Media and Society* 7(3) 311–332.

Vered, K. O. (2002) "Televisual Aesthetics in Y2K: From Windows on the World to a Windows Interface," *Convergence* 8(3) 40–60.

Villi, M. (2006) "Photo Messages and the Ritual View of Communication," paper presented to the *Mediatutkimuksen päivät (National Conference on Media Research)*, Helsinki, Finland.

Vosgerau, J., K. Wertenbroch, and Z. Carmon (2006) "Indeterminacy and Live Television," *Journal of Consumer Research* 32 (March) 487–495.

Wakeford, N. (2003a) "Research Note: Working with New Media's Cultural Intermediaries. The Development of Collaborative Projects at INCITE," *Information, Communication and Society* 6(2) 229–245.

Wakeford, N. (2003b) "The Embedding of Local Culture in Global Communication: Independent Internet Cafes in London," *New Media and Society* 5(3) 379–399.

Wakeford, N. (2004) "Pushing at the Boundaries of New Media Studies," *New Media and Society* 6(1) 130–136.

Wang, J. and B. J. Calder (2006) "Media Transportation and Advertising," *Journal of Consumer Research* 33 (September) 151–162.

Wang, T. L. (2002) "Whose 'Interactive' Channel? Exploring the Concept of Interactivity Defined in Taiwan's 2000 Presidential Election Online Campaigns," *Asian Journal of Communication* 12(2) 50–78.

Warde, A. (2005) "Consumption and Theories of Practice," *Journal of Consumer Culture* 5(2) 131–153.

Wei, R. (2006) "Lifestyles and New Media: Adoption and Use of Wireless Communication Technologies in China," *New Media and Society* 8(6) 991–1008.

Wei, R. and V.-H. Lo (2006) "Staying Connected While On the Move: Cellphone Use and Social Connectedness," *New Media and Society* 8(1) 53–72.

Wellman, B. (2004) "The Three Ages of Internet Studies: Ten, Five and Zero Years Ago," *New Media and Society* 6(1) 123–129.

Westphal, M. (1999) "Hermeneutics as Epistemology" in J. Greco and E. Soza (eds.) *The Blackwell Guide to Epistemology*. Oxford: Blackwell, pp. 415–431.

Wiklund, H. (2005) "A Habermasian Analysis of the Deliberative Democratic Potential of ICT-Enabled Services in Swedish Municipalities," *New Media and Society* 7(5) 701–723.

Willett, J. (ed.) (1979) *Brecht on Theatre*. London: Methuen.

Williams, D. (2003) "The Video Game Lightning Rod: Constructions of a New Media Technology, 1970–2000," *Information, Communication and Society* 6(4) 523–550.

Williams, D. (2006) "Why Games Studies Now? Gamers Don't Bowl Alone," *Games and Culture* 1(1) 13–16.

Williamson, J. (1978) *Decoding Advertisements: Ideology and Meaning in Advertising*. London: Marion Boyars.

Willmott, H. (1994) "Social Constructionism and Communication Studies: Hearing the Conversation But Losing the Dialogue" in S. Deetz (ed.) *Communication Yearbook* 17. Beverley Hills: Sage, pp. 42–54.

Wilson, T. (1993) *Watching Television: Hermeneutics, Reception and Popular Culture*. Cambridge: Polity Press.

Wilson, T. (2001) "On Playfully Becoming the 'Other': Watching Oprah Winfrey on Malaysian Television," *International Journal of Cultural Studies* 4(1) 89–119.

Wilson, T. (2004) *The Playful Audience: From Talk Show Viewers to Internet Users*. Cresskill, NJ: Hampton Press New Media and Policy Studies.

Wilson, T. (2006) "Processing Local Understanding/Perceiving Global Media: Reading Convergent Text Across Cultures," *Australian Journal of Communication* 33(1) 53–72.

Wilson, T. (2007) *Global Media: Malaysian Use*. Kuala Lumpur: University Book Stores/August Publishing.

Wilson, T., A. Hamzah, and U. Khattab (2003) "The Cultural Technology of Clicking in the Hypertext Era: E-Journalism Reception Research in Malaysia," *New Media and Society* 5(4) 523–545.

Wilson, T. and Y. Suraya (2004) "The Tourist Gaze Goes On-line: Rojak (Hybrid) Reception Theory Structures of Ludic Looking," *Tourist Studies* 4(1) 69–92.

Wilson T. and H. P. Tan (2005) "'Less Tangible Ways of Reading': Multicultural Explorations of Online International News Sites," *Information, Communication and Society* 8(3) 394–416.

Wilson, T. and H. P. Tan (2006) "Television's Glocal Advertising in Veridical Product Narrative: A S.E. Asian Reception Study of Consumer Alignment/Alienation," *Consumption, Markets and Culture* 9(1) 45–62.

Wolf, M. J. P. (2006) "Games Studies and Beyond," *Games and Culture* 1(1) 116–118.

Woodlief, A. and Cornis-Pope, M. (n.d.) "On the Reading Process: Notes on Critical Literary Philosophy and Pedagogical Practice." www.vcu.edu/engweb/home/theory.html. Accessed March 22, 2004.

Yee, N. (2006) "The Labor of Fun: How Video Games Blur the Boundaries of Work and Play," *Games and Culture* 1(1) 68–71.

Yoon, K. (2006) "The Making of Neo-Confucian Cyberkids: Representations of Young Mobile Phone Users in South Korea," *New Media and Society* 8(5) 753–771.

Yoon, T.-J. and M. Ok (2007) "Watching and Shopping: Television Audiences' Experiences with Home-Shopping Channels in Everyday Lives," paper presented at the International Association for Media and Communication Research Conference, UNESCO, Paris.

Zhong, Y. and Q. Wang (2006) "Cannibalizing the Chinese 'Watching Mass'," *Journal of International Communication* 12(1) 23–36.

Zhou, B. (2006) "Audience Research Trends in Mainland China: An Analysis of Three Major Journalism and Mass Communication Journals, 1985," *Asian Journal of Communication* 16(2) 119–131.

Zwick, D. and N. Dholakia (2006) "The Epistemic Consumption Object and Postsocial Consumption: Expanding Consumer-Object Theory in Consumer Research," *Consumption, Markets and Culture* 9(1) 17–43.

Index